THE
HIDDEN SCROLLS

THE HIDDEN SCROLLS

CHRISTIANITY, JUDAISM, & THE WAR FOR THE DEAD SEA SCROLLS

NEIL ASHER SILBERMAN

A Grosset/Putnam Book
Published by G. P. Putnam's Sons
New York

The author and publisher gratefully acknowledge permission to reproduce extracts from the following copyrighted material:

The Dead Sea Scrolls in English by Geza Vermes (Penguin Books 1962, Third Edition 1987) © Geza Vermes 1962, 1965, 1968, 1975, 1987. Reproduced by permission of Penguin Books, Ltd.

"The Messiah at Qumran" by Michael O. Wise and James D. Tabor, *Biblical Archaeology Review* 18:6 (November/December 1992). Reproduced by permission of Michael O. Wise.

"The Hubris of Antichrist" by David Flusser, *Immanuel* 10 (1980). Reproduced by permission of David Flusser.

"The New Halakhic Letter (4QMMT) and the Origins of the Dead Sea Sect" by Lawrence H. Schiffman, *Biblical Archaeologist* 53 (1990). Reproduced by permission of Lawrence H. Schiffman.

A Grosset/Putnam Book
Published by G. P. Putnam's Sons
Publishers Since 1838
200 Madison Avenue
New York, NY 10016

Book design by H. Roberts

Library of Congress Cataloging-in-Publication Data
Silberman, Neil Asher, date.
    The hidden scrolls : Christianity, Judaism, and the war for the Dead Sea scrolls / Neil Asher Silberman.
        p.   cm.
    "A Grosset/Putnam book."
    Includes index.
    ISBN 0-399-13982-6
    1. Dead Sea Scrolls—Criticism, interpretation, etc.—History. 2. Dead Sea Scrolls—Relation to the New Testament. 3. Qumran community.   I. Title.
    BM487.S49   1994
    296.1'55—dc20   94-18417 CIP

Printed in the United States of America
1   2   3   4   5   6   7   8   9   10

This book is printed on acid-free paper.
∞

CONTENTS

PREFACE

This book will offer an alternative version of the Dead Sea Scrolls story. It will suggest that many of the hundreds of ancient Hebrew and Aramaic texts found in caves by the northwestern shores of the Dead Sea must not be read solely as purely religious writings, but also as a powerful message of rage against empire—a direct and timeless challenge to the injustices and inequalities imposed by the powers that be. The context for this protest movement was political and economic, not only spiritual; throughout the first century of the Common Era, a growing proportion of the population of the small province of Judea joined in an ever-more violent movement of resistance against the imperial rule of the world's only superpower, the Roman Empire.

For Christians, this was the era of the missionary efforts of the early Apostles; for Jews it was the last period of ancient Jewish political and territorial autonomy, after which local synagogue worship replaced centralized Temple sacrifice. Yet I will argue that the essential message of the Dead Sea Scrolls reflects one of the most widespread of all the politico-religious movements of first-century Judea—the revolutionary, messianic faith of the Elect of Israel with its call to Holy War against foreign conquerors and collaborators. Far from being the work of isolated, otherworldly monks living in a desert monastery (as many scholars maintain), the scrolls give voice and authority to the aspirations of the forgotten majority of the Judeans, who embarked on a risky, even suicidal, armed rebellion that raged on for four full years, from 66 C.E. until the destruction of the Temple of Jerusalem in 70, and even then, fitfully continuing until the fall of Masada in 74. Many of these ancient texts express the timeless dreams of a subject people who would no longer allow themselves to be brutally exploited, alienated, and dispossessed.

As we have seen in our own times, the feverish apocalyptic visions of cultists, survivalists, and religious separatists—each with their own distinctive violent visions of Armageddon, an unshakable faith in the Victory of Light over Darkness, and searing hatred for all whom they identify as sinners or traitors—can have a frightening impact on events in the here and now, not just in the World to Come. Indeed, the angry message of the scrolls often seems eerily close to the chanted accusations of modern Islamic fundamentalists condemning "seekers after smooth things" among their most westernized coreligionists. They also have much in common with the tirades of modern cult leaders and born-again visionaries, who bellow out condemnation for the fornication, idolatry, and moral pollution of these Last Days.

For the last forty-five years, the world's most respected scroll scholars have concentrated almost exclusively on the scrolls' language and literary genres, without recognizing—without wanting to recognize—the radical message they contain. The apocalyptic literature of the Dead Sea Scrolls represents a long-lost yet authentic expression of the biblical religion, embodying messianic expectations shared by the large segments of the Judean population who rose in the ill-fated revolt against Rome. For centuries, the message of the scrolls was reinterpreted or was branded as heresy by both the rabbis and the early Church Fathers who eventually established a modus vivendi with Rome, surviving through accommodation and compromise. The adherents of the revolutionary messianic movement were killed, enslaved, or scattered. Yet as this book will attempt to explain, the vast treasury of ancient texts from the caves in the Judean Desert may provide us with a glimpse at the forgotten, radical message that lies hidden at the heart of both Judaism and Christianity.

This account of the discovery, interpretation, and struggle for control of the Dead Sea Scrolls could never have been written without the valuable contributions of many people at every stage of the work. As will become evident in the chapters that follow, the main narrative of this book is based on extended conversations I conducted with some of the most important characters in the Dead Sea Scrolls story—all of whom patiently and graciously answered countless technical questions, shared with me private reminiscences, and offered their differing perspectives on the historical significance of the Qumran literature.

Among these scholars, I owe special thanks to Professor Lawrence Schiffman of New York University for his generosity, enthusiasm, and kind invitation to attend Dead Sea Scrolls symposia in Philadelphia and New York; to Professor John Strugnell of Harvard University for sharing with me his incomparable knowledge of the personalities and historical turning points of the scrolls project and allowing me to read preliminary drafts of his own memoirs; and to Hershel Shanks, founder and editor of *Biblical Archaeology Review,* who provided me with his own perspective on the latest developments in the scroll story and drew my attention to overlooked facets of the earlier history of the scrolls.

Dr. Emile Puech of the Ecole Biblique et Archéologique in Jerusalem generously took time from his busy schedule to accompany me to the Rockefeller Museum to examine and discuss some especially important Cave 4 manuscripts. Archbishop Athanasius Yeshue Samuel of the Syrian Orthodox Church of America and Canada—still an active and charismatic leader of his community—shared with me his reflections on the discovery that changed his life. My thanks also go to Director Amir Drori of the Israel Antiquities Authority; to Professor Emanuel Tov, editor-in-chief of the Dead Sea Scrolls Publication Project; and to Curator

Magen Broshi of the Shrine of the Book. Last but certainly not least, I want to express my gratitude to Professor Robert Eisenman of California State University, Long Beach, who discussed with me at length his historical hypotheses about the Qumran community and provided me with copies of documents and correspondence related to the struggle to gain open access to the unpublished Qumran texts.

A full listing of the scholars I interviewed during my research can be found at the end of this book. My deepest thanks go to all of them, though of course none bears any responsibility for the opinions I express or the historical interpretations I have adopted in this book. Readers will note that I have made extensive use of extracts from my transcripts of many of these taped conversations in my reconstruction of the Dead Sea Scrolls story. In most cases, I have reproduced the speaker's words precisely as recorded; in only a very few instances have I made slight changes in the grammar or style to make the spoken word more easily readable as printed text.

The bibliographical notes I have included at the end of the book serve a double purpose: to offer sources for further reading to general readers and to provide a general essay on the sources I have utilized in arriving at certain admittedly controversial historical conclusions. In the interest of keeping the bibliography useful to general readers, I have cited only a few works that are highly technical or have been published in obscure sources. For the fullest published bibliographies of Qumran studies, see Fitzmyer, *The Dead Sea Scrolls: Major Publications and Tools for Study,* and Tov, "The Unpublished Qumran Texts." In light of the accelerating pace of Qumran publication, however, many new bibliographical items are added every year, making published listings incomplete almost as soon as they appear.

In most cases where I have quoted directly from the scrolls, I have utilized the English translations of Geza Vermes from his book *The Dead Sea Scrolls in English.* The sources of other translated extracts can be found in the bibliographical notes. Readers should be aware that the words that appear between square brackets [ ] have been restored by the translator as likely reconstructions of words or phrases in damaged parts of the scroll. Words that appear between parentheses ( ) do not appear in the original text but have been added for clarity of translation.

Regarding chronological terminology, I have used the accepted, neutral terms "Common Era" (C.E.) and "Before the Common Era" (B.C.E.) in place of the traditional B.C. and A.D., whose religious associations would be out of place here.

Finally, a word about the title: In late 1947, when Professor Eleazar Lipa Sukenik of the Hebrew University first recognized the importance of several ancient Hebrew manuscripts recently discovered by the Taamireh bedouin in the Dead Sea region, he gave them the Hebrew name *Megillot ha-Genuzot,* the "Hidden" or "Concealed" Scrolls, in his belief that the documents had been deposited in antiquity in a *geniza,* or repository for worn or damaged sacred writings. The later adoption of the common name "Dead Sea Scrolls" for these ancient manuscripts removed the concept of intentional concealment. My choice of the title for this book is meant to re-emphasize the conscious action that led to the deposit of the scrolls in Qumran Cave 1.

As in my previous book, I want to express my appreciation to Janet Amitai for her superb research assistance and continuing editorial advice and administrative support. My thanks also go to Susan Berman, who also helped me with early interviews and archival research. The staffs of the Sterling Memorial Library of Yale University and of the Yale Divinity School Library offered their usual efficient assistance. On my research trips to Jerusalem, I was helped greatly by the staff of the Israel Antiquities Authority, especially Ayala Sussmann, director of publications; Chief Curator Ruta Peled; and Dr. Ronny Reich of the department of archives.

Steven Weinstock, friend and media guru, offered invaluable input and encouragement. And, as always, Steve Horn served as my dependable historical, philosophical, and medical advisor.

My incomparable literary agent, Carol Mann, has—once again—has earned my deepest respect, appreciation, and thanks.

Working with copy editor Timothy Meyer at the Putnam Publishing Group has been a pleasure; I want to offer him my gratitude for a job excellently done.

It is no exaggeration to say that this book would have never come to be—and certainly would never have reached its present form—without the constant encouragement and invaluable editorial insights of Jane Isay, publisher of Grosset Books. Any thanks I express here are not nearly enough to repay her fundamental contribution to this project.

Lastly, I want to offer my love and appreciation to friends and family who showed their usual understanding to me during yet another season of intensive book-writing. And to Ellen and Maya—who had to live with a husband and father, who, for months on end, spoke of little but scrolls and scholars—I can only hope that this book, now finally finished, will justify their patience and continuing confidence in me.

—N.A.S.
Branford, Connecticut
May 10, 1994

THE
HIDDEN SCROLLS

1

A Way in the Wilderness

Here is my vision: Two thousand years ago in the desolated, devastated province of Judea, some faithful people (whose precise number or names we can now never know) made a gesture of astonishing faith and optimism to reach out to us across the centuries. The time was one of horror and suffering. The Roman Tenth Legion, clanking arrogantly across the countryside, raising high the loathsome symbol of the wild boar on their idolatrous battle standards, was systematically surrounding and conquering the last few strongholds of the Jewish Revolt, unhesitatingly executing all who would offer resistance and condemning most of the survivors to a life of slavery. Compliant Jewish priests, turncoats, and collaborators were settled by the Romans in specially designated towns and villages—places that we might today call re-education camps. At the same time, tens of thousands of Judeans who had surrendered or been captured in earlier operations were even now being concentrated in Mediterranean port cities to be sold in the slave markets of Crete, Ostia, Ephesus, and Sardinia as prostitutes, mine workers, or human fodder for the wild animal shows.

The Holy Temple in Jerusalem, once the heart of the nation

and the scattered people of Israel, lay in smoking ruins. The city of Jerusalem, embellished as the crowning jewel of Herod's kingdom, was now a stinking, charred quarry and graveyard through which only wild dogs and human scavengers roamed. But down by the shore of the Dead Sea, in the silence of the wilderness, far from the cities and camps of the Occupying Power, some surviving Jews proved that they had not abandoned their faith that God would—some day—wreak his holy vengeance on the Romans, on the Jewish collaborators, and indeed on all the wicked people of the world. Gathering together some precious scrolls of scriptures, hymns, and prophecies of the coming Day of Judgment, he, she, or they carefully wrapped them in linen fabric (one of the pieces was embroidered with the symmetrical plan of the ideal Israelite Temple), and placed them for safekeeping in tall pottery jars.

The path up to the cliffside was steep and rocky. The tall jars in which the scrolls were placed were heavy, but this was a mission of faith. High above the destroyed settlement of Secacah was a natural cleft in the hard, brown limestone—one of hundreds of natural caves in the cliff face which the settlers here had used for decades as living places, hiding places, and *genizot,* or sanctified places for the disposal of damaged or worn-out religious texts. This particular cave was deep and narrow; fragments of biblical books and mystical speculation, worn-out leather phylactery cases, and broken pottery lay scattered on the dirt floor of the cave. But this deposit was not meant as a routine, reverent disposal; it was a bold testimonial of religious identity and belief. With perfect faith that some day people would return to this place and find the scroll jars—and that those people would be able to read their impassioned message—the anonymous survivors of the great war between the Jews and the Romans left their precious documents inside the narrow cave.

The documents they bequeathed to the future had been carefully selected from the hundreds of texts that had been written, read, and studied by the members of this community. There was the Book of Isaiah, with its vision of sin, suffering, and the divine redemption of the people of Israel. There was a copy of the law code by which the Community had maintained its sanctity during the time of ever-deepening troubles by voluntarily separating itself from the Men of Falsehood and faithfully walking in the Way of Light. There were the penitential psalms written by the Community's leader, the Teacher of Righteousness, declaring gratitude to God for personal salvation and for the sure knowledge that the Wicked would, in the end, be destroyed for their sins. And there was the "Rule of War on the unleashing of the attack of the Sons of Light against the company of the Sons of Darkness, the army of Belial," a scroll of detailed instructions for the conduct of the final, decisive Holy War, to be waged at the End of Times.

Among the other documents left for the future was a poignant commentary on the Book of Habakkuk, in which the horrible events of these recent days of Roman sacrilege and genocide were explained as the fulfillment of the oracles of the ancient prophet—and a sure sign that divine vengeance was coming, even if its advent would be painfully delayed. "On the Day of Judgment," the last line of the text read, "God will destroy from the earth all idolatrous and wicked men." Scattered here and there in the caves of the nearby cliffside were the traces of other Hebrew and Aramaic scripture, oracles, and testimonies, and they, too, were part of this community's legacy. They were scrolls and fragments of hundreds of works of law, oracles, poetry, and visions that had been buried, hidden, or borrowed by other members of this community over many decades. All these manuscripts, taken together, might be read as the recorded faith of a community of alienated, dispossessed Jewish priests and their followers who remained true to the strictest possible interpretation of the biblical laws. They also remained true to the hope for national redemption from the yoke of the people they called the Kittim—and we call the Romans—idolatrous invaders from across the sea "who trample the earth with their horses and beasts."

Almost a century before (at about the time later gospel writers would place the birth of Jesus of Nazareth), the spiritual founders of this community had established a wilderness camp here by the shore of the Salt Sea opposite the Land of Moab, at a site they knew as Secacah—the "Covered" or the "Hidden"—a place mentioned in the Book of Joshua and given to the Tribe of Judah as an eternal inheritance. At the time of the Community's arrival, the place was just a ruin. But during the period of Judean political independence under the Maccabees, before the coming of the Romans, Secacah had been an outpost of the Maccabean kingdom. And because its earlier occupants were faithful Maccabean soldiers and had apparently made an impression on travelers through the region, the cluster of buildings on the white plateau overlooking the seashore was also known as the "Fortress of the Pious Ones." Thus, settling at this place with its scriptural and patriotic associations, the group, numbering only a few dozen people (who variously called themselves the Community, the Sons of Zadok, the Elect, the Poor, the Way, and the Sons of Light), constructed their place of voluntary exile. They vowed to themselves and their God to "make a way in the wilderness," in the words of the Prophet Isaiah, "to separate from the habitations of ungodly men," and play a central role in the terrifying events that were soon to engulf the world. A few years after their community was destroyed and their manuscripts hidden, the Jewish turncoat historian Josephus Flavius mistakenly (perhaps intentionally) described this priestly group and their lay followers throughout the country as the pious, pacifist Essenes. But they were certainly not docile monks and mystics, no matter what Josephus said. They were to become the angry imams of their people, the rage-filled voice calling for resistance to the innovations and to the influence of the Great Satan from the West.

The Great Satan was, of course, the Roman emperor, whose numberless agents, bureaucrats, enforcers, and stooges in Judea and throughout the Mediterranean had the blasphemous gall to declare their leader a son of god and savior of all humanity. Of course this son of god and savior was just a front man for a system of exploitation and conquest that made the metropolis of Rome an urban black hole of wealth and power into which all the riches of its empire would eventually spin. Even in the relatively poor land of Judea, the effects of the New World Order were unmistak-

able, as small landholders, progressively forced into debt by taxation and natural disasters, were compelled to seek their livings as
tenants, migratory workers, or day laborers in the rapidly expanding cities. And it was there that they came into contact (albeit at a
respectful distance) with those Judeans—large landowners, high
priests, successful merchants, and royal functionaries—who were
happy to bow and scrape to the Romans, in the name of profit and
political moderation, and in the interest of what they called
modernity.

In fact, King Herod, ruling from 37 to 4 Before the Common
Era, (B.C.E.) had made a mockery of all the ancestral laws of the
Covenant of Sinai by erecting magnificent temples to Augustus in
Greek cities and by squandering his country's wealth in his lavish
donations to the idolatrous Olympic Games. In Jerusalem,
Herod's magnificent rebuilding of the Temple of the God of Is-
rael resulted in a spectacular structure which was—in its most authentic and spiritual essence—little more than an empty shell.
Herodian princes and princesses swapped husbands, wives, and
jockeyed for dynastic position. The High Priests of the Temple of
Jerusalem appointed by Herod were little more than manipulable
yes-men from wealthy Jewish families of Egypt and Mesopotamia,
servants more of the king than of God. Thus the three snares of
Belial, the Prince of Darkness—riches, fornication, and defilement of the Temple—had ensnared the high and the mighty of
Jerusalem, which had itself become nothing more than a City of
Vanity. The rulers of the last of the Maccabean kings may have
been self-serving and lacking on occasion appropriate piety, but
Herod and his loathsome son Archelaus (both descended from
Edomites who had been forcibly converted to Judaism) had de-
stroyed all righteousness from the land.

It was at this time of darkness that the Sons of Zadok renewed
habitation of the ruins of Secacah. They restored the cisterns,
watchtower, assembly rooms, and workshops built decades before
under the patronage of the Maccabean kings. And after the death
of Herod and the direct annexation of Judea to the Roman Empire, this small group enjoyed a fairly untroubled communal exis-

tence (as far as we can tell), living far from the scenes of urban unrest and imperial regimentation. Down by the Dead Sea, they cultivated land that was apparently too parched and poor to be worth the trouble of the tax collectors; they raised flocks, gathered in holy assemblies, and produced their characteristic tools, pottery vessels, and literature of rage. As the times grew darker for their fellow Judeans, they looked forward ever more fervently to a glorious time of redemption, to be ushered in by the appearance of God's messiahs, or anointed ones, who would bring justice and vengeance to the earth with their terrible swift swords.

Though distinctive in their piety and communal discipline, the group that settled at Secacah was part of a larger movement of national resistance. Though the historian Josephus Flavius, writing in luxurious surroundings in Rome about the events in Judea of this period, was always at pains to minimize the revolutionary tendencies of his people, his descriptions of the increasing unrest in Judea through the first century of the Common Era (C.E.) unwittingly betray the truth. His grim anecdotes of charismatic prophets and messiah figures, public hysteria, and the customary cruel execution of would-be saviors in first-century Judea appear again and again. Simon, Athronges, Judas, John the Baptist, Jesus of Nazareth, Theudas, and the mysterious "Egyptian" were just some of the leaders and preachers mentioned by Josephus who ended up beheaded or nailed to a cross.

Under the rule of Roman officials with names like Pontius Pilate, Cuspius Fadus, Antonius Felix, and Gessius Florus, the Sons of Zadok may have been known as spiritual leaders—not recluses—adapting and elaborating ancient traditions of messianic fulfillment to the nation's aspirations for independence. They may have urged and promoted a subtle strategy of political noncollaboration through the ever-stricter application of the traditional purity laws. Through the divine inspiration claimed by their Teacher of Righteousness, Community members were given a glimpse of God's secret timetable for redemption—which could be checked against the terrifying, dislocating omens and events of their own times. And even after the Teacher was persecuted and killed by the Jerusalem establishment, the community at Secacah continued making their way in the wilderness, seeing in even their most painful misfortunes the unmistakable fulfillment of ancient prophecy.

History has shown that this kind of gospel of rage against empire must at some point explode from silent anger to violent rebellion. And in that sense, the prophecies and admonitions of the Sons of Zadok were translated into action with the eruption of a great national rebellion against the Roman Empire in 66 C.E. The Temple was purified of its quisling priests and the dutiful daily offering for the well-being of the emperor ceased. The long-expected Holy War finally got underway as the Kittim brought their forces from the north and the south to wage war against God's people, and God's people arose to fulfill their destiny. But no savior arose to lead the Sons of Light into battle. After a series of stunning military victories at the start of the rebellion, the Jewish independence movement degenerated into a bloody struggle for power between opposing, mock-pious warlords. The zealous gospel of redemption through absolute submission to God's law—not earthly power—was betrayed by the rebel leaders' hunger for power. In time, God's enemies, the Sons of Darkness, conquered the land and laid waste to many cities. They leveled the city of Jerusalem, and the luxurious villas where the Judean aristocrats had toasted their good fortune. The Temple was destroyed, and the Holy Vessels—which were desecrated by the greedy grasp of the opposing rebel factions—were carried away to Rome, including the golden Menorah. Yet even this holocaust and Abomination of Desolation were seen by some survivors as clear signs of God's power to punish the Wicked. The real Day of Judgment could not be far away.

Were it not for the scrolls left behind by the members of the Community at Secacah, we would never have had a glimpse of what it meant to be on the receiving end of Roman civilization—and to be determined to fight its encroachments with the weapons of tradition, no matter what the cost. Theirs is a voice from the wilderness camp, the ghetto, and the barricade that even today points an accusing finger at all of us who see in ancient and modern empires only order, logic, and efficiency. They reveal in their passion—and in their retreat into a reformulated fundamentalist tradition—the anger of people who refuse to become the raw material for *other* peoples' dreams. Yet the great irony was that in those latter days dreamt of by the members of the Community, when their precious scrolls would be recovered and opened, these writings would come into the possession of timid, straitlaced scribes who were skilled at deciphering ancient texts, parsing verbs, and distinguishing literary genres, but had absolutely no inclination to take the message of the scrolls seriously. The scholars' guiding creed was academic respectability, not resistance to unjust power. In their ivory towers and university campuses, these men (and very occasionally, women) made careers for themselves, gave lectures, and slowly—very slowly—began to publish the contents of the scrolls. The message from the past had indeed been recovered, but in the process of translation something powerful was lost. The "Dead Sea Scrolls" became a harmless public fascination. But their revolutionary passion and outrage against injustice had been, consciously or unknowingly, stripped from them.

For many years, the Dead Sea Scrolls were for me just an innocent childhood fascination. The small reproduction clay scroll jar brought back from Israel by my grandfather in the late 1950s is an archaeological relic of my early interest in the scrolls. It still stands on my daughter Maya's night table among the snow globes and souvenir silver bells from Colonial Williamsburg and Niagara Falls. Yet even now that souvenir jar evokes for me those childhood stories of bedouin boys discovering an ancient treasure in the wilderness—which is probably as close to an authentic biblical vision as any child of the 1950s or 1960s was ever likely to get.

In college in the late 1960s, as I began to study the Dead Sea Scrolls as an undergraduate student of the history of religion, I saw in the esoteric doctrines and apocalyptic poetry of the Dead Sea Scroll community an attractively iconoclastic contrast to the canonical books of the Old Testament. In the age of be-ins, sit-ins, and communes, I became fascinated by the faith of a group of desert recluses who had rejected the official worship of the Jerusalem Temple and who focused all their hopes on the imminent, cataclysmic End of the World. Yet now as I look back, academic study of the Dead Sea Scrolls—all its superficial mystical and nonconformist associations notwithstanding—was really quite an unimaginative intellectual pursuit in those days. Even though sixties rebelliousness was creating upheaval and turmoil in so many scholarly disciplines, the conventional, nonpolitical interpretation of the Dead Sea Scrolls, as it had crystallized in the 1950s, remained largely unchallenged. No one except the handful of members of the official International Team of editors knew the full extent of the documents of the Dead Sea collection, and the few texts known at the time were read as a purely religious doctrine, in a way that was hardly less canonical than the Bible itself. And when the time came for me to write a senior thesis on the Dead Sea sect's bizarrely fascinating interpretation of the Book of Nahum, I, too, faithfully towed the party line.

Like a faithful seminarian I visited and briefly spoke with two of the leading scrolls scholars: Professor Frank Moore Cross at the Semitic Museum on the Harvard campus, and Professor John Strugnell at the Harvard Divinity School. There was almost a mystical quality (or maybe just a celebrity mystique) that seemed to cling to these men. They were among the small group of experts invited to Jordan in the early fifties who, with their own hands, had begun to piece together ancient texts from the thousands of parchment fragments recovered from the caves of Qumran. Occasionally, at scholarly conferences, they would offer tantalizing hints of future revelations from the large numbers of still-unpublished documents. They were a powerful clique, an academic aristocracy. And few ever thought of questioning their authority.

Indeed, their conventional interpretation of the scrolls themselves subtly reinforced the importance of conformity, not rebellion. From the enormous jigsaw puzzle of scroll fragments, Cross, Strugnell, and the others had crafted a saga-fable of a self-righteous group of ancient Jewish pietists who were dedicated—

not in the time of Jesus, but at the time of the great Maccabean uprising around 165 B.C.E.—to freeing Judea from the rule of the Seleucid Empire and the local Hellenized aristocracy. But seeing the Maccabean leadership eventually crown themselves kings of Judea and adopt Hellenistic trappings—so the standard explanation went—these religious rebels left Jerusalem around 125 B.C.E. to establish a remote monastery in the wilderness, where they could practice what they believed was the true biblical faith.

What followed was a two-century-long story of an isolated monastic community, which was almost uniformly identified by scholars as a settlement (perhaps the main settlement) of the ancient Essenes. Although this group's doctrines and beliefs, as revealed in the scrolls, were superficially similar to those of early Christianity—in the prominence of messianism, dualism, baptism, and communal life—the Dead Sea Scroll sect, so the scholars determined, represented little more than an evolutionary dead end. Father Josef Milik of the Dominican Ecole Biblique et Archéologique in Jerusalem, who was one of the most influential scroll editors, left no doubt as to his own religious allegiance, when he summed up the ultimate impact of the scrolls in his 1959 book *Ten Years of Discovery in the Wilderness of Judea,* which I had been assigned to read as an undergraduate text. "Although Essenism bore in itself more than one element that one way or another fertilized the soil from which Christianity was to spring," Milik wrote, "it is nevertheless evident that the latter religion represents something completely new which can only be adequately explained by the person of Jesus himself."

The scrolls' main significance was therefore perceived as an illustration of religious evolution. Most scholars saw the beliefs of the Essenes as expressed in the scrolls as religious insights that were slightly more advanced than mainstream Judaism, insights on the way (as conceived in the simplistic terms of unilinear evolution) to becoming Christianity. But it was *not* Christianity, just a brief aberration. It was a religious branch that bore no fruit. While waiting for the End of Times and divinely aided triumph over the forces of Darkness, the Dead Sea sect—so the standard explanation concluded—penned their scrolls, performed their ablutions, and remained serenely uninvolved in the turbulent politics of the times. Since the scholars directing the study had little interest in the connections between religious expression and political action—past or present—they could not imagine their ancient scroll writers lifting their heads from the tightly written lines of Hebrew scripture to contemplate or even react to the Roman oppression that was pressing down ever more heavily on their kinsmen and townsmen in all the places that they had left. And so the scholars explained that while the rest of the Judean people eventually rose in revolt against the corrupt Roman administration, the scroll sect maintained its life of seclusion to the very end. Like cloudy-headed intellectuals with tenure and therefore no need to worry about the present while contemplating the apocalyptic future, the Qumran center was destroyed and its helpless members massacred when Vespasian's legions marched through the lower Jordan Valley in the spring of 68 C.E.

This story came to be gospel to all respectable biblical scholars and religious historians. For all their vividness, the scrolls' specific End of the World visions were seen as just so much feverish nonsense. Like the "Get Ready for Armageddon" warnings of the door-to-door Jehovah's Witness missionaries in our own times or the peasant revolts and public hysterias of medieval Europe, the fervor for the End of the World has always threatened and unsettled all sober, respectable citizens. And here, the academic study of the Dead Sea Scrolls ironically provided a calm reassurance that these apocalyptic expectations were just a passing mania, significant only in their later transformation and universalization in the spiritual Kingdom of God of established Christianity. In behavioral terms, the study of the scrolls was the opposite of the rage that filled the poetry and prophecy of the ancient documents. The scholars' discourse was civil, unemotional, analytical, and filled with the jargon of tweedy academics who were themselves voluntary exiles from the rough-and-tumble of life beyond the ivy walls.

I never questioned the traditional interpretations, even when I was working for the Israel Department of Antiquities in the early

1970s, when my interest shifted from the ancient texts to the archaeological finds. It was an exciting time to be involved in archaeology in Jerusalem. With the eastern part of the city conquered by Israel in 1967, excavations were underway throughout the Old City, vastly expanding our information about Jerusalem at the time of Jesus and at the time of the Great Revolt against Rome. The massive, toppled stones of the Herodian Temple and the charred ruins of the wealthy villas in the Upper City were the kinds of vivid reminders that were being daily revealed. And at the headquarters of the Israel Department of Antiquities, newly shifted to the stately Rockefeller Museum opposite the battlements of the Old City, I came closer to the archaeology and secrets of the scrolls themselves. In the turreted white stone building—that Hershel Shanks would later dub "The Dead Sea Scrolls Prison"—was the basement labyrinth of storerooms and laboratories that held the greatest treasures of fifty years of Holy Land archaeology.

Just off the main hallway of the basement level, with its walls lined with wooden shelves for disinterred ossuaries and sarcophagi of generations of ancient Jerusalemites, was the mysterious closed room where the thousands of unpublished scroll fragments were stored in metal file drawers, pressed between glass plates. I remember the room's bone-chilling coldness even in the midst of raw and rainy Jerusalem winters, and I remember the eerie yellow light installed there to prevent the fading of the ancient manuscripts. But my memories were from fleeting glimpses through the half-opened doorway because, even then, only the small circle of scholars appointed under Jordanian auspices was permitted free access to this holy of holies of the world of the Dead Sea Scrolls.

For me, the archaeological finds from Khirbet Qumran, the ancient site found near the scroll caves, were far more evocative than the dark, crumpled pieces of inscribed leather on which the scholars continued to work. The archaeological finds from the site of the Qumran—or, as the French Dominican excavators preferred to call it, the Essene settlement—were arranged on shelves in a special storeroom. Here were the pots and pans and bowls and inkwells created and used by the people who wrote the Dead Sea

Scrolls. Here were the bulky storejars smashed in antiquity but now glued back together and arranged in rows. Here were the dozens of identical porridge bowls, each one carefully wrapped in yellowed Jordanian newspaper, that were discovered in the "pantry" off the room that the excavators had identified as the monastery's "refectory." Yet these finds remained mute and forgotten. The director of the excavations, Father Roland De Vaux, had not seriously dealt with this material after formulating his initial, sweeping theories about the history of the Qumran community. Promises of the eventual detailed publication of the finds were frequent and plentiful, but I never saw any other scholar in the storeroom, and the pottery simply collected dust. At the time, though, it hardly mattered, for the Qumran artifacts were not scientific evidence as much as they were sacred relics in the cult of the famous and ever-fascinating Dead Sea Scrolls.

By the late 1980s, however, the peaceful silence of Qumran studies was broken. A highly publicized campaign to "free" the scrolls from the control of a small circle of scholars created an atmosphere of tension and suspicion and became an international *cause célèbre*. Supermarket tabloids and mass-circulation dailies, which usually concentrated on sex, violence, and celebrity gossip, now speculated on the possibility that explosive religious secrets lay among the unpublished Hebrew and Aramaic documents. Why else would they be kept unpublished for so long? And they reportedly contained secrets about the early history of Christianity that the Vatican—or alternatively, the government of Israel—wanted permanently suppressed. *The New York Times, Time,* and *Newsweek* meanwhile pontificated on scholarly ethics, ancient Jewish messianism, and the history of first-century Judea with the same self-important punditry that they used for matters of state.

The public attention, focused brightly on the scholars involved in the scroll story, sparked a series of soap-operalike sensations. After months of sniping and bickering with the rising chorus of protestors (many of whom were Jewish), the chief editor of the Dead Sea Scrolls publication project, an Oxford-trained Harvard professor named John Strugnell, gave an embarrassingly frank interview in 1990 in which he called Judaism a "horrible religion" and proudly defined himself as an "anti-Judaist." In the inevitable public uproar, Strugnell was excoriated from pulpits and in angry editorials, and was soon institutionalized for a severe bout with manic-depression and relieved of his official post. The walls of scholarly privilege had begun to crumble. After forty-five years of control by an official publication team, large numbers of unpublished scroll fragments would soon be made available to all scholars. The Huntington Library in San Marino, California, unilaterally removed all restrictions on a duplicate set of scroll photographs it possessed. Professor Robert Eisenman of California State University at Long Beach, one of the most outspoken critics of the old order, was the first to pore through the precious microfilms. Hershel Shanks, crusading publisher of the *Biblical Archaeology Review,* who had spearheaded the campaign for free access to the scrolls, was hailed in the press and on television as a champion of intellectual freedom. But in the academic community, among the respected scholars who had devoted their lives to the study of the scrolls, the outcome of the struggle was seen as a grave defeat. Shanks and Eisenman were seen as agents of chaos who had threatened the traditional scholarly pecking order. They had dared to challenge the deference that had always been accorded to those privileged few who were the official editors of the scrolls.

Foolishly, and mistakenly, I had never paid much attention to the Dead Sea Scrolls uproar. Whenever an archaeological sensation— like the search for Noah's Ark, the existence of Atlantis, or the Curse of Tutankhamen—suddenly starts turning up in the pages of the supermarket tabloids between UFO sightings and celebrity diets or starts popping up in angry made-for-TV shouting matches, I usually reach for the remote control. So I assumed that the three magic words—Dead Sea Scrolls—had merely become a media prop, just an empty symbol for "ancient" and "mysterious." Everyone seemed to know vaguely what the Dead Sea Scrolls were, but hardly anyone had a clue about what they meant. Most people believed—and still believe—that they had something to do with

Jesus, and almost everyone had gotten the impression that *all* the scrolls have been long suppressed. But none of this had any basis in reality as far as I understood it. So whenever a news story appeared about the "suppression" of the scrolls and the topic came up in casual conversation, I tended to ignore the whole thing.

Some of it was due to hasty personal judgments. I had known Hershel Shanks for more than a decade as an enthusiastic and tireless promoter of his glossy, widely circulated *Biblical Archaeology Review*, and I suspected that this whole scrolls business was, for him, primarily a successful publicity campaign. As far as Robert Eisenman was concerned, I had met him briefly in the mid-1980s, when I was living in Jerusalem, and there was something about the way that Eisenman portrayed himself as a despised outsider that initially rubbed me the wrong way. Eisenman's crusade to liberate the scrolls was later covered in the thickly perfumed pages of *Vanity Fair* and in a nonfiction thriller called *The Dead Sea Scrolls Deception*, a book that touted Eisenman's unorthodox theory of Dead Sea Scrolls origins. When I read through the book's dubious accusations of an Israeli-Vatican conspiracy to suppress the scrolls, I dismissed both it and the value of Eisenman's historical theories. But at the time, with my opinion dulled by the old, conventional story, I didn't realize how Eisenman's critique of the established scrolls scholars was part of a far broader and more powerful challenge to the historical and spiritual authority of the Jewish and Christian religious establishments.

Through 1992, while the national press was making hay out of the Dead Sea Scroll story, Eisenman and a colleague, Michael Wise of the University of Chicago, were hard at work on their own translations and interpretations of fifty long-restricted texts. They gave their book the most unscholarly title *The Dead Sea Scrolls Uncovered*, adding to their transcriptions an implicit dig at the selfishness of the scholars who had kept those texts covered for so long. Eisenman and Wise also added a no-holds-barred commentary that linked the Dead Sea Scrolls to rage, revolution, Jewish nationalism—and to the supposed secret militant roots of early Christianity. Most serious scroll scholars had disdainfully dismissed this radical reinterpretation and had by this time gotten their fill of Eisenman's arrogance, activism, and insolence. The 1992 New York Academy of Science conference on the Dead Sea Scrolls was therefore destined to be the scene of the showdown in which eighteen of the most respected scrolls scholars in Israel, England, and America would try their best to silence or at least humiliate him.

In an official statement signed by the scholars and faxed to newspapers and academic institutions all over the world, the Eisenman-Wise book was branded as an insidious misrepresentation, in its claims that it presented documents that had been "withheld for over thirty-five years." The signatories now angrily claimed that a significant number of the book's transcriptions were rehashes of previous publications or directly plagiarized. The statement went on with a list of damning charges of false claims, dishonesty, deception, and finally, in an ominous tone of High Church orthodoxy, with the accusation that "the volume abounds with errors and imprecisions in the transcription of the Hebrew and Aramaic documents and in translating and interpreting them."

Every now and then, the drowsy boredom of academic conferences is dispelled by moments of high drama. The chairman of the opening session of the 1992 conference, Professor Eric Meyers of Duke University, first read the contents of a letter from Jerusalem explaining the current policy of the Israel Antiquities Authority regarding the use of photographs of unpublished Dead Sea Scrolls fragments and explaining that the Eisenman-Wise book was a clear violation of the rules. Then Professor Lawrence Schiffman of New York University, a tall, black-bearded scholar, the chosen spokesman of the accusers, read a long, passionate essay of indictment, complete with a list of apparent specific instances of plagiarism—with detailed bibliographical citations of each. In one particularly telling example, he even demonstrated how the Eisenman-Wise book reproduced another scholar's handwriting mistake. The verdict seemed already decided; Schiffman's final words were of ringing, outright condemnation, declaring that Eisenman and Wise's behavior was a slight to serious scholars everywhere.

Other statements followed, attempting to counter the charges. Professor James Robinson of the Ancient Biblical Manuscript Center sent in a statement calling for an end to the era of scholarly possessiveness. Professor Norman Golb of the University of Chicago, one of the conference organizers, suggested that the disciplinary charges were just a transparent cover for what amounted to intellectual censorship. Next Michael Wise rose to present a polite and respectful refutation, going over all of the charges against him and Eisenman, one by one. But they all proved to be poor and unconvincing spokesmen for academic rebellion compared to Robert Eisenman. A stocky, combative figure, he had not been invited to sit on the stage with the main participants in the discussion but stepped to the microphone set up in the aisle for comments from the audience. Everyone knew that *he* was the main target, and he rose to meet the challenge, his slight stutter repeatedly breaking through his rage.

"The strangest thing here," Robert Eisenman observed sarcastically and angrily as he gripped the microphone and glared across the faces of the respectable scholars gathered before him, "is that I am always called idiosyncratic and a maverick. They all know very well that I don't read their works. I never read their works because I don't want my brain to be addled, quite frankly. I'm not invited to their conferences, and I don't get their handouts. And when I submit my papers to them, they don't publish them. So ethics or whatever," he continued with pointed, angry irony, "to hear that I have borrowed other people's work *staggers* me. Everybody in this room, everybody in the world knows that my theories don't resemble anyone's theories. I don't borrow from anybody and that is the most preposterous accusation. You see, if you are going to dream up an accusation, you couldn't dream up a falser one, as far as I am concerned."

Eisenman then spoke with unembarrassed pride, not shame, of his recent book. "What is so thrilling to me personally," he insisted, "is to get to the point of being first out there with an inter-pretation. That's what I really loved about this volume; for the first time we were going to be able to comment first. Because if you have been following my ideas, you know that I have been saying all along that an *editio princeps*—an official edition—also subtly slides in an official interpretation that to a docile and unsuspecting pub-lic becomes orthodoxy. And I have said that the reason I par-ticipated in the facsimile edition"—he noted, referring to his earlier publication with Shanks and Robinson of scroll photo-graphs without official authorization—"was to level the playing field, to get away from the official interpretations of the texts—to let a thousand voices sing. So when this chance came to be out there first with the fifty best documents from the unpublished cor-pus—something like that is how we privately described the kinds of things we were doing. Frankly, I felt that most of that material was unpublished. I was really astonished by Michael's publication notes. I thought he was very generous there. He gave credit beyond what any ordinary mortal should be called upon to do."

Eisenman delighted in showing his impatience with the kinds of footnotes and attributions that so many mediocre scholars con-fuse with scholarship. For him, the importance of the Dead Sea Scrolls was earthshaking, revolutionary, not just a matter of re-spectfully reproducing the main conclusions of others, with the addition perhaps of a newly dotted "i" or a newly crossed "t." What Eisenman was suggesting was both blasphemous and revolu-tionary: that both Christianity and Judaism as we now know them are fraudulent debasements of an earlier messianic faith. He was convinced that both Christianity and Rabbinic Judaism had sur-vived and gained adherents primarily because they were systemati-cally stripped of all the teachings of the earlier Jewish messianic movement that questioned or threatened the status quo. Put sim-ply, Eisenman was asking the world to look back and see that our understanding of the early history of Judaism and Christianity was a calculated misrepresentation, fostered and disseminated by priests and rabbis willing to ensure their own survival through smarmy accommodation or even conspiracy with the powers that be. The Dead Sea Scrolls, miraculously discovered after 2,000 years, offered modern scholars direct evidence of the events of New Testament times, untouched by the bonfires of the Inquisition or the ecclesiastical censor's pen. Yet the scholars failed to see what Eisenman did. "What was staring them in the face," he later insisted to me, "was the actual, authentic messianic literature of Palestine."

His voice tightened and his tone grew more angry. "I never looked at anyone's work. I don't *care* about these people's work. I do not look at it in order to get inspiration. I go to the first sources. I'm interested in the principal sources. I consider Professor Schiffman's attack—I consider that a complete slander. He knows that very well."

Yet Eisenman wanted to get to the heart of the matter, to move from a discussion of mere bibliographical matters to a discussion of religious history. For he was convinced that the fifty documents he and Wise had published provided the indisputable evidence that the people of Qumran were the earliest "Christians"; that the scrolls represented the historical reality of a violent first-century nationalistic messianism that was subsequently systematically suppressed in the writings of the Church Fathers and by the sages of Rabbinic Judaism. One of the texts he and Wise had published was a fragment of Hebrew poetry, listed officially as 4Q285. The fragmentary text, only slightly bigger than a large postage stamp, referred to a messianic redeemer, descended, like Jesus, from the Davidic line.

Eisenman and Wise had reconstructed the broken text to suggest that this messianic figure was distinguished by his suffering, "pierced," and ultimately slain by his enemies. When reported in *The New York Times*, this discovery caused a public sensation, for it was seen as the missing link between Judaism and Christianity. Some of the most prominent mainline scholars, adamant in their insistence that the Dead Sea sect and Christianity were quite different, convened a special seminar at Oxford and concluded that Eisenman and Wise were in error: The text should be read that the Davidic Messiah would *kill*, rather than be killed by, his enemies. Eisenman, of course, realized that few scholars supported his identification of a Jesus-like character in the scrolls, but he was gratified that serious debate about this long-secret text had been provoked. "You know, the public knows we found the Pierced Messiah text," he told his accusers. "Whether we interpreted it right or not isn't the point."

Eisenman glared silently at a heckler in the audience and then continued as if nothing had happened. "So we found the Pierced Messiah text. Everybody knows that, we found the Messiah of Heaven and Earth text. I was the first one to publish the Qahat text . . . We also found those extra passages in the Genesis Florilegium and reconstructed a beautiful text superior to the Oxford reconstruction of it . . . We have been finding these texts all along. We reconstructed a beautiful text called the Children of Yesha, the Children of Salvation text. We found that marvelous masturbation text. We didn't need anyone's help in finding the two copies of the last column of the Damascus Document, and we developed it with our own translation. Now I submit to you if we could do all that, do you think we needed to rely on these people's work for these other things? I submit we couldn't have needed to rely, we could do it ourselves. As far as I am aware, we did do it ourselves."

Over and over in the coming year, I would hear from Eisenman his belief that the scholarly establishment was out to get him—out to destroy his credibility and the power of his ideas. He put it succinctly in his closing statement: "Our last point is about whether this has to do with transcriptions or scholarship, or whether it has to do with an old establishment attempting to reassert control over the field again to go back to the old situation of official editions." Comparing the viciousness of the attacks against him to other cases of disputed authorship in scroll studies, he concluded that the animosity arose primarily against "the new translations and the new interpretations, the new spin that we—Professor Wise with his own hypothesis, and me, with the Jewish-Christian one—are giving these things."

"We got out there first with it and that infuriates a lot of people. They feel that by discrediting us, they discredit our interpretations. I submit that it won't work. The game is up, Mr. Schiffman. Even though you have joined the official team, you remember what you were termed according to my view of you in the *Vanity Fair* article. And you told me you didn't know what a 'running dog' was. In any case, I submit that the game is up, that there are no more official editions, no more teams. What we have is free competition and free thinking." Eisenman finally ended his passionate defense of the serious charges against him. "And that's where we should have been in the first place."

In the lobby of the auditorium, on the opening day of the conference, I had approached Robert Eisenman directly. He was standing alone while the other scholars chatted in small groups. To tell the truth, even though I had been impressed with his presentation and wanted to talk with him further, I felt uncomfortable as I stood with him in the small outer lobby, fearing that the more respectable scholars would assume that I had gone over to the enemy. I had learned all too well in earlier interviews of the depth and the breadth of the hostility to Eisenman; bringing up his name without the requisite disavowal was usually regarded as a reason for suspicion or a symptom of emotional distress. Eisenman had been publicly accused of being just a "minor" scholar— which was little more than an expression of disdain for his scholarly affiliation, California State University at Long Beach. It was certainly not based on a serous evaluation of his ideas. The eloquence with which he had delivered his defense against the charges of plagiarism and his utter unconcern with currying other scholars' approval led me to see almost immediately that this was a personality I could not afford to neglect. So we struck up a conversation. We set a time to get together and, with the clear intimation that I should keep the meeting quiet, he handed me a card with the name and address of his West Side hotel.

I had expected Eisenman to be relatively tight-lipped about his legal and professional problems, but he readily opened up the details of his earlier career to me. He had placed the two big volumes of unauthorized scroll photos on prominent display on the coffee table of his hotel suite. Utterly uncontrite and even proud of his role in breaking the scroll monopoly, he launched into a long autobiographical monologue. I had previously only known him from a distance, but now I got a glimpse of his personality—as the younger brother of the internationally acclaimed architect Peter Eisenman, who had apparently always received far more attention than he. Intellectually, Robert Eisenman was hard to characterize. His Columbia Ph.D. was not in biblical literature or history, but in Islamic law. He had previously studied Hebrew and Near Eastern history at New York University, and after a period of post-doctoral study in Israel, he had become something of an academic jack-of-all-trades. Yet there was something more than a younger son's craving for attention or a marginal scholar's self-promotion in his recounting of his own intellectual achievements and deepening interest in the Dead Sea Scrolls.

As we walked out into a blustery December night and stopped for dinner at an ominously empty Indian restaurant on Columbus Avenue, Eisenman described the genesis of his unique scroll theories with angry clarity. His historical theories required a complete mental shift of gears. I had come to New York with the highest regard for the scholars that Eisenman had been relentlessly attacking and had been convinced that Eisenman was nothing more than a troublemaking gadfly. Yet as we talked, I recognized how Eisenman honed in precisely on the dubious assumptions, shaky logic, simplistic readings of ancient sources, and pseudo-scientific dating methods for handwriting that supported the whole superstructure of Qumran research. In the face of professional ostracism, he had spoken with conviction, refusing to be humbled. He showed that he had not the slightest interest in stealing the work of others, and while others waffled or equivocated, he had maintained his integrity.

Through the rest of the week, I sat impatiently and with increasing boredom listening to what the respectable scholars had to say. The same old arguments were put forward placing the origin of the sect in the context of anti-Hasmonean protest, and declaring that the Qumranic idea of the messiah was quite different from that of Christianity. Except for Eisenman's paper (which was greeted with titters) and Wise's paper (which was overshadowed by his forced statement of contrition), few of the papers addressed the scrolls' significance for understanding first-century Judean society as it hurtled toward its own apocalyptic war. And by the end of the conference, Eisenman's passionate conviction that our society's conventional ideas about the origins of Christianity and Rabbinic Judaism were fictional, self-serving fables—and that many of the most prominent scroll scholars were mere lackeys for the establishment—finally began to make sense to me.

In the chapters that follow I will try to try to reconstruct the history of Dead Sea Scroll interpretation and focus on the crucial moments when subtle preconceptions and conventional religious sensibilities—both Jewish and Christian—clouded the conclusions of mainstream scholarship. It is a story far more gripping than any Vatican conspiracy dreamed up by the tabloids and far more enlightening than the rehash of conventional scholarship that is dished up warmed-over in the religion sections of *Time* and *Newsweek* and in the science section of *The New York Times*. The study of the Dead Sea Scrolls is and has always been neither theology nor science but an exercise in almost pure religious metaphor. One merely had to scan the audience of scholars assembled at the New York conference to see that there were virtually no sociologists, philosophers, or social critics among them. Their chief qualifications for heaping disdain upon Eisenman and his theories was their vastly superior skill at analyzing biblical Hebrew grammar or parsing Aramaic verbs. Certainly they could chastise Eisenman and Wise for errors of transcription and perhaps even for utilizing the literal decipherments of others, but what of the larger significance of those documents? What more did these respectable and respectful academics know of the rage of the apocalyptic outsiders who wrote the scrolls, who withdrew from a society that had betrayed them and spent the rest of their days dreaming and scheming in quiet anticipation of the divine wrath that would rain down upon their enemies at the End of Days?

*   *   *

The Way in the Wilderness has endured through the ages as a viable, if desperate, avenue of political action—appearing again and again as the central hope of the displaced, the dispossessed, the homeless, and those with nothing to lose. Through the ages, peasants have left the lord and the manor to build New Jerusalems in waste places; pietists and refugees have abandoned all that is familiar; crusaders, pioneers, and cultists have departed from lives of not-so-quiet desperation to conquer new worlds and construct for themselves their own City on the Hill. Rarely have these exiles succeeded in their expectations, for the Way in the Wilderness must eventually lead to a fateful choice between submission or death.

The frontier and desolate places chosen by such voluntary exiles are sometimes the birthplace of powerful spiritual insights that precariously strike the balance between their violent, rage-filled nightmares and their utopian dreams. Those who withdraw from the society of power and greed and ambition see redemption as the result of righteousness and human effort. Yet the grim satisfaction of the utopian in seeing the left-behind world decay and crumble can never completely square itself with the innocent piety of communal greenhouses, workshops, and living quarters. They too represent a vestige of the earthly order that must—by the heartless calculation of the apocalyptic—be destroyed. This paradox of construction and destruction poised on the knife edge is the heart of the message of the scrolls. Again and again, the overwhelming feelings of oppression imposed by arriving empires that change the order of life and culture and move people around like chess pieces brings forth those groups who will make a way for themselves in the wilderness.

The Dead Sea Scrolls are the voice of some of those who would not submit to the inevitability of Roman power—and by extension, who would not submit to a system in which peoples were treated as objects, natural resources, or available draft animals, whose only value was to keep the empire's coffers full. As usual, great expense was lavished on the public monuments to the inevitability of this imperial order, and they are the monuments so beloved of tourists to Israel even today. At Caesarea by the sea, the seat of the governors of Palestine, a massive restoration project is underway to link the ancient amphitheater with the other ancient temples and warehouses of Herod's harbor; at Beth Shean (ancient Scythopolis) in the northern Jordan Valley, the columns and the statues of the forum are being erected once more at the behest of the Ministry of Tourism and the delight of the local labor exchange. And beneath the modern courtyards and villas of the Jewish Quarter of the Old City of Jerusalem, the residences of the last High Priests of Jerusalem have been lovingly restored to give visitors a glimpse of their splendor and elegance.

But where are the archaeological monuments to the passion and rage of the national uprisings against the Romans? Where can one go in Israel to see an archaeological monument that makes some sense of the resentment of people whose way of life was disrupted by the sweeping changes in economy and culture—and by the accumulation of vast estates worked by tenant farmers and dedicated to the profit of others, others who revelled in the ways of Greece and Rome? Even at the sites of Masada and the stronghold of Gamla, where archaeologists have been able to pinpoint the grisly evidence of death and destruction that marked an end to the rebellion, the larger context for the sacred rage and willingness to fight the Romans to the death remains undiscovered. How do the pieces of the archaeological puzzle fit together? How can a connection be made between Gamla and the Romanized city of Sepphoris in the Galilee with its theater and wealthy residences, between Masada with its simple synagogue and Caesarea with its massive temple to the deified Emperor Augustus? This was more than pure religious conflict: It was the collision of two worlds. The Roman triumph over the Jewish rebels in 70 C.E. and again in 135 marked the permanent establishment of a system of exploitation which could not tolerate the existence of any group that would refuse to accept its logic or even its inevitability.

Both Christianity and Judaism arose in this moment of triumph for the forces of Roman order, and we are today all heirs, for better or for worse, to the cultural surrender and spiritual accommodation that the establishment of those religions signified. Maybe we cannot see what went on in the Roman province of Judea because we live today in a world of ever-intensifying and expanding industrial development that ultimately cannot tolerate the existence of what we brand as primitive or backward without transforming it into a quaint curiosity or wiping it out. Both Rabbinic Judaism and Christianity abandoned the violent passion of the earlier messianic movements of Judea; they abandoned the hope that all must physically and completely separate themselves from the forces of Darkness and await the coming Judgment Day.

The scrolls' visions, like those of latter-day apocalyptists Jim Jones and David Koresh, of Islamic jihad and West Bank Kahanists, can become pornographies of violence, acted out with a horrifying relish for blood. Alternatively, these visions can become the starting point for more mystical hallucinations and otherworldly journeys; a way in the alienated wilderness of the psyche of the individual. In their unrelenting apocalyptic message, the scrolls give a voice to a group that felt dispossessed and disenfranchised in a world turned upside down. They give voice to a rage against invaders and contempt for collaborators interested only in personal gain. They wrap their community in a defensive cocoon of national laws and traditions. They express the hope for a day when this upside-down world will be righted, when the wicked will suffer for their wickedness, and when the Poor will be recognized as the Elect of God. The Way in the Wilderness is a declaration of war against the settled order, a direct challenge to the powers-that-be.

The struggle for the Dead Sea Scrolls has stakes that are enormous. It can challenge some of our society's deepest and most cherished religious understandings; it calls into question the right of academic specialists to set our society's intellectual agenda; and it proposes a disturbing and radical revision of our understanding of the history of both Judaism and Christianity. Yet for more than forty-five years, the Dead Sea Scrolls have been fought over by many jealous claimants, each with a view of the texts' historical or religious significance that they believed was the definitive one.

This conflict of interpretations has fueled a bitter struggle for exclusive intellectual control and physical possession, in which the scrolls have become little more than the stage props for the public disputes of opposing political and religious ideologies. Since their composition more than two thousand years ago by the pious Sons of Zadok, the scrolls' message has been repeatedly twisted, reframed, and reinterpreted by others. And in that sense, the Dead Sea Scrolls have been stolen again and again.

2
DISCOVERY
AT QUMRAN

There is something mysterious and a bit unsettling to outsiders about the hot and barren coast of the Dead Sea. Even in winter, the midday heat there can be oppressive, and when the wind dies down, an unpleasant, sulphurous smell from the Dead Sea's bitter waters hangs in the air. Away from the main road, the silence is eerie, with craggy brown limestone cliffs baking under a relentless sun and a brilliant, cloudless sky. Down by the greasy, gray water and the muddy, black beaches, there is hardly a sign of any vegetation, except for the tough old thorns among the rocks and the thickets of reeds that clog the few fresh water springs.

This is the surreal stage on which some of the most important scenes of the Dead Sea Scroll drama were enacted. From a single small cave in the cliffside came the first seven ancient rolls of leather, preserved by this region's extraordinary aridity. At the foot of the cliffs on a white chalk cliff overlooking the seashore, at a site called Khirbet Qumran, the Dominican archaeologists uncovered what they believed to be the meeting rooms and workshops of the Essene settlement. And over the years many other caves have been discovered in the vicinity of Qumran, containing the fragmentary remnants of the religious literature, rule books, psalms, and even prophetic interpretation of a group of radical, rage-filled Jews who awaited the arrival of the Anointed of God precisely in the period and within hiking distance of the places where John the Baptist proclaimed the imminence of redemption and of the city where Jesus of Nazareth preached to his disciples and was crucified.

Though you can now drive to Qumran from Jerusalem in a rented car or cruise in air-conditioned, tourist-coach comfort, this region, with its salt-encrusted tablelands, floodwashed gullies, towering limestone cliffs, and dark, jagged caverns, has long been perceived by western travelers, pilgrims, and explorers through the hazy lens of biblical myth. It was not far from here, according to the Book of Genesis, that the people of Sodom and Gomorrah were incinerated by fire and brimstone. Only a few miles to the north, according to the Book of Joshua, the walls of Jericho supposedly toppled from the Israelites' loud trumpet blasts as they began their campaign to drive out the Canaanites and conquer their Promised Land. And it was in this rugged region that David and his band of renegades escaped from the wrath of King Saul.

The scrolls have absorbed some of this aura of legend; over the years, the circumstances and even the date of the original discovery have become the subjects of colorful fables. That's why it's so important in any examination of the affair of the Dead Sea Scrolls to start at the beginning—at the moment of discovery. And while dismantling the tall tales of an innocent bedouin boy, a Bethlehem shoemaker, and a Syrian archbishop may be simple, it is far more difficult to understand what really went on. Most of the traditional stories can be shown to be false, inaccurate, or outright deceptions. And when you peel back the layers of misrepresentation and cultural misunderstanding, you discover that the saga of the Dead Sea Scrolls, as conveyed to the public, consists, like the biblical stories themselves, of a small historical kernel and a heaping helping of self-serving ideology.

For the sake of the historical record—and in the interest of showing how thoroughly the Dead Sea Scrolls story has been saturated with subtle political and religious messages—it is important to remember that the traditional version of the discovery is little more than an Arabian Nights fairy tale. The dates and even the main characters have been so stripped of their historical identities and context that they would not seem out of place in a bedtime storybook. I do not mean to single out any particular retelling of the discovery story because *all* of the most widely read authors of the 1950s—Burrows, Allegro, Milik, Cross, Wilson, and Yadin— betray in their narrative a subtle condescension toward both the intelligence and the motives of the bedouin.

As the standard story goes, a single bedouin boy (sometimes two) was wandering with his mixed flock of sheep and goats some distance north of the fresh water spring of Ain Feshkhah, when, noticing that one of the animals had strayed from the others, he idly tossed a rock into the small opening of a nearby cave. "Instead of the expected smack of rock against rock," wrote the scholar Frank Moore Cross—with a vividness of prose that is conspicuously absent from his descriptions of the explorations of Western schol- ars—"he heard a shattering sound. He was frightened and fled. Later, presumably when the fear of *jinn* or hyenas finally gave way to the lure of buried gold, he and his companion Ahmed Mu- hammed returned and crept into the cave and found decaying rolls of leather in one of a number of strange, elongated jars em- bedded in the floor of the cave." This and the other stories go on to relate a comedy of errors by which the ancient scrolls, plucked from their ancient hiding place by the innocent shepherd, finally made their way through a series of middlemen and shady antiqui- ties dealers into the hands of competent archaeologists.

Most of the major actors in the opening acts of the Dead Sea Scrolls drama are dead, so to find out anything novel you have to rely on faded and often confused memories of aged priests, clerks, and scholars who have spent the last forty-five years embellishing the importance of their peripheral roles. None of the actual dis- coverers is now living, and the way of life of the Taamireh (usually pronounced Ta-AM-ra) tribe is now almost totally changed. Nowa- days most of the Taamireh have ended their wanderings and set-

tled down in clusters of low stone houses on the southeastern outskirts of Bethlehem.

In the cruel, demeaning jibes of outsiders, it is often said that
each of the larger houses in the Taamireh neighborhood represents the proceeds from the sale of a scroll. But today the days of
scroll hunting are long over, and it is not easy for a stranger to pick
out a Taamireh man from the rest of the population in Bethlehem. While many of the Taamireh women still wear traditional
bedouin dresses and appear at the weekly open-air market to sell
fresh produce, the men of the tribe now work mostly in construction, local factories, and stores. Only a few tribal members still
wander toward the Dead Sea with their sheep and goat herds. And
as these few shepherds and their flocks walk along the side of the
highway, sporadically whipped by the exhaust gusts of the passing
air-conditioned tour buses on their way to Masada or the health
spas near En-Geddi, they represent the last vestiges of a lifestyle
that had gone on here for hundreds of years.

Despite the fact that many chroniclers (among them, Burrows, Milik, and Wilson) have placed the discovery of the first
group of scrolls at Qumran in the spring or summer of 1947, the
actual date was apparently several months before that. The sea-
sonal movements of the Taamireh tribe toward the Dead Sea region at that time were not haphazard but carefully synchronized
with the needs of their flocks. In the summer dry season, they
would pitch their camps on the outskirts of Bethlehem in the hill
country, where they could sell mutton, wool, and milk to the
townsmen, and graze their flocks in the stubble of the newly har-
vested fields. In the winter, when the cold rains returned, members of the tribe would drive the flocks eastward down to the
warmth of the Jordan Valley and the shores of the Dead Sea. Thus
it is probable that the discovery of the scrolls took place in the
winter, or more precisely, November or December of 1946.

And the discovery was not due to the miraculous luck of a
single lonely bedouin shepherd boy, but to the cooperation of
three Taamireh cousins: Khalil Musa and Juma'a Muhammed

Khalil were grown men, and Muhammed Ahmed el-Hamed (who went by the colorful nickname *edh-Dhib*, "the Wolf") was still a teenager. According to repeated interviews conducted by the American scholar John Trever in the early 1960s, the three had gone down to the Dead Sea shore with their flocks, and while wandering with the sheep and goats along the foot of the steep limestone ridges Juma'a Muhammed noticed a small opening in the cliff face, tossed in a stone, and heard the sound of breaking pottery.

This was not the act of a bored shepherd but of an experienced hunter for antiquities. Juma'a, like many other members of his tribe, knew exactly what he was looking for when it came to ancient artifacts, long before the winter of 1946. Even a quick glance at the reports of the early archaeologists working in this region shows that the name of the Taamireh comes up again and again. Over the years the Taamireh had proved far more skillful, thorough, and daring in finding ancient artifacts in the ravines and caves of the Dead Sea region than the Western archaeologists who lived (and still live) with the conceit that their motives are somehow more idealistic and less self-serving than those of the bedouin.

So as far as archaeology was concerned, the Taamireh were, by the late 1940s, not scavengers but entrepreneurs. As early as the 1930s, the Taamireh had begun to offer for sale ancient coins and pottery to the Jewish workers at the potash plant at the northern end of the Dead Sea. For a few more piastres they were willing to take the Jewish workers to see caves that contained "books from the time of your kings." (That second offer was never accepted, as far as I know). Archaeological artifacts had clearly become for the Taamireh a welcome new source of sustenance in otherwise barren territory. Some of the tribe members also worked as hired laborers for the French consul—and noted prehistorian—Rene Neuville in his explorations of the caves of Wadi Khareitun southeast of Bethlehem. And because Neuville was always ready to purchase artifacts that the Taamireh had found at other locations, they began applying fairly systematic techniques of excavation for their own benefit, techniques not far below the technical standards of some of the university-trained archaeologists of those days. In at least one case of enterprising excavation, a group of the Taamireh had carefully removed the earth from a cave layer by layer—with one of the diggers maintaining a notebook with records of which soil layers contained the richest concentrations of artifacts.

Thus when Juma'a heard the sound of breaking pottery in the cave to the north of Ain Feshkhah, he probably had a fairly good idea of what he had found. But by the time he had summoned his cousins to help boost him up to the high, narrow cave entrance, darkness was falling. And the next day, the three men had to leave the immediate area to water their flocks at the spring of Ain Feshkhah, about two miles to the south. It was only two days later that one of the three—the teenager Muhammed edh-Dhib—returned to the cave and found not the usual small pottery vessels but a number of tall jars with covers. He opened at least two of them and took out three brittle leather rolls, some of them wrapped in linen, which scholars would later identify as the Habakkuk Commentary, the Community Rule, and the Great Isaiah Scroll.

According to their later recollections, Juma'a and Khalil Musa were angry at edh-Dhib for going back to the cave without them, and they claimed the scrolls for themselves. They also recalled that they stashed the manuscripts away in a sack and left it hanging on a tent pole in the Taamireh camp for several weeks. But Juma'a and Khalil clearly considered these scrolls to be worth something; had they been as bumpkinish as they are usually depicted, they would simply have thrown the dirty old scrolls away. But on their next trip to Bethlehem, they brought the scrolls to Ibrahim Ijha, a carpenter and woodworker, who occasionally dealt in antiquities. While it is easy enough to flatter ourselves that the value of the scrolls should have been evident to any well-educated person, Ijha was justifiably skeptical about the find. The fact is that even later, after the scrolls were shown to several supposed experts, they were dismissed as either tattered modern Torah scrolls or worthless forgeries.

These manuscripts were not, after all, the usual saleable oil lamps, jars, coins, or jewelry that found a ready market among the pilgrims and tourists who came to visit the Church of the Nativity. Besides, they were written in Hebrew and tensions in Palestine between Arabs and Jews were rising. When Ijha brought the bedouins' scrolls for an appraisal by one of Bethlehem's most experienced antiquities dealers, Feidi al-Alami, he received a stern warning that the bedouin had probably stolen them from a synagogue and that he had better get rid of them before he got into serious trouble with the authorities. That, too, could have been the end of the matter, but when Juma'a came back to Ijha's shop about a month later, in April, he retrieved the unwanted scrolls, indignantly dismissed the frightened shopkeeper's warning, and made his way to Bethlehem's open-air market place.

That Bethlehem market is even today still bustling with local shoppers. Its merchandise varies widely, from old furniture and appliances to old clothing, squawking chickens, and fresh vegetables. And on that particular day in April 1947, the market also featured three of the original Dead Sea Scrolls. The next walk-on part in the on-going drama was played by a man named George Isaiah (Shaya, as he was known in Arabic), who would prove to be as important a figure in the story as any Harvard professor or Israeli general. Shaya, a member of the Syrian Orthodox community of Jerusalem, made his living selling shoes, cloaks, and other dry goods to the Taamireh and the other bedouin tribes in the Bethlehem area. In the marketplace, Shaya met Juma'a (with whom he had done business) and he learned of Juma'a's discovery. Shaya, too, was convinced that the scrolls might be worth something, and he persuaded Juma'a to go with him to the shop of another member of the Syrian Orthodox community—a cobbler named Khalil Iskander Shahin, whom everyone knew simply as "Kando."

It is another common misconception that the bedouin brought the scrolls to Kando because they stupidly assumed that the leather rolls might be useful to a cobbler as raw material for insoles or sandal straps. That is just another Dead Sea Scrolls fable, for anyone who has seen the scrolls or read the early descriptions of their brittleness must know that this is a ridiculous claim. Kando, though uncertain of the scrolls' value, was willing to take a calculated business risk. And he would grow rich beyond his wildest dreams on account of that decision. Proposing to act as an agent (for a 33 percent commission), Kando took the scrolls and gave Juma'a and Musa Khalil a cash advance of five Palestine pounds—about $20—as a sign of good faith. Kando had an idea of someone who might be interested: Mar Athanasius Yeshue Samuel, the Jerusalem Syrian Orthodox community's bright, ambitious, and charismatic forty-year-old archbishop, who was fascinated by ancient manuscripts.

It is important to stress that this was not the first time that such documents were discovered, even from caves in the immediate region of the Dead Sea shore. I have already mentioned the rumored discoveries of "ancient books" by the Taamireh bedouin as early as the 1930s, but the recorded discoveries of ancient documents in this region go back many centuries before that. The Church Father and biblical scholar Origen, who visited Palestine in the early third century C.E., reported the discovery of an ancient manuscript "together with other Hebrew and Greek books in a jar near Jericho." Some six hundred years later, around 800, Timotheus, the Nestorian Patriarch of Seleucia, reported even more details about a subsequent manuscript discovery, the circumstances of which uncannily foreshadow those of the discovery of the Dead Sea Scrolls.

"We have learned from trustworthy Jews," wrote Timotheus to a friend and colleague, Sergius, the archbishop of Elam in Mesopotamia, "that some books were found some years ago in a rock dwelling near Jericho. The story was that a dog belonging to an Arab out hunting, while following game, went into a cave and did not come out again; its owner went after it and found a chamber in the rock containing many books. The hunter went off to

Jerusalem and told his story to the Jews, who came out in great numbers and found books of the Old Testament and others in Hebrew script; and, since there was a scholar well read in literature among them, I asked him about many passages quoted in our New Testament as coming from the Old Testament but found nowhere in it, neither in copies amongst the Jews nor in those amongst Christians. He said: 'they are there and can be found in the books discovered there.' "

That was an astounding suggestion—that there had been in antiquity a Hebrew scriptural tradition quite different from that of the canonical Old Testament. From the next century, around 950 C.E., came more information about newfound manuscripts. Yakub al-Qirqasani, a historian of the breakaway Jewish sect of the Karaites, briefly described the doctrines of a Jewish group he called the *Maghariyah,* the "cave people," because their doctrines (which he described between his accounts of the beliefs of the Sadducees and the early Christians) were contained in ancient books that they had hidden in a cave. But the discoveries apparently stopped sometime in the Middle Ages. By the nineteenth century, all knowledge that the caves of that hot and forbidding area contained ancient manuscripts was lost to all—except perhaps to the local bedouin.

If the discovery of the Dead Sea Scrolls would prove in some respects to be a comedy of errors, the Shapira Affair was a tragedy. In 1882, a Jerusalem antiquities dealer named Moses Wilhelm Shapira appeared suddenly and proudly in London, claiming that he had come into possession of ancient manuscript fragments from the Book of Deuteronomy that had been found in a cave by bedouin near the eastern shore of the Dead Sea. While the British Museum initially agreed to purchase the "World's Oldest Bible" for the astounding sum of a million pounds sterling, Shapira's Deuteronomy fragments were eventually branded as cunning forgeries and completely discredited. In the face of the public humiliation, Moses Shapira committed suicide.

Today, when you walk along Christian Street in the Old City of Jerusalem through the hanging forests of bedouin dresses, keffiyehs, and T-shirts, past the stacked pyramids of enameled metal ashtrays and mass-produced pottery, it is not easy to find the small shop—really just a two-roomed cell overlooking the Pool of Hezekiah—from which Shapira sold fine antiquities to both museums and wealthy tourists, and which became a shuttered, notorious landmark after his death. The story of his discovery of the ancient manuscripts rings strangely true in light of the later Dead Sea Scroll story, which, of course, was not to occur for another sixty-four years. According to Shapira's published accounts, he was informed that a bedouin had by chance discovered blackened strips of parchment wrapped in cloth when he happened to take shelter in a cave near the outlet of the Wadi Mujib on the eastern shore of the Dead Sea. Shapira was clearly intrigued by this story and, in the course of a series of secret meetings with the bedouin, he purchased fifteen of the manuscript fragments. The text they bore was a previously unknown version of the last speech of Moses on Mount Nebo and a variant form of the Ten Commandments. They differed dramatically from the canonical version in the Book of Deuteronomy in that they were shortened, rearranged, and interwoven with quotations from other biblical books.

To be honest, there is much that is still mysterious about Shapira's manuscript fragments. Their whereabouts today are unknown (some accounts say they were destroyed in a fire in the home of a collector who had acquired them), and the photographs taken at the time show only black leather with no letters visible. A drawing of the text made at the British Museum shows archaic Hebrew characters that look like they had been haltingly copied from a stone-carved inscription rather than flowing from a scribe's experienced pen. However, that might have more to do with the draftspersons at the British Museum, for, in the 1880s, the collections were filled with stone inscriptions and no truly ancient Hebrew manuscripts were known. And the fact was that Shapira had been involved in the sale of forgeries before. But what was really at stake in the whole Shapira affair went far beyond mere paleography or the suspicion of a Jewish antiquities dealer's motives. The idea that the text of the Bible was fluid and not based directly and unerringly on God's revelation was an insult to many scholars' deepest religious faith.

Although it is perfectly clear that Shapira's manuscripts were not as old as he claimed them to be—around 850 B.C.E. was the date that he estimated—the discovery of the Dead Sea Scrolls has, as we shall see, allowed another possibility to surface. The use of archaic Hebrew letters came to be a form of patriotic expression at the time of the Maccabean kings, and later during the Jewish Revolts against Rome. And at the same time there was a wide range of religious literature circulating among the Jewish population, in which a free rewriting of the Bible was regarded as a sign of divine revelation, not heresy. But all these insights lay far in the future, and before the deal with the British Museum could be consummated Shapira was condemned by an imperious French scholar named Charles Clermont-Ganneau, and soon branded as nothing more than a sly Jew in the popular press. For him the shame was unbearable and, driven to destitution in an unsuccessful campaign to prove that the scroll fragments were genuine, he took his own life. That is an act that seems out of character for a schemer just out for money and fame.

Had poor Shapira lived in the twentieth century, his fate might have been different. But then, who can be sure? When Archbishop Samuel offered his scrolls for inspection to the scholars and experts, several of them warned him that his documents were probably forgeries and that the whole matter could turn out to be just another Shapira affair. Yet the intellectual atmosphere and political context of *this* manuscript discovery was very different from that of the nineteenth century. The reality of textual evolution had caught on in biblical studies. Scholars paid as much attention to the details of letter forms as they did to the literary contents. And most important of all, the political situation in Palestine was moving toward a situation where tangible mementos of the Jewish past would possess a powerful emotional impact. Whether Shapira's earlier discoveries were genuine is not the real question. The real question is: Would the Dead Sea Scrolls found by the bedouin and purchased by Archbishop Samuel ever have come to the world's attention if the imperious skepticism of the early scholars had prevailed?

Like every other part of the landscape of the Dead Sea Scrolls story, the appearance of St. Mark's Monastery in the Old City of Jerusalem has been changed by time, war, and urban development. But it is still possible to follow the path that Kando and George Shaya took to show the scrolls to Archbishop Samuel. Winding your way down a narrow, stepped street in the Armenian Quarter in the direction of the Jewish Quarter, you finally reach a sharp leftward angle, where, tucked inconspicuously into the corner is a medieval stone gateway surmounted by a garish modern mosaic of St. Mark. The electric doorbell beside the heavy metal door summons one of the deacons, who opens the door slowly and suspiciously. Few tourists now come to visit the church, the library, or even the underground room which Syrian tradition believes was the scene of the Last Supper. For the congregation of St. Mark's is the last bastion of a dwindling community that finds itself surrounded and besieged by strangers on all sides.

The living quarters for the priests and the residence of the archbishop are located up a steep stairway from the entrance courtyard; the church sanctuary, with its icons, elaborate altarpiece, and ancient Syriac inscriptions is directly ahead. There are today few parishioners to share in the worship; since 1948 most of the Jerusalem Syrian Orthodox community has gone off to find new homes and livelihoods in Canada and the United States. Yet St. Mark's continued existence, though flickering like the candles on the altar, represents a living link to the earliest days of Christianity. Not only is the church built on one of the traditional sites of the Last Supper (and possibly also of the meeting place of the Council of Jerusalem, presided over by James the Just, the brother of Jesus), but the Syrian Orthodox community itself traces its origins back to the original Christian community founded in Antioch by St. Paul.

The complex fifth-century C.E. theological disputes about the human and divine nature of the person of Christ that led to the eventual secession of the Syrian Orthodox Church from the Byzantine Church (in the sixth century under Jacob Baradaeus) are convoluted and hard to follow for outsiders; suffice it to say that the Syrians have always considered themselves to be the only true keepers of the Christian flame. The language of their liturgy is Syriac—a form of Aramaic that is probably close to that spoken by Jesus and his disciples—and the Syrian Orthodox priesthood prides itself in erudition when it comes to the subtleties of ancient doctrine as revealed in each monastery's large collection of ancient Syriac manuscripts. Though we have become used to equating sound scholarship with accredited universities and formalized doctoral dissertations, there is no reason naturally to assume that some junior professor in a department of religion is fundamentally more perceptive about ancient texts than a bright young Syrian Orthodox priest.

Athanasius Yeshue Samuel, who had come to Jerusalem as a child with his mother from northern Syria in 1920, was one such priestly scholar. Soon after entering the church, he was assigned to the library at St. Mark's, and his skill in handling, reading, and identifying ancient documents was so good that in 1939 he was dispatched by his archbishop to accompany an English scholar, Boyd Alexander, in search of ancient Syriac manuscripts in the library of St. Catherine's Monastery in Sinai. So there is no reason to portray Samuel—as some popular accounts of the scroll story attempt to—as a sly and calculating figure, interested only in the money he believed the scrolls would bring. Though appointed Syrian archbishop of Jerusalem at the relatively young age of forty in the previous December and saddled with many new responsibilities, Archbishop Samuel, with his raven-black beard and his infectious enthusiasm, was honestly fascinated by the rolls of inscribed leather that his parishioners Kando and George Shaya brought him soon after Holy Week 1947. Immediately noting that the parchment of the scrolls was far more brittle than that of even the oldest New Testament manuscripts in the library, Samuel made an intuitive calculation that proved to be surprisingly accurate. Samuel's decision to buy the documents was made almost immediately, but the purchase was not finalized until midsummer, after long and complex negotiations, directed by Kando for his bedouin clients. Not that the agreed sum was by any means enormous: Samuel agreed to purchase the scrolls for twenty-four Palestine pounds, then approximately equivalent to $100. Kando then gave two-thirds of the proceeds to Juma'a and Khalil Musa. He kept the equivalent of about $35 for himself.

Today Archbishop Samuel no longer ministers to the dwindling flock at St. Mark's Monastery. Now in his mid-eighties, he lives in a comfortable split-level ranch house on a quiet suburban street in Lodi, New Jersey, and serves—as he has since 1949—as the primate of the Syrian Orthodox Church in Canada and the United States. Though his famous beard is now white and his movements are slow and deliberate, he still wears the archbishop's robes and heavy golden cross so familiar from the early photos— and he is still as loquacious as ever about the scrolls. I went to see him for the first time the day after Christmas 1991, and he greeted me with a broad smile and a firm handshake. With his housekeeper already boiling Turkish coffee in the kitchen, Archbishop Samuel invited me into the living room, where he had set out some scroll memorabilia on a low table: a large photo facsimile of the Great Isaiah Scroll and the few genuine scroll fragments he still possessed.

I had a long list of questions that I wanted to ask him—about Kando, the bedouin, the discovery, but the archbishop had a question he wanted to ask me first.

"Did you see the *Nova*?," he asked me, referring to the recent episode of the PBS science series that highlighted the conflict over the Dead Sea Scrolls. In addition to an opening montage of old photos that told the story of the scrolls' early wanderings, the documentary featured extensive interviews with the current disputants in the scrolls controversy, including Hershel Shanks, Larry Schiffman, and Norman Golb. "I saw it also," the archbishop said with a weak smile, trying to hide his embarrassment. "I made a copy of it. They wrote me a letter. They said when we were making the film, we didn't know how to locate you and now we located you, but it's too late, the film is ready. So I watched it," he continued, "and saw myself and how young I was at the time. How many years ago was it?" He paused to make a silent calculation. "Yes, it's been forty-four years."

The irony of the archbishop's latter-day snubbing is that the scholars who now so eagerly jostle for position to give on-camera interviews about the importance of the scrolls bear an uncanny resemblance to those scholars who had only disdain for Archbishop Samuel and his crazy ideas in the summer of 1947. Once again—as was the case with the standard stories about ignorant bedouin—the storybook buffoon turns out to be the story's real hero. For despite all their explanations, equivocations, and rationalizations, most of the scholars on the scene—even those who supposedly specialized in the study of ancient manuscripts—simply got it wrong.

Samuel first turned for a professional opinion to Stephan Hanna Stephan, a St. Mark's parishioner who served as assistant librarian in the Palestine Archaeological Museum. Stephan (whom acquaintances remember as a sour-faced little man with a bad disposition) looked over the leather rolls and declared them to be modern forgeries. A Dutch priest, J.P.M. van der Ploeg, who was in Jerusalem for a year of study and who had often visited the library of St. Mark's, identified the largest of Samuel's scrolls as a copy of the Book of Isaiah; another seemed to him to be a collection of prophetic quotations, but he was not willing to vouch for their antiquity. In August of the same year, two experts from the Hebrew University Library came by to see the scrolls and mistakenly identified them as medieval—unusual and perhaps worthy of study—but not earthshaking by any means. As a last resort, Samuel brought the scrolls in the early autumn of 1947 to his ecclesiastical superior, Patriarch Ignatius Aphram, in the northern Syrian city of Homs. And even though the patriarch advised Samuel to forget the whole matter, the young archbishop persisted, fully convinced of the value of the scrolls. In October, Dr. Tuviah Wechsler of Hebrew University, who identified (yet again) the large scroll as the

Book of Isaiah, tried to convince the archbishop of the absurdity of his claims for the antiquity of these things.

Wechsler's words were right on the mark, though he certainly didn't intend them that way. "If that table were a box," he said, pointing to the surface where the archbishop's scrolls were displayed, "and you filled it full of pound notes, you couldn't even measure the value of the scrolls, if they are two thousand years old as you say!" The truth was apparently beyond the comprehension of the established scholars. It was only the Syrian Orthodox Archbishop Athanasius Yeshue Samuel who had the imagination to see. Other doubters would come forward in later years to claim that the scrolls were not nearly as important as some people said. But Archbishop Samuel has always been faithful. "I knew that they were ancient," he told me himself as he leaned forward in his easy chair in the living room in Lodi. "I knew that it wasn't a lie."

The Dead Sea Scrolls in their Shrine of the Book at the Israel Museum are today as much a political symbol as Rome's Colosseum or Philadelphia's Liberty Bell. For in the State of Israel, the drama of their discovery has always been juxtaposed in metaphorical terms with the founding of the Jewish State. Despite the heretical, anti-authoritarian message that runs through the Qumran literature, the building that houses the scrolls is an example of an Establishment institution, part of the landscape of power in western Jerusalem. As you stand in the plaza of the Shrine of the Book, you can hardly avoid noticing the modernistic structure that houses the Knesset, and beyond it the office buildings for the various government ministries. That juxtaposition of past and present, of temporal power, ancient manuscripts, and spiritual message, is certainly not coincidental. For during the last forty-five years, the Dead Sea Scrolls have acquired a certain sanctity in Israel. And the Shrine of the Book has become a chapel of relics dedicated to the miracle of national rebirth.

How that happened is due to something of a comedy of errors. For by the autumn of 1947, there were *two* rival groups of ancient manuscripts circulating in Jerusalem. Juma'a's discovery in the cave near Qumran was to be just the beginning. For once Archbishop Samuel had expressed his interest in buying the scrolls, Kando sought additional merchandise. Sometime in the spring or early summer of 1947, he dispatched George Shaya on an expedition, accompanied by Juma'a and Khalil Musa, to find the original cave. The journey of the two bedouin and the Syrian dry goods peddlar down to the Dead Sea in a hired taxi must have been hilarious, though certainly not to the participants. You can almost imagine the angry, uncomfortable taxi driver sitting impatiently behind the wheel of his car parked by the side of the road, cursing and sweating in the sweltering heat while his three passengers got out and hiked their way up to the cave.

Yet the haul proved to be worth the effort. George Shaya and Khalil Musa dug away the dirt on the floor of the dark and stuffy cave amid shattered jars and hundreds of parchment fragments, to retrieve four more documents. In contrast to the other group (then still in the hands of Kando), three of the four were in relatively poor condition. Two of them were crumpled and matted rather than rolled, and one had a damp, gooey end—obviously in an advanced state of decay. By now, however, the antiquities grapevine had been apparently humming around Bethlehem and there was considerable interest in the scrolls. Returning from the Dead Sea, Shaya took one of the scrolls for his share in the renewed expedition (it was the gooey one—later to be identified as the Genesis Apocryphon—and would eventually be sold with the first group to Archbishop Samuel). Juma'a and Khalil Musa, for their part, apparently found a new and more lucrative outlet; they sold the other three scrolls to the dealer Feidi al-Alami, who had now become convinced of the possible value of ancient scrolls.

Rarely have national treasures been sold at such bargain basement prices. Al-Alami paid seven pounds (not quite $30) for the three documents that turned out to be the Scroll of the War of the Sons of Light Against Darkness, the Thanksgiving Hymns, and another Isaiah scroll. In addition, he purchased the two tall jars in which the scrolls had been hidden for about seventy-five cents apiece. Hoping to get a big-city price for these acquisitions, al-Alami contacted an associate in Jerusalem, an Armenian named Nasri Ohan, who had an antiquities shop in the Christian Quarter, opposite the Lutheran Church. Now this is how the connection to Israel was made, for Ohan had for years done business with Professor Eleazar Sukenik of the Hebrew University, and when the matter came to Hebrew manuscripts, Ohan gave Sukenik a call. And unlike the scholars consulted by Archbishop Samuel, Sukenik recognized immediately from the fragments that Ohan showed him that the scrolls were of unimaginable importance, and he quickly made arrangements to buy them from Feidi al-Alami.

Sukenik was not a conventional scholar. Largely self-taught (he had only two years of formal university training), his greatest talent was being in the right place at the right time. A dedicated Zionist, he had made a conscious decision years before to make his fame promoting "Jewish" archaeology. His achievements in that field were numerous: he had excavated a significant number of ancient synagogues and tombs. But one particular area of expertise enabled him to recognize the scrolls' value. In excavating and studying dozens of inscribed stone ossuaries, in which the bones of the Jewish inhabitants of the first centuries B.C.E. and C.E. were deposited, he was well aware of the distinctive Hebrew letter forms of that period. The letters on the scrolls were strikingly similar. And while Archbishop Samuel had only an intuitive feeling about their proper dating, Sukenik could rely on demonstrable archaeological facts.

The story of Sukenik's trip on an Arab bus with Ohan to al-Alami's house in Bethlehem is usually described as a dangerous mission, for the day of the journey was November 29, 1947—the day that the United Nations General Assembly voted to partition Palestine. Certainly, in light of the bloody violence that was to erupt between Jews and Arabs in the months that followed, Sukenik's decision to go to the Arab town of Bethlehem, taken against the advice and warnings of his wife and son Yigael Yadin (who was then serving as the chief of operations for the Haganah), has to be admired as a sign of his conviction about the value of the scrolls.

That night, Sukenik returned home with two scrolls—the War Scroll and the Thanksgiving Hymns—and the two jars taken from the cave. About a month later, he was able to acquire the poorly preserved Isaiah scroll. Sharing news of his great discovery with President Judah Magnes of the Hebrew University, Sukenik gained an important ally. Magnes was so impressed with the discovery of ancient Hebrew writings from the Second Temple period that he provided two hundred pounds from university funds for the purchase of the manuscripts. That sum was still quite modest, but it was an indication that the going price for scrolls was clearly on the rise.

At this time, Sukenik knew nothing of Archbishop Samuel's manuscripts. But by late January 1948, Samuel was getting discouraged by his own prospects, since he had so far found no one who believed in the antiquity of the scrolls. Among the archbishop's closest advisors, Anton Kiraz, who had driven him to Syria in the previous autumn, now suggested Sukenik as a potential buyer for the scrolls. Back in 1945, Professor Sukenik had excavated an ancient tomb on Kiraz's property; perhaps the professor would be interested in examining the archbishop's discovery. A meeting was arranged at the Jerusalem YMCA and Sukenik immediately saw that Samuel's four scrolls were in even better condition than his own. Seeking time to study them further and perhaps to confer with some colleagues, Sukenik received Kiraz's permission to keep them for a few days.

Had life in Jerusalem been normal, there is no question that Sukenik could have easily raised an unprecedented sum to purchase these scrolls on behalf of Hebrew University. But at this time, when both Arab and Jewish inhabitants of the city were beginning to fear for their very existence and the overland links between Jewish Jerusalem and the outside world were being slowly cut off, money to purchase antiquities was understandably difficult to raise. Yet that was not the real reason for the termination of contacts between Sukenik and Samuel and the return of the borrowed scrolls to him. Another of Samuel's close friends and advisors—Brother Butros Sowmy of St. Mark's—warned the arch-bishop that, in light of the increasingly violent conditions in Jeru-salem, he should avoid further dangerous contact with the Jewish professor and take the scrolls for an evaluation to the more neu-tral American Schools of Oriental Research.

Nothing in the further history of the scrolls story contradicts Mark Twain's assertion that Americans have always been the most credulous Holy Land pilgrims, bringing with them the innocent arrogance of prim and proper Protestant missionaries. In the war-torn academic year of 1947–48, there were only two students at the American School in Jerusalem: John Trever and William Brown-lee, both of them earnest Midwesterners who had come to pursue their biblical studies with perhaps less intellectual brilliance than abundant Sunday School faith. The school's annual professor, Dr. Millar Burrows of the Yale Divinity School, was away on a trip to Baghdad when Brother Sowmy and Archbishop Samuel came call-ing, and John Trever was the only one there to welcome them. "Trever had two things going for him," Professor Frank Moore Cross of Harvard recalled. "One was naivité. He wasn't used to seeing forgeries. He hadn't been in that part of the world very long. Most of all he was a very impressive photographer. The com-bination was providential."

It was providential because Trever and then Brownlee—who returned to the school from an errand to the post office—became convinced that the archbishop's scrolls were really quite ancient once they had leafed through some books in the library about the development of Hebrew scripts. At once Trever set to work, with the archbishop's permission, photographing the documents in the basement of the school. The film was expired, the conditions were difficult, but Trever managed to take the clearest color photos ever made of the Great Isaiah Scroll, the Manual of Disci-pline, and the Commentary on Habakkuk—all of which Trever and Brownlee managed to identify and study at least briefly after the return of Professor Burrows from Iraq. Trever also had the presence of mind to send a few copies of his photos to Professor William Foxwell Albright at Johns Hopkins, the undisputed doyen of American biblical archaeology. Albright responded immediately and enthusiastically to the American scholars: "My heartiest congratulations on the greatest MS discovery of modern times!"

With the violence intensifying every day in Jerusalem as the weeks ticked toward May 15th and the end of the British Mandate, Burrows, Trever, and Brownlee made preparations to return to the United States. But before they did, they managed to persuade Archbishop Samuel to sign an agreement guaranteeing the American Schools of Oriental Research the exclusive right to publish photographs of the scrolls. Burrows also apparently made some unofficial assurances that he would help the archbishop find a suitable buyer or institution to house the scrolls and support the work of his church. With seductive visions of prosperity and acclaim in America dancing before him, Samuel agreed to the warm scholarly embrace of Burrows, Trever, and Brownlee. An appropriate press release was drafted and sent off to the ASOR headquarters in New Haven. And on April 11, 1948, the existence of the Dead Sea Scrolls—including the oldest biblical texts ever discovered—was revealed to the world.

When Professor Eleazar Sukenik, on the western side of embattled Jerusalem, was shown the American statement, he exploded with anger. He suspected that his abortive negotiations with Anton Kiraz had been sabotaged by the Americans. Sukenik's furious letters to America, and his frantic attempts to enlist the aid of Prime Minister David Ben-Gurion in declaring that the archbishop's scrolls should be the rightful property of the newly established State of Israel, achieved no results, however. At this time of war, other priorities took precedence. And Archbishop Samuel himself had, in the meantime, left Jerusalem with the scrolls. The details of his understanding with the Americans were probably never set down in writing, but it is clear that he saw that his future lay in the United States. Appointed Apostolic Delegate to North America by Patriarch Ignatius Aphram, he arrived in New York in January 1949 with two clear objectives: to expand the activities of the Syrian Orthodox Church in the New World and to make the most of his scrolls.

Trever and Burrows hurried to New York to meet him, and over the next two years they accompanied Samuel to highly publicized exhibitions of the scrolls—at the Library of Congress, the Walters Art Gallery in Baltimore, the University of Chicago, and Duke University. In 1950, the first of the promised ASOR publications appeared, with a volume containing Trever's photographs of the Isaiah scroll. In the next year came a full publication of the Manual of Discipline and the Habakkuk Commentary. Sukenik, for his part, also put out a series of reports both on the three scrolls that he had purchased from Feidi al-Alami *and* of the brief transcriptions he had made of portions of the archbishop's scrolls during the few days they were in his hands. Ordinarily this would have been seen as a crude breach of scholarly etiquette—the unauthorized publication of a manuscript being studied by somebody else. In fact, a similar event—but forty years later—would become the essence of the scrolls controversy. But Sukenik was truly convinced that he had made a gentleman's agreement with Anton Kiraz and that all the scrolls rightfully belonged to him.

Sukenik made that position clear in a face-to-face meeting with John Trever in New York City in the spring of 1949. Trever, who is now retired with his wife in southern California, remembered this meeting vividly when I spoke with him in the summer of 1993. The meeting began quite cordially, Trever recalled, but slowly the passion mounted as Sukenik listened to John Trever's pride in having "discovered" the scrolls. Trever was at that time working for the International Council of Religious Education, traveling around the country promoting the new Revised Standard Version of the Bible, and it is not difficult to imagine how Sukenik quickly became impatient with Trever's polite conversation about Christian youth groups and Sunday schools. This young American—with only the most rudimentary knowledge of Jewish history—was now standing in the way of Sukenik's obtaining what he believed was a precious national heritage. To this day, Trever recalls the unpleasant climax of the meeting with an innocent lack of understanding. "He just blew up at me after he had been very polite for quite a while," Trever told me. "I could see the tension building up and then he said, 'You had no right to get involved in any of this!' "

Eleazar Sukenik died in 1953 and did not live to win the battle for the scrolls, but they would all eventually be united in Israeli Jerusalem. The reason was that by the time of Sukenik's death, Archbishop Samuel had recognized the emptiness of Professor Burrows's promises and the utter inability of John Trever, despite all his noble intentions, to do anything for him. For once the scrolls had been published and the scholarly laurels had been obtained by the Americans, it was far more difficult to find a buyer for the scrolls. Sukenik, of course, had kept up a steady stream of threats of lawsuits against any potential purchaser. And in the meantime, the government of Jordan (now in occupation of the Qumran region) joined the angry claimants. Needless to say, Archbishop Samuel was getting desperate; he had gambled his future on the scrolls. By the spring of 1954, he was ready to try almost anything and, following the advice of his closest American confidant, a successful wholesale plumbing distributor named Charles Manoog, he placed a fairly inconspicuous announcement in the classified advertising section of *The Wall Street Journal* on June 1, 1954:

> "THE FOUR DEAD SEA SCROLLS"
>
> Biblical manuscripts dating back to at least 200 BC are for sale. This would be an ideal gift to an educational or religious institution by an individual or group. Box F 206, The Wall Street Journal.

The idea that the scrolls would be merchandised like apartments for rent or used machinery always gets a laugh when the story of the Dead Sea Scrolls is presented. But the fact is, that ad in *The Wall Street Journal* led directly to the sale of the scrolls.

By yet another twist of fate, General Yigael Yadin, former Israeli chief of staff and son of Professor Sukenik—who had just completed his doctoral dissertation on the Scroll of the War of the Sons of Light Against the Sons of Darkness—was in New York on a lecture tour just at that time. Alerted to *The Wall Street Journal* ad by an acquaintance, he set to work with the help of the Israeli consul-general in New York, Avraham Harman, to open anonymous negotiations for the purchase of the scroll through middlemen. A price was duly arrived at—$250,000 for all four scrolls—and Archbishop Samuel and Charles Manoog drove into Manhattan with the ancient documents. After the scrolls were inspected and certified to be authentic by Dr. Harry Orlinsky, the contract was signed and the money was transferred. Yadin eventually gained the financial support of a New York industrialist and philanthropist, D. Samuel Gottesman, to underwrite the purchase, but the subsequent shipment of the scrolls to Israel was to be kept a secret, at least initially. But Yadin could not restrain his excitement. On the afternoon of July 4, 1954, he telephoned Professor Albright at Johns Hopkins. Albright immediately dashed off a letter of congratulations. "How happy your father would be at this development, since all his efforts were unsuccessful! These priceless documents belong at the Hebrew University with the other scrolls from Qumran."

John Trever, then teaching Bible at Morris Harvey College in Charleston, West Virginia, had a different opinion when he learned the news some months later from Millar Burrows at Yale. The news that the scrolls had been secretly sold to the Israelis was a bitter and disappointing pill. Even after the American Schools of Oriental Research, having concluded the publication of the documents, broke off their official connections with Samuel, Trever tirelessly traveled throughout the country trying to find appropriate buyers for the archbishop's scrolls. His idea was to raise funds to establish a foundation that would place the scrolls on display in a renovated exhibition hall in St. Mark's Monastery. In fact, he was on the verge of persuading the International Jaycees at their 1954 convention to support this interfaith project when he received Burrows's letter that the scrolls were now on their way to Israel.

"I was trying to use every opportunity I could to find ways to get financial support for the publication of these materials," he told me of his continuing efforts. "There were all these different groups that were struggling to find a way to purchase these things and"—he hesitated for a split second and then pressed ahead with his innermost thoughts and recollections—"so I was trying to find a way that would keep it out of the control of the Jews. Now I was not doing that because of anti-Semitism," he assured me. "It was simply because of the way they had treated me. I felt that they really didn't have a right to do anything with these things." Even more galling to Trever must have been the fact that the announcement of the acquisition of the scrolls made in Israel, on February 13, 1955, was a state occasion, with Prime Minister Moshe Sharett thanking Yadin on behalf of a grateful nation for returning these precious documents to their proper place in Jerusalem.

Almost immediately, an Israeli government commission was appointed to plan and construct a special exhibition hall attached to the National Library on the new Givat Ram campus of Hebrew University. The location was later shifted to the site of the new Israel Museum compound opposite the Knesset, and the flamboyant, symbolic design for the Shrine of the Book, by architects Frederick Kiesler and Armand Bartos, became one of West Jerusalem's most recognizable landmarks. Its central, subterranean exhibition hall would be surmounted by a grotesquely gigantic representation of the cover of the clay jar that Feidi al-Alami had purchased just a few years before from Juma'a Muhammed and Khalil Musa for about seventy-five cents. In the meantime, Yadin and his late father's assistant, Nahman Avigad, supervised the unrolling and decipherment of the mysterious fourth scroll, which proved to be a colorful retelling of some stories from Genesis. But the main significance of the Dead Sea Scrolls for the State of Israel was, as John Trever had recognized, in the realm of national ideology.

Yadin expressed it succinctly in his popular 1956 book, *The Message of the Scrolls*. "I cannot avoid the feeling that there is something symbolic in the discovery of their scrolls and their acquisition at the moment of the creation of the State of Israel," he observed. "It is as if these manuscripts had been waiting in caves for two thousand years, ever since the destruction of Israel's independence, until the people of Israel had returned to their home and regained their freedom . . . and just as a Christian reader must be moved by the knowledge that here he has a manuscript of a sect whom the early Christians may have known and by whom they may have been influenced, so an Israeli and a Jew can find nothing more moving than the study of manuscripts written by the People of the Book in the Land of the Book more than two thousand years ago."

Back in New Jersey, Archbishop Samuel, no longer in possession of the ancient documents, tried to build a new life for himself as best he could. With the $250,000 he received from the sale of the scrolls, he could travel, preach, and contribute to the growth of the Syrian Orthodox church among the growing numbers of immigrants to America. In 1966, he published an autobiography, *The Treasure of Qumran: My Story of the Dead Sea Scrolls,* whose melodramatically framed scenes and breathless dialogue betray the pen of an American ghostwriter as well as his own. Then slowly, the archbishop dropped out of the public limelight as the first group of scrolls became ever more firmly associated with the State of Israel and subsequent scroll discoveries were made.

Does he have regrets today about all that has happened? "At that time, I wish I knew what I know now," Samuel told me with a chuckle, "so it would be an entirely different situation. I would have never gotten rid of them. But at that time I was here, I needed money for my churches, to form dioceses, and to bring church people to the United States. In some ways, I helped my church, and I'm glad about that." And there was an even larger significance that the archbishop is not afraid of stressing. "You see, I'm happy because God gave me a very special mission," he told me with a broad, confident smile that was neither naive nor sentimental. "He chose *me* to be the one to bring these scrolls to the world."

So what exactly was the historical and religious significance of the seven scrolls purchased from the Taamireh by Archbishop Samuel and Professor Sukenik, published by the American Schools of Oriental Research in 1950 and 1951, and brought back to Israel in 1954 through the efforts of General Yadin? So far I have been describing the struggle to possess them as if they had an obvious value that could be easily appraised and given a fair-market price like ancient gold jewelry, coins, or statuary. Even if the Dead Sea Scrolls had not become the focus of nasty, international rivalry, no art gallery or auction house in Manhattan, London, or Zurich would have been likely to snap up these smelly, rotting rolls of leather. For these are antiquities whose appreciation requires far more than the connoisseurship of even the most discriminating collector or curator of ancient art. On some of them, to be sure, the Hebrew calligraphy is clear and artful, but it still falls far short of the elaborate, masterful hands of the far better preserved illuminated Hebrew manuscripts of medieval times.

There is, of course, the scrolls' importance for biblical studies, though that is naturally a matter more of concern to religious historians and church-goers than to lovers of beautiful antiquities. Before the discovery of the scrolls, the next oldest biblical manuscript known to scholars was almost a millennium younger. Known as the Aleppo Codex, it was written in Tiberias around 950 C.E., and was preserved for centuries in the main synagogue of the Syrian city of Aleppo. After being badly damaged by fire in an anti-Jewish riot in 1947, it was secretly purchased by intermediaries and brought to Israel in 1956. But this manuscript, despite its age, contained a version of the scriptures identical to that of modern Hebrew Bibles, namely the Masoretic, or "Traditional," text. The Great Isaiah Scroll from the Dead Sea cave is different. For all the self-righteous pontificating of fundamentalist preachers about the immutable, unchanging Word of God to be found in the Bible, this document shows quite conclusively that the biblical text was still fairly fluid before the destruction of Jerusalem in 70 C.E. Not that there were any mind-boggling differences that would be immediately apparent to the layperson—no hidden stories or blasphemous twists. But the grammatical and syntactical differences in the Isaiah Scroll were significant enough for thirteen of its variant readings to have been incorporated in the Revised Standard Version of the Bible—which is still the English translation used by most mainstream Protestant denominations.

Far more stunning than minor textual changes are the creative liberties taken with traditional biblical stories by the author of the scroll known to scholars as the Genesis Apocryphon. Small, half rotted, and the ugliest of the original documents (it was described as looking like a damp cigar by several of those who saw it), it was not unrolled during the seven years that Archbishop Samuel possessed it, and its full text was not deciphered until its opening in 1955 in Jerusalem. Today the leather has darkened considerably and it is impossible to make out more than a few letters with the naked eye. But when unrolled, it contained twenty-two columns of text written in Aramaic (the everyday language of Judea and most of the Near East after the decline of Hebrew for all but religious uses), and it retold several stories from the Book of Genesis with surprisingly sensuous detail.

In terms of romantic writing, the Genesis Apocryphon is far more lively than the Bible, at least in one case. In Genesis 12:10–20, the dangers of Abraham and Sarah's journey to Egypt to escape famine in the Land of Israel are described in graphic detail. In the biblical version, Sarah's beauty almost immediately catches the eye of some Egyptian courtiers who "praised her to the Pharaoh," leading to Sarah's forced conscription into the royal harem, followed by the expectable plague on the Pharaoh's family, and the precipitous deportation of Abraham and Sarah back to the Negev, from whence they had come. It has often been said that erotic literature is more forceful when a great deal is left to the imagination, but the author of the Genesis Apocryphon apparently did not agree. Following what may have been a well-known folk tradition, he identified the chief Egyptian courtier (anonymous in the biblical story) as a man called Harkenosh and provided him with vivid dialogue, describing in surprising detail just how alluring the illegal immigrant woman Sarah had appeared to him.

... And beautiful is her face! How ... fine are the hairs of
her head! How lovely are her eyes! How desirable her nose
and all the radiance of her countenance ... How fair are
her breasts and all her whiteness! How pleasing are her
arms and how [desirable] all the appearance of her hands!
How fair are her palms and how long and slender are her
fingers! How comely are her feet, how perfect her thighs!
No virgin or bride led into the marriage chamber is more
beautiful than she; she is fairer than all other women.
Truly, her beauty is greater than theirs. Yet together with
all this grace, she possesses abundant wisdom, so that whatever she does is perfect.

Here is a text that clearly does not fear to improve on the Bible if
there's a better or more vivid tale to be told. Scholars have long
been struck by the freedom with which the scrolls often expound
and elaborate on the scriptures as if the authors were convinced
that they were still the recipients of direct inspiration from God.

That inspiration sometimes manifested itself in a more violent, angry manner as seen so clearly in the document that Sukenik called The War of the Sons of Light Against the Sons of
Darkness, a beautifully written scroll more than thirteen feet in
length. It describes in great, gory detail the battle plan, arms, tactics, and prayers to be used in the great campaign of the Sons of
Light in their triumph over the forces of evil in the world. The war
itself would last fifty years, the scroll related, with six years of
preparation, twenty-nine years of campaigns against various nations, and every seventh year devoted to rest. The Sons of Light,
marching to fulfill God's plan for the universe, would be led at
first by figures called the High Priest and the Prince of the Congregation, and at the crucial moment they would give way to the
leadership of no one less than the Archangel Michael.

Another of the first group of scrolls also foretold the imminent extermination of the wicked; Sukenik gave it the mislead-
ingly serene name "The Thanksgiving Hymns." It has nothing to
do with pious pilgrims, their hands clasped in silent, humble worship, but contains a series of rage-filled condemnations against the

wicked and an assurance of their destruction at the End of Times. The scroll, retrieved on the second visit to the cave by Shaya and Khalil Musa, was found crumpled and decaying, with additional fragments scattered nearby on the cave floor. It was apparently already worn and damaged when it was hidden—thus leading Sukenik to believe that the cave was a *geniza,* or place of disposal, for sacred texts. Whether not that is correct, this scroll was, in its original form, large and impressive, nearly two feet in height and more than twenty feet long.

Written in biblical Hebrew, it consists of psalmlike poems that speak of the power of God and the completeness of his creation, even down to the preordination of every event of human history. The writer, whose voice serves as the narrator, expresses his gratitude to God for having permitted him to glimpse the details of the divinely preordained plan. Because of that revelation he has the power to persevere and be righteous and to gather faithful followers around him, despite the rampant iniquity of the times. In fact, God has steeled the writer in his struggles with the "congregation of Belial," who had forced him into exile. God had also protected him from the traitors within his own community. The personal tone of this document and the autobiographical details it seemed to reveal about the author led Sukenik to make a direct connection with a figure known from another ancient work, in quite a different context.

In 1896, a Jewish scholar named Solomon Schechter was dispatched on behalf of Cambridge University to rummage through the dusty *geniza* of the Ibn Ezra synagogue in Cairo in search of valuable manuscripts. Several years before, a Hebrew manuscript of the apocryphal book of the Wisdom of Ben Sira (previously known only in its Greek translation as Ecclesiasticus) had been obtained through antiquities dealers from apparently the same source. The find of the Hebrew original of the work had caused a scholarly sensation, and with a letter of introduction from the Chief Rabbi of England to Cairo's Grand Rabbi, Schechter was permitted to spend several weeks selecting and removing documents from the stuffy, dusty, dark chamber in the synagogue's upper story—that was filled with decaying paper and parchment and infested with insects.

Schechter's haul was thirty bulging bags of ancient manuscripts (he had consciously decided to ignore all printed material) that contained about 140,000 pages, fragments, or handwritten notes. When brought back to Cambridge and studied more intensively, the collection provided important evidence of the life of the medieval Jewish community of Egypt, valuable information on trade and political history, and a number of previously unknown religious texts. The material was primarily medieval, but Schechter noted one particular text with interest that seemed to provide connections with a much earlier historical period. It was represented by two fragments: one, consisting of eight double-sided pages, dated by the handwriting to the tenth century C.E.; and an additional double-sided leaf dating a century or two after that.

The work apparently embodied the teachings of an extinct Jewish sect that existed while the Temple in Jerusalem was still standing and was led—at least for a short time—by a saintly, priestly figure identified only as "The Teacher of Righteousness." The precise dates for the founding of the sect was uncertain. Although the text said that it took place 390 years after the conquest of Jerusalem by the Babylonians (and would therefore place it at 196 B.C.E.), such chronological figures were known to be highly unreliable and might be more symbolic than literal. Whenever the events occurred, however, religious differences between the sect and the rest of the nation led them to go into exile in the "Land of Damascus" under the leadership of the Teacher of Righteousness where they established a New Covenant. The Teacher was seen by his followers as a messianic figure who received direct revelations from God. Yet he was apparently killed at the hands of his enemies and was expected to rise again at the End of Times.

The identity of the sect responsible for this "Damascus Document"—as this text later became known—was long a source of contention. The group called itself the Sons of Zadok, but the theories of its true identity varied widely from Sadducees to Jewish Christians to Samaritans to anti-Roman rebels. None of the distinctive practices of the sect, however, seemed to match any ancient Jewish group that was known. Their special hatred was directed toward a group called "the Builders of the Wall" for their injustice, duplicity, and violence, and also against the "Kings of Greece" (though some suggested that this might be a poetic reference that included Roman emperors as well). Most of all, the sect protested the defilement of the Jerusalem Temple, which was most probably the reason for their exile. To Schechter's mind, there was at least one ancient Jewish sect that could be excluded. "For whatever difficulties the present unsatisfactory state of our MS. may place in the way of the student, and whatever doubts may prevail as to the meaning of this or that passage, one thing is certain," he noted in his 1910 transcription and translation. "We have to deal here with a sect decidedly hostile to the bulk of Jews as represented by the Pharisees."

Already in February 1948, in his private conferences with Judah Magnes, Sukenik was suggesting that the authors of the Dead Sea Scrolls might be closely related to the mysterious Damascus Document sect, and that both of them should be identified with the Essenes. The ancient authors Josephus Flavius, Philo of Alexandria, and Pliny the Elder had all left intriguing (and not completely compatible) descriptions of this religious movement in Judaism, which was in many ways the strictest and most exacting of all known Jewish sects. While some Essenes were permitted to marry, others were strictly celibate. But they formed themselves into tight-knit communities, where special religious rites were kept secret from all but those who had undergone a period of initiation. Christian scholars had always noted the similarity of some Essene practices to those of the early Christians—notably the holding of all property in common, communal meals, and the importance of baptism. But now the connection between the scrolls and the Essenes was made even stronger with the decipherment and study of another scroll called at first the Manual of Discipline.

This scroll was among the four that Archbishop Samuel took

with him to America and was named by Burrows, Trever, and Brownlee—during their hurried study of the scrolls in Jerusalem—after the "Manual of Discipline" of the Methodist Church. Of course any resemblance between this harsh, monastic document and the constitution of the Methodists was purely coincidental. The text, later and more appropriately called the Community Rule by other scholars, proscribed the rules for admittance to the community (called the *Yahad* in Hebrew), detailed the strict code of community discipline, and described the sacred banquets in which all members were required to participate. The parallels to the ancient descriptions of the Essenes were striking, as was the fact that Pliny the Elder had placed the community of Essenes near the shores of the Dead Sea. That was the last piece of the puzzle in the construction of what came to be the dominant hypothesis. And it is amazing how over the last forty years most of the scholars who dealt with the scrolls came to nearly identical conclusions about the identification of the authors (the Essenes) and the date of the founding of the sect and the appearance of the Teacher of Righteousness (in the second century B.C.E.).

By the agreement of virtually all scholars, the scroll known as the Habakkuk Commentary contains the most important evidence for reconstructing the history of the Dead Sea sect—and for determining the religious significance of the scrolls. On display today in its humidity-controlled and light-shielded case in the Shrine of the Book, it certainly is not much for the layman to look at. Its opening column is split down the middle and its bottom edge is scalloped from decay and deterioration. Even when it was complete and in good condition, it was not particularly impressive—never more than seven inches wide and only about five feet long. On paleographical grounds, it is dated to the late first century C.E., not long before the Great Revolt against Rome and the deposit of the scrolls in the cave. And that creates a serious problem, because from the time of the initial interpretation of the Damascus Document in the early years of the twentieth century, most scholars have placed the origin of the sect and the life of the Teacher of

Righteousness in the second century B.C.E., around the time of the Maccabean Wars.

First some background about the Book of Habakkuk, because it was so obviously important to the Dead Sea sect. The literary form is that of a dialogue between the prophet and God that ostensibly takes place in Judea, in the tense and uncertain time just before the Babylonian conquest, around 600 B.C.E. The prophet cries out to God in protest of the violence and the wickedness that goes unchecked in the land. "For the wicked surround the righteous, so justice goes on perverted."

God responds that he is "doing a work in your days that you would not believe if told." He is raising as an instrument of his own divine wrath the Chaldeans, "that bitter and hasty nation who march through the breadth of the earth, to seize habitations not their own." God offers a horrifying portrait of the Chaldeans' terrible earthly power: "Their horses are swifter than leopards, more fierce than the evening wolves; their horsemen press proudly on. Yea, their horsemen come from afar; they fly like an eagle swift to devour. They all come for violence; terror of them goes before them. They gather captives like sand. At kings they scoff, and of rulers they make sport. They laugh at every fortress, for they heap up earth and take it. Then they sweep by like the wind and go on, guilty men, whose own might is their god!"

The prophet then poses the obvious question: Will God allow his instruments of wrath to devour even the few righteous people that survive in this sinful time? "Why dost thou look on faithless men and art silent when the wicked swallows up the man more righteous than he?" The prophet puts himself in an allegorical watchtower to await the answer of God. God replies that the ultimate judgment is coming even though it is now delayed. The wicked man shall, in the end, die for his sinfulness and the righteous man shall live. And then, having received this divine reassurance, the prophet himself pours bitter scorn on the Chaldeans, in the form of a triumphal ode that will be pronounced by the nations that have been oppressed by them, and it is as close to a revolutionary hymn as anything you might see coming from the peoples' revolutions of the twentieth century. He condemns the plundering of peoples with a series of prophetic accusations that foretell destruction for the Chaldeans' plunder, greed, ostentatious splendor, cruelty toward their subjects, and idolatry.

This all-purpose oracle contains within it the eternal rage of the oppressed nations under a tyrannical conqueror, and so it has been used from pulpits and speakers' podiums for hundreds of years. The date of its original composition is uncertain. Although its subject is the Chaldeans (better known today as the Babylonians) who destroyed Jerusalem and exiled most of its population in 586 B.C.E., a number of modern commentators have underlined the metaphorical dimension of the prophecy and have suggested that the "Chaldeans" are used here as a masked term for the Hellenistic conquerors and that the work was composed sometime after the conquests of Alexander the Great in the fourth century B.C.E. Whatever the time of its composition, the Dead Sea Scroll sect considered this oracle to have an enormous significance for their own times. In the Habakkuk Commentary—as in a number of other works of biblical interpretation later found among the Dead Sea documents—the author quotes a verse or two of scripture, then follows it with a unique interpretation, which is identified as a *pesher,* a rare Hebrew-Aramaic term used in the Book of Daniel for the mystical meaning of dreams.

In the scrolls, the *pesher* is an exegetical technique that explains the "hidden" meaning of a selected passage of scripture, finding prophetic fulfillment in contemporary personalities and events. It is not much different from the technique of modern evangelists and assorted TV preachers, who see in such events as the establishment of the State of Israel, the fall of the Soviet Union, or the outbreak of the AIDS epidemic sure signs that the End of the World is at hand. Yet the problem with the Dead Sea Scrolls' *peshers* is that, being highly poetic and metaphorical, they are also highly ambiguous. That is apparently how the authors wanted it, for in their rage against the established Jerusalem priesthood and in their hopes for its imminent destruction, they ran the risk that all heretics run of being accused of revolutionary sedition by the powers that be. Thus, with very few exceptions, this and the other Dead Sea Scrolls refer to the events and personalities of the times with poetic titles that, though veiled, are often cruel, mocking, and filled with contempt. Thus besides the Teacher of Righteousness, the Sons of Light, the Sons of Zadok, and the Community of the New Covenant—who are obviously the heroes of the story—there is the Wicked Priest, the Man of Lies, the Scoffer, the Seekers after Smooth Things, and those Who Build the Wall—who are obviously the bad guys.

In the latter-day interpretation of the Dead Sea sect, the Wicked Priest and the Man of Lies are equated with the wicked of Judea, whom God is planning to exterminate. A people called the Kittim ("They come from afar, from the islands of the sea, to devour all the peoples like an eagle which cannot be satisfied") are equated with the Chaldeans. And in the interwoven lines of scripture and interpretation, the main events of a long struggle between the Teacher of Righteousness and the Wicked Priest emerge.

At first, the Wicked Priest was apparently not so wicked, "but when he ruled over Israel, his heart became proud." After a period in which he plundered the people, he died a painful death, and his ill-gotten wealth was delivered into the hands of the Kittim. But before his death, there was a dramatic confrontation between the Wicked Priest and the Teacher of Righteousness. According to the interpretation, the Wicked Priest "pursued the Teacher of Righteousness to the house of his exile, that he might confuse him with his venomous fury." The precise end of the story is not described in this document, but from other references to the death of the Teacher of Righteousness, it was almost certainly bad. The commentary ends on an optimistic note, if a desperate yearning for Armageddon can be called optimism; for "on the Day of Judgment God will destroy from the earth all idolatrous and wicked men."

Almost immediately after the publication of this document, scholars set to work trying to match up the main actors of this drama with figures known from history. Eventually, something of a consensus emerged. Though the script of the document was dated to the first century C.E., a majority of experts insisted on seeing in the text veiled references to events of the second century B.C.E. Thus even though most agreed that the "Kittim" were the Romans (based on the references to their being like eagles and sacrificing to their standards), the confrontation between the Wicked Priest and Teacher of Righteousness was placed at a time when there were no Romans around. Linking the story of the exile of the sect under the leadership of the Teacher of Righteousness to the putative Hasidean schism, most scholars saw the Wicked Priest as one of the Maccabean priest-kings. The scholars therefore reached back to the second century B.C.E. and pointed the finger of accusation at, variously, Jonathan, Simon, or John Hyrcanus.

Indeed, what is so strange in this consensus scroll interpretation is that it leaves the events of the first century C.E., with their wicked priests, would-be messiahs, rampaging Roman armies, and the destruction of Jerusalem utterly uncommented on. Nearly all agree that the sect that wrote the scrolls remained in the wilderness until the arrival of Vespasian's search-and-destroy mission in the Jordan Valley in the spring of 68 C.E.—which is the time when most agree that the scrolls were deposited in the caves. Yet is it conceivable that a sect that devoted so much literary effort to commenting on religious intrigue and disputes in Jerusalem—and that prided itself on having access to divine revelation and knowledge of the apocalyptic battle that would soon unfold between the Sons of Light and the Sons of Darkness—would have restricted their subject matter to grievances of the time of their great-great-great-great grandparents? Would they remain entirely silent about the apocalyptic significance of the arrival of a terrifying new Chaldean army, which, with the complicity of a corrupt, sycophantic priesthood, conquered, plundered, and eventually massacred the people of the land?

But that is how the story is told to the hundreds of thousands of tourist-pilgrims who come to the Shrine of the Book every year. It all comes across as a rather tame story of the ancient Jewish sect that lived in monastic isolation, quite uninvolved in the struggles that led to the Great Revolt against Rome—at least until the Romans came down to the Dead Sea shore and quickly wiped them out. The important element for most Jewish visitors to the Shrine of the Book is the fact that the sacred texts of this innocent group slaughtered by the Romans have been reclaimed and proudly exhibited by their returning descendants, the founders of the State of Israel. For Christians, these documents bear witness to the historical milieu in which Christianity was to emerge. Written around the time of Jesus' earthly ministry, they reflect the familiar motifs of the coming of the Final Days, the importance of faith, and the necessity of baptism for washing away sin. Sadly, the scrolls have been transformed from potent religious texts into mere relics: tangible tokens that are meant to be venerated, not studied, and for which small clay reproduction scroll jars are offered for sale to the faithful as souvenir icons of the Dead Sea Scrolls' perceived sanctity.

Architecturally, the Shrine of the Book contributes to this mindless veneration. In the circular domed form of its central exhibition hall, it resembles a classic Byzantine *martyrium* where the relics of the saints were enshrined in a circular hall at the end of a long ceremonial way. And so it is that today's visitors, entering the shrine's dark tunnel with expectation, first see a series of documents (which are tersely labeled and are actually from the Bar Kokhba Caves) and then pass through a portal guarded by the two tall clay jars retrieved from the Qumran Cave 1 by the bedouin. From there, visitors enter the cavernous dome, with the various documents ranged around the outer walkway. In the center is a soaring, absurdly huge Torah handle on which the Great Isaiah Scroll was meant to be the centerpiece. And this is the greatest misrepresentation in this hall of pretended sanctity. For in planning the focal point of the exhibition hall, the architects revealed their utter ignorance of the character of ancient manuscripts. Although the Isaiah Scroll was meant to be unrolled, face-out, around the centerpiece Torah, the brittle, inward-rolled document would have bent backwards and snapped instantly. So the centerpiece of the Shrine of the Book continues to be based on a deception: A faded Xerox copy now occupies the place where the most sacred document of the State of Israel is supposed to be found.

Xerox copy or not, the Last Testament of the Community was transformed into a relic. Though the modern religious meaning of the scrolls was hazy, and scholarly assessments of their historical importance based on simplistic readings and enormous leaps of faith, the scrolls and their shrine, standing opposite the Knesset building in the capital of Israel, became profoundly patriotic artifacts. Yet the first finds of what we now call the Dead Sea Scrolls were only part of the picture. The publicity generated by the discovery and the money made from the sale of the first seven scrolls persuaded the Taamireh to resume their searching through the caves of the Dead Sea region, and their activities brought forth a new haul of discoveries. By that time a new political reality had cast its shadow on the war for the scrolls: The caves and the nearby ruins were now in territory controlled by the Hashemite Kingdom of Jordan, cut off and at war with the State of Israel.

Beginning in January 1949, the Department of Antiquities of Jordan and the French Dominican Ecole Biblique et Archéologique in the Jordanian sector of divided Jerusalem began a partnership of exploration and research on a growing mass of manuscript fragments and archaeological finds uncovered in territory now under the control of Jordan far greater in quantity and no less important in historical connections than the original seven scrolls. If the political atmosphere between Israel and Jordan had been different, there is a possibility that the study of the two groups of Dead Sea Scroll materials could have gone on cooperatively, and perhaps the historical conclusions would have continued to be refined. But that conclusion is purely hypothetical. For reasons of modern Middle Eastern politics, international finance, and personal ambition, the scholars in Jordan would maintain tight control over the dissemination of details of the new discoveries. Insiders, establishment figures, and government appointees now controlled the study of the scrolls on *both* sides of the barbed-wire border that divided Jerusalem. And despite the wealth of material soon to be uncovered in the other caves of the Qumran area, the natural conservatism of the Dead Sea Scroll scholars and the durability of the dominant Essene Hypothesis would continue—for many years—to mask the revolutionary message of the scrolls.

3

THE INNER CIRCLE

Professor John Strugnell now lives alone and humbled, toppled from his post as chief editor of the Dead Sea Scrolls Publication Project by his own innocence, his continuing battles with manic depression, and his inability to anticipate the unfeeling cruelty of those who have power to wield. Now in his mid-sixties, he walks slowly and painfully with a cane up and down the three steep flights of stairs leading to his small Cambridge apartment, his solitary house of exile, just across the street from the Harvard Divinity School. Though he no longer teaches his famous seminars on the scrolls to masters classes of eager graduate students and is consigned to the bizarre and embarrassing status he calls "indefinite sabbatical," Strugnell is still among the most senior scroll scholars in the world. More than that: Strugnell's life story, with its ups and downs and pride and ultimate disaster, is an inseparable part of the scroll saga, stretching from his arrival in Jordanian Jerusalem in the summer of 1954 as a bright-eyed young Oxford scholar to his ignominious removal as editor-in-chief of the Dead Sea Scrolls project in December 1990. John Strugnell's identity is still shaped by his membership in a select fraternity of scholars who jealously guarded their exclusive access to the vast bulk of scrolls for almost forty years. Never numbering more than a dozen men from Europe and North America, they became known to detractors as the Inner Circle, and to themselves—perhaps a bit grandly but certainly proudly—as the International Team.

Since the autumn of 1991 and the opening of the Dead Sea Scroll photo archives to all interested scholars, the original team members no longer have a monopoly on the study of the hundreds of unpublished scroll fragments. They no longer have the privilege of parceling out to their favorite graduate students exclusive publication rights for important documents or the prerogative of refusing access to unpublished documents to scholars who they, for personal or professional reasons, look down upon. For almost forty years, embittered outsiders and critics alternatively ascribed the arrogant behavior of the insiders to clandestine theological motives (the censorship of potentially explosive "religious secrets") or to mere selfishness. But the story of the International Team must be seen in a political context; their story is also one of a colonial frame of mind that was vigorous and perhaps persuasive while Great Britain and France still harbored realistic pretensions of overseas empires, but petulant and petty once those empires began to die.

The team's glory days took place in the Hashemite Kingdom of Jordan in the 1950s and early 1960s, when the small circle of scholars brought in from Europe and America to serve as experts naturally assumed that their franchise was exclusive and that their superiority and competence were obvious to all. Yet the world changed, the Middle East changed, and the International Team refused to notice. Even today, John Strugnell looks back fondly to those far-off days of Jordanian rule in Jerusalem—"in those days when things were quiet and we thought God was in his heaven and the king was on his throne," as Strugnell puts it—and when civility, respectability, honor, and even elegance typified an expatriate Dead Sea Scroll scholar's life.

Like the European empires themselves, this scholarly imperium would eventually crumble. And the colonial joys that Strugnell once cherished in Jordanian Jerusalem remain out of reach in the seedy surroundings of Cambridge, Massachusetts, in the 1990s, with its urban grime, muggers, and homelessness. Strugnell is now forced to find self-justification in a kind of lonely nostalgia; while he readily condemns the selfishness of other scholars and the hidden political agendas of Israeli officialdom, he jokingly shrugs off all those inevitable vices as they were practiced in the close vicinity of the Hashemite court. Before I got to know Strugnell, I would have joined most others in ascribing this mind-set to an animus against Israel—understandable perhaps from his long experience in Jordan and dismissible perhaps as just another one of those familiar, empty litanies of allegiance that Western scholars often feel compelled to recite in all the nations of the modern Middle East. But I eventually found Strugnell's perspective both honest and unembarrassed. When he shared it with me through a haze of cigarette smoke, historical erudition, and witty self-deprecation, it made sense, naturally and innocently.

I had feared confronting Strugnell for months before I made the first contact. From the time of his now infamous interview in the Israeli daily *Haaretz* in November 1990 (in which he proudly identified himself as an "anti-Judaist," expounded on the theological reasons why all Jews should convert to Christianity, and expressed his disapproval of Zionism, as having been based "on a lie"), Strugnell had been made by the press into a larger-than-life bogeyman for anyone who had even a passing interest in the scrolls. No less intimidating to me were the stories of his drinking and his manic depression which forced him into hospitalization in those dizzying final days of 1990, when the first real break in the power of the Inner Circle/International Team was made. Strugnell seemed, from a distance, to be a very dangerous character, with his air of Oxford superiority and publicly expressed attitude that his opponents and rivals were merely fleas, morons, or incompetents who had not the decency to leave to the true Qumran scholars the very serious and exacting work of deciphering the Dead Sea Scrolls.

How would he react to me, a Jew, a prober and interviewer without a proper scholarly pedigree? I carried around his phone number for months before I took the initiative and dialed it, to hear his halting, reedy Oxford accent over the telephone. In fact, he was exceedingly friendly and helpful. He responded that he would be pleased to meet with me and discuss the history of the Dead Sea Scroll project, for he, too, was involved in a similar investigation. He was writing his own memoirs and would be happy to help in any way he could. So in late July 1992, on a scorching hot day, I drove to Cambridge to find Strugnell a bit grayer and a bit more dishevelled than he appeared in the standard press photo. He was obviously in some physical discomfort, huddled in his third-floor walk-up with the window air conditioner going at full blast. The drawn blinds blocked the glare from the pavement and the windshields in the Harvard Divinity School parking lot. This was not the heat of the Dead Sea summer, but the stuffy, dank world of a man who had been abandoned by most of his colleagues—even some of those who had worked with him for almost forty years—lest Strugnell's unfortunate statements about Jews and Israel endanger their own positions in an age of politically correct academia.

The floor-to-ceiling bookshelves on one of the walls of Strugnell's sitting room groaned with the weight of a vast library of scripture, scholarly periodicals, and literary and historical works. On a table pushed against the front window was a small portable television, an ashtray filled to its brim with the twisted butts of Marlboro 100s, a half-empty bottle of soda water, and a bulky, square microfiche reader, to view the newly published photographs of the scrolls. Taped to the wall by the front window was a newspaper photograph of Menachem Begin shaking hands with Anwar Sadat. Strugnell waved me toward the overstuffed sofa, just under the roar of the window air conditioner, while he sat down, stiffly and painfully, by the table and lit up another long cigarette. We spoke of modern Middle Eastern politics, of the history of archaeology in Palestine and Israel, of Victorian travel literature, and, of course, of his own role in the story of the scrolls. I found Strugnell's honesty about himself and about the unspoken politics of Dead Sea Scroll study surprising, yet welcome. And we began by discussing the personalities and roles of two of the other main characters of the scroll story: the English-born director of the Jordanian Department of Antiquities, Gerald Lankester Harding, and the director of the Ecole Biblique et Archéologique in Jerusalem, the Dominican Father Roland De Vaux.

It is an understatement to say that Harding, the gaunt, tight-lipped colonial official with a romantic attachment to bedouin life, and De Vaux, the charismatic, volatile priest from a prominent, conservative Parisian family, were an unlikely couple. But in the earliest days of scroll discovery and study, they emerged as efficient partners, brought together by historical circumstance to administer the antiquities of the newly annexed area of the Hashemite kingdom, to stop the bedouin plunder, and to supervise the preservation and eventual publication of the Qumran manuscripts. Through the 1950s, as scholars all over the world began their study of the original seven documents (photographs and transcriptions of which had all been published by 1955), Harding and De Vaux began to acquire—on behalf of the Palestine Archaeological Museum—the fragments of many more scrolls both through purchases on the antiquities market and by continuing archaeological excavations and surveys in the area of Qumran. In early 1949, soon after the end of the first Arab-Israeli war, they located and jointly directed an excavation of the first scroll cave, recovering a great deal of smashed pottery and other artifacts and hundreds of scroll fragments, some even belonging to the seven original scrolls. In late 1951, they began excavations at Khirbet Qumran, and through the spring of the following year they directed a search of the hundreds of nearby crevices and caves.

Yet it was in September 1952, once again due to the entrepreneurial spirit of the Taamireh bedouin rather than the preconceived plans of the archaeologists, that the greatest Dead Sea manuscript discovery was made. The story of the discovery of Cave 4 (Caves 2 and 3 had in the meantime been located and excavated by the archaeologists) is perhaps no less apocryphal than the tales of the original discovery. Yet this one at least credits the Taamireh with some skill and ingenuity. According to the most common version, some members of the tribe were sitting around a campfire when a Taamireh elder recalled his discovery—many years before—of a cave containing antiquities hidden in the steep side of the limestone plateau of Khirbet Qumran. Since the archaeologists had so far not searched this area, several of the Taamireh located the hidden cave, lowered themselves into it, and started to dig. They may have been experienced antiquities hunters, but no previous experience could have prepared them for this find. Scraping away a dusty, acrid layer of dirt and bat dung mixed with a few potsherds, they came upon a hard-packed layer of thousands and thousands of manuscript fragments.

The Taamireh immediately set to work digging out the mass of parchment scraps from the bottom of the bell-shaped cavity, while others stood guard on the surface above. Their good fortune was beyond all expectations, and this time, when they brought the first boxes of inscribed fragments to Jerusalem, they were not greeted with the skepticism and disdain that Ahmad Muhammed and Khalil Musa faced when they tried to find buyers for the first group of scrolls. In early September, they called at the Ecole Biblique and offered De Vaux a large group of fragments, for which De Vaux immediately paid 600 dinars, apparently borrowed from the Ecole's operating funds. It was clear to him that a major new discovery had been made in the Qumran area and he alerted Harding, who immediately dispatched mounted police to the site. The Taamireh therefore fled before the end of their excavation, and by the end of September, De Vaux and a young scholar from the Ecole, Abbé Josef Milik, went down to Qumran to remove the last few hundred fragments from the plundered floor of the cave. Nearby they discovered two smaller caves, now called Cave 5 and Cave 6, both containing some inscribed material.

With most of the fragments from Cave still in the hands of the Taamireh, Lankester Harding was determined to continue his policy of official purchase. Yet in light of the enormity of the Cave 4 discovery, it was clear that Harding's standing payment rate of a dinar (equivalent to a pound sterling) per square centimeter would soon bankrupt the museum. In September and October of 1952 alone, he and De Vaux acquired more than 11,000 square centimeters of scroll fragments directly from the bedouin—and subsequently from Kando, the Bethlehem merchant, who once again became their commercial agent and middleman. Harding began to dash off urgent letters to every archaeological and philanthropic institution he could think of, "in the hope that people interested in Biblical matters might be persuaded to make contributions to enable the rest of the material to be rescued from dispersal or even oblivion." A few contributions trickled in, but fortunately the government of Jordan came to the rescue, providing an emergency guarantee of 15,000 dinars so that the new discovery might be acquired by the Department of Antiquities.

The tangled financial arrangements for the acquisition of the scrolls would become even more complex in the coming years with the increasing involvement of foreign institutions and the changing legal status of the Cave 4 fragments themselves. And it would be nearly forty years before the enormous variety and significance of the literary works discovered in Cave 4 at Qumran would become generally known. The discovery of the first seven scrolls in 1946 and 1947 was just a tiny sample of the hidden Dead Sea literature. Although the copies of Isaiah from Cave 1 were trumpeted around the world as the world's oldest biblical manuscripts, Cave 4 contained at least fragmentary copies of every single book of the Old Testament—perhaps with the exception of the books of Nehemiah and Esther—and even those exceptions are still under scholarly dispute.

No less important were the original Hebrew texts of apocryphal books previously known to scholars only from Greek, Latin, Slavonic, and even Ethiopic translations—in addition to dozens of poetic and liturgical texts that were previously unknown. In the boxes of fragments bought from the Taamireh or excavated by the archaeologists were what eventually were estimated to be approximately 800 manuscripts. Whereas the Commentary on Habakkuk from Cave 1 was regarded as an intriguing and important piece of historical evidence, Cave 4 included commentaries on Isaiah, Micah, Zephaniah, Hosea, Nahum, Genesis, and Psalms. There were numerous Aramaic expansions of biblical stories as had been found in the Genesis Apocryphon. There were prayers, hymns, and visions; calendars, laws and legal opinions, financial accounts, and even horoscopes. There were more copies of the "Manual of Discipline" and of the "Damascus Document," which had been previously known only from the Cairo *geniza* text. In short, the thousands of manuscript fragments found in Cave 4 would represent an unimaginably significant historical treasure, once they were pieced together, deciphered, and transcribed. Cave 4 was a unique, overstuffed time capsule filled with firsthand evidence for understanding one of the most important periods in the religious development of the western world.

But how was that treasure to be treated? Would it be viewed as precious, uncontaminated evidence of a time and a place and a mind-set, and therefore serve as the starting point for an independent historical investigation of the period? Or would a religiously based inclination to accept the traditional stories as gospel undercut the independence of the analysis? The undeniable fact is that virtually every other source of written information we possess about the period of the birth of Rabbinic Judaism, the life of Jesus, and the birth of Christianity has been gleaned from literary works passed down from generation to generation—the Mishnah, the Talmud, the New Testament, the works of Josephus Flavius, and apocryphal works like the Book of Jubilees and the Book of Enoch—all of them subject to hundreds of years of correction, deletion, and censorship. So long as religious manuscripts had to be painstakingly copied by hand, word after word, verse after verse, by both Jewish and Christian scribes, there was ample opportunity to alter the historical record if the reality was found to be distasteful or heretical. Naturally, in periods of religious persecution or revival, some ancient works were proscribed altogether and consigned to the bonfire. Others were rewritten to conform to the current orthodoxy. Before the discovery of the Dead Sea

Scrolls, we possessed only documents that were so heavily edited for ideological and religious reasons that they were, in a sense, more properly records of continuous ecclesiastical censorship than pristine documentary evidence of first-century Judean society.

That is not to say there was no truth to be found in the New Testament stories; in the references in rabbinic literature to the personalities, customs, and events in Judea before the destruction of the Temple; or in the elaborate accounts of Josephus Flavius, whose physical descriptions of Jerusalem, Masada, and other Judean and Galilean landmarks have proved uncannily accurate by recent archaeology. It is, rather, that the larger historical context of all these sources is open to question. The Gospel writers were clearly not journalists or dispassionate observers but committed adherents of a faith in the salvation offered by Jesus Christ, Son of God and resurrected Messiah. They, and the generations of Christian copyists and commentators that came after them, had no interest in diluting the proselytizing power of the gospels with inflammatory political details. Likewise the rabbis sought to demonstrate that the triumph of Pharisaic Judaism was the natural and inevitable culmination of a Judaism that had already existed before the destruction of the Temple. The scattered details of other sects, beliefs, and legal opinions are rarely framed in a complimentary light. And such was the case with the writings of Josephus Flavius, written originally to flatter and justify the actions of his Roman patrons, to whom he defected during the course of the Jewish Revolt against Rome.

Could the hundreds of documents from Qumran Cave 4—when placed alongside the other Dead Sea discoveries—offer a radically different version of familiar events? Could they reveal the beliefs, hopes, and expectations of Judean groups who did not survive the brutal Roman suppression? Could they place Christianity and Pharisaic Judaism in a completely different light? It would take years of study and scholarly discussion before coherent answers could be given to any of those questions. The challenge would prove to be more than a technical one. The growing body of recovered Dead Sea manuscripts could offer a glimpse at the forgotten, suppressed, and otherwise unknown beliefs of dispossessed, radicalized, and rage-filled Jews, who were convinced that the End of Times had actually begun. The scrolls could offer new understandings of the ancient Jewish concept of the messiah and of the relationship of the Kingdom of God to the Empire of Rome. In 1952, a wide range of interpretive possibilities was still open to use the Dead Sea Scrolls to challenge tradition, to serve as eloquent evidence of a quite different religious reality. There is no question that the original team of scholars handled the literal transcription and grammatical analysis of the Dead Sea Scrolls with consummate skill. Yet there was always something missing. Unfortunately, even tragically, the wider historical meaning and powerful message expressed in the Dead Sea Scrolls was suppressed for decades—not necessarily by any conscious conspiracy but by a combination of scholarly nearsightedness, personal possessiveness, and intellectual arrogance.

Today when you skim through the yellowed pages of Père De Vaux's frequent reports of work in progress published in the *Revue Biblique* in the early 1950s and leaf through the large, heavy volumes of Oxford University Press's *Discoveries in the Judaean Desert of Jordan,* you have to admire the amount and quantity of work that Harding and De Vaux managed to accomplish with resources that were admittedly sparse. In the aftermath of the 1948 War, Jordan experienced a severe economic downturn and continuing political instability; antiquities were not high on the list of Jordanian national priorities. In 1952, the permanent staff of the Palestine Archaeological Museum consisted of an administrator, a few watchmen, a restorer, and a photographer. As a result of this shortage in manpower, Père De Vaux—as president of the Museum trustees—had enlisted the aid of two young clergymen scholars from the faculty of the Ecole Biblique, Father Josef Milik from Poland and Father Dominique Barthélemy from Switzerland.

By the time the finds from Cave 4 began to arrive at the museum, Milik and Barthélemy already had their hands full cleaning, sorting, mounting, transcribing, and translating the few hundred fragments recovered from Caves 1, 2, and 3. But now, instead of a few hundred fragments, scroll material was coming in every day by the fistful, by the boxful—big pieces, tiny pieces, pieces of ripped and folded scrolls. Sensing the enormity of the discovery and the challenge of both acquiring and processing it, Harding dashed off letters to all the archaeological colleagues he could think of in Europe and America, hoping to raise funds for the purchase of all the fragments in the hands of the bedouin and for the proper study and publication of the ancient documents as well. Conferring with De Vaux, he began to search for qualified scholars who would be willing to come to Jordan for an extended period of work at the Palestine Archaeological Museum to help clean, piece together, and publish the thousands of fragmentary ancient Hebrew and Aramaic scrolls. And through the personal intercession of Professor Carl Kraeling, director of the University of Chicago Oriental Institute, and—far more important—a confidant of John D. Rockefeller, Jr., Harding obtained approximately $30,000 from Rockefeller to support the work of six scholars (two from America and four from Europe) to undertake the decipherment of the Cave 4 fragments. By the fall of 1953, the work was in full swing.

At this point in the historical record, John Strugnell began his own story. And in the course of our discussions in his apartment in Cambridge, he, now as an older man, recalled for me the serendipitous, almost offhand way he had became involved in the project in the spring of 1954. He was at that time a twenty-four-year-old graduate student at Oxford, one of the small circle of protégés of the world-renowned Old Testament scholar Godfrey Driver. During the previous summer, Harding had begun to solicit recommendations from Driver about likely candidates for work in Jerusalem, and at the time Driver had given Harding the name of another of his students, a cocky young biblical scholar named John Marco Allegro, to join the International Team. But now, a year later, more help was needed. "It was at the end of a seminar"—Strugnell remembered of Driver's first mention to him of the Dead Sea Scroll Project—"he asked me to stay behind. He asked me about my plans because I was very interested in studying theology later on, and he asked if I would be willing to intriculate a year or two in Palestine."

For all the later talk about the International Team's members being uniquely qualified for their positions, Strugnell readily admitted to quite a different reality. "If you ask me what I had heard about the Dead Sea Scrolls, it was very little because they were not in the examination schedule at Oxford, and I was confined to that canon," he admitted. "Of course I heard occasional mention of the scrolls while I was studying by one of my teachers. Chaim Rabin, was in fact editing at the time the Damascus Document, which is related. But they were not part of the essential syllabus." When his examinations for the year were completed and he had formally accepted the offer of employment in Jerusalem, Strugnell asked Driver for suggestions on background reading to prepare him for the task ahead. "I saw that there were only four or five documents that were published," Strugnell continued, "so I went and bought them and read them on the plane coming out, and I thought that this was just going to be a problem in Hebrew. As to the theological business, I had a certain question, but at the moment I thought it was going to be like any other group of papyri."

Thus started the adventure for the young man whose closest previous connection with the modern Middle East—as he noted with irony—was the fact that he faced the portrait of T. E. Lawrence every evening at supper in the dining hall of Jesus College. Yet once his exams were completed and the details of his employment in Jerusalem were settled (he was to receive seventy dinars per month from the Palestine Archaeological Museum), Strugnell left England and, after stopping briefly in Italy, proceeded on by plane to Beirut. His final destination was the tiny Jerusalem airport, near the village of Kalandia. Strugnell's first memory of Jordan still remains with him, the vividness perhaps intensified with time. "Waiting at the airport was a beautiful girl, a member of the tourist staff who was there to greet everybody. Absolutely stunning," he recalled. But his real greeter was Yusuf Saad, Harding's assistant at the Palestine Archaeological Museum, who guided the young Englishman through customs and drove him to the American Schools of Oriental Research in Jerusalem, where he would stay for the first few months. And it was there at the American School that Strugnell first met one of his fellow team members, Monsignor Patrick W. Skehan of Catholic University in Washington, who had been appointed during the previous year.

In his recollection of his initial conversations with Skehan and later with team members Abbé Josef Milik and Abbé Jean Starcky at the museum, Strugnell admitted a certain uneasiness. "I was at this time a Protestant, very suspicious of Catholics walking around in cassocks and scarlet scarves." But that feeling began to dissolve with his first meeting with Père Roland De Vaux. "We had tea together at the Ecole Biblique and that's where De Vaux gave me his own view of all the background. I asked who the scrolls belonged to and if we could be thrown out of the country, and De Vaux gave me a scholarly and political orientation." It was then, Strugnell noted, that he first got detailed information on the legal and political status of the project—and the source of the funding for the project itself. "De Vaux answered my political questions. He said that this is an international museum and an international project authorized by the museum and financed by Mr. Rockefeller." Strugnell then recalled asking more pointed political questions about the team's position in Jordan, to which De Vaux replied that practically speaking their position was strong, "but of course it was always possible that political mania could come over us, but I have usually found that it is short-lived."

"He had a personality that grabbed you," Strugnell recalled of De Vaux at this and subsequent meetings—and that is an opinion I find to be shared by everyone who met him. With his white Dominican habit, unruly gray beard, horn-rimmed glasses, and animated manner of a born raconteur, De Vaux was an unforgettable character. More important, he was a natural organizer and leader. "He incorporated me into his team," Strugnell noted with obvious admiration. "If he told me to do something I would have done it without question. All along I had regarded these people as members of an erroneous religion but great scholars. There were long discussions with them over matters of religion that prepared the ground for my ultimately becoming Catholic, I suppose."

Harding proved to be another model. "I met Harding about four days later," he remembered, noting that as director of antiquities Harding's main office was in Amman and that he used to come to Jerusalem for the scroll business and the museum business about once a week. The contrast with De Vaux could hardly have been sharper. "He was a very different kind of man," Strugnell noted, "a windswept man. No fat on him at all. He was full of culture. We discovered in our first conversation that we must have met before because he had been at a small London concert where William Walton's *Façade* was performed; it was only performed once and I was there too. So this was a sign of what a small world it was. He was a man of culture. He was the answer to Edward Said's idea of orientalism, because he was perfectly orientalized—a perfect Arabic speaker, all his friends were Arabs, yet there was no doubt when you talked to him that he was an Englishman." He was also, according to Strugnell, a complete agnostic. "If you ever wanted to guarantee the complete nonprejudice of our group," he insisted, "it was that Harding had control over it."

At the time of Strugnell's arrival at the museum, the large-scale scroll project had been going on for almost a year. Strugnell was, in fact, the last to be appointed of the original group, joining his old classmate Allegro, Monsignor Skehan, Dr. Frank Moore Cross of the McCormick Theological Seminary in Chicago, Dr. Claus-Hunno Hunzinger of Göttingen, Abbé Jean Starcky of the Centre Nationale de la Recherche Scientifique in Paris, and Abbés Milik and Barthélemy, who were already there. The team members worked in a large room in the museum, in which long tables were set up and upon which thousands of fragments, mounted between glass plates, were spread out to be fitted together into individual documents. The task resembled the assembling of a gigantic jigsaw puzzle—or perhaps *hundreds* of jigsaw puzzles—whose indeterminate number of pieces were jumbled, shriveled, torn, in some cases rotted, or in many cases completely lost.

Before long, Strugnell got into the rhythm of the work with the other team members. Though he had no experience in paleography (the study of ancient handwriting styles was "not a subject studied at Oxford at all," Strugnell admitted), he soon showed talent in distinguishing the handwriting of individual scribes and recognizing distinctive parchment textures, so he could join the others in walking up and down the long tables, scanning the thousands of unidentified fragments, finding new "joins" for the texts that had been assigned to him.

Once the team members began to assemble individual documents from the mass of fragments, the wide range of the literary genres became clear. In Cave 1 at Qumran, there had been examples of several distinct genres: the Isaiah Scroll (quite close to the received Hebrew text of the Bible); the Habakkuk Commentary (a metaphorical interpretation of the biblical oracles); the Genesis Apocryphon (an Aramaic expansion of stories from the Book of Genesis); and the Manual of Discipline, the War Scroll, and the Thanksgiving Hymns (all unknown Hebrew works that were presumably written by members of the Qumran sect). Cave 4 yielded examples of all these types in great quantity. And this enormous quantity soon gave rise to an informal division of labor. The two Americans on the team, Frank Cross and Patrick Skehan, took the biblical texts. Allegro took the biblical commentaries and related documents. Starcky took all the documents in Aramaic. And Milik took the apocryphal Hebrew texts and works that were hitherto unknown.

Milik, having more than his share of material, set aside certain groups of material for Strugnell to work on when he arrived in the summer of 1954. Among them was a long legal text that would later become famous as 4QMMT and would become the centerpiece of the eventual struggle for control of the scrolls. From an initial twenty or so plates of joined fragments, Strugnell eventually expanded his share to well over a hundred—by identifying more pieces that fit into the gaps in the original documents, by identifying new texts among the unclaimed fragments, and by just taking others which seemed interesting. "In terms of manuscript fragments"—Strugnell laughed at his overt colonial reference—"it was like the Europeans dividing up Africa."

The work in the "Scrollery" was interesting, and Strugnell slowly developed a love for the slow pace of life in Jordanian Jerusalem. In fact, he proudly revealed to me that he had been the one to give the Scrollery its name; it was meant merely as a British schoolboy joke in the beginning—a parody of the name of Owl's new home, "The Wolery," in *Winnie the Pooh*. Yet the name stuck and the parody was forgotten, as the International Team developed a familiar routine. "We would work every day from nine to twelve and in the afternoon from three to six. Lunch and siesta was from noon to three. I would have lunch at the American School, I was staying there at first. When I moved in with an Arab family, I used to lunch at the National Palace Hotel. It was the nearest decent restaurant from the museum and one where I could meet with English-speaking Arabs and gradually Arabic-speaking Arabs, who would speak Arabic to me. It was a very civilized place in those days. If you ordered a bottle of wine and only drank half of it, they would put it in the refrigerator for the next time."

During my first conversations with Strugnell, I couldn't resist posing an intentionally provocative question. Although the International Team was meant to be nondenominational, all of the team members invited to Jordan were Christians, even though Strugnell had admitted that there was no lack of Jewish students with Driver at Oxford. In fact, Strugnell recalled that about half of his classmates were Jews. And in looking over the scholarly publications in the first years of scroll research, it is clear that there was no lack of Jewish candidates for team membership had the leaders of the project really wanted to make it as international and ecumenical as they claimed.

Strugnell recalled and sympathized with the overwhelming situation that faced De Vaux and Harding. They were confronted with the sudden responsibility of preserving one of the century's great archaeological discoveries in a delicate political climate. De Vaux was in Jerusalem as a foreign resident whose status and influence in Jordan was dependent on his political connections, and Harding was, after all, an official of the Jordanian government. His first priority was to purchase the thousands of fragments still in the hands of the bedouin and, despite the restricted government budget, he had managed to persuade the Council of Ministers to place funds at his disposal for the acquisition of the bulk of the Cave 4 scrolls. With regard to the recruitment of the team of scholars, the political realities of the Arab-Israel conflict were so obvious they never had to be openly discussed.

While doing research in Jerusalem I had come across a letter in the files of the Department of Antiquities that illustrated the uncomfortable situation. In November 1952, Sir Thomas Kendrick of the British Museum had replied to an urgent appeal from Harding with a telling reference to a Jewish member of the British Museum, who was skilled in the handling and decipherment of ancient Hebrew manuscripts. Sir Thomas wrote to Harding on November 8, 1952, that while the British Museum was ready and even anxious to purchase at least some of the manuscripts, the idea of sending an expert was, unfortunately, out of the question. Since the British Museum staff member best equipped to deal with the material was Jacob Leveen, Sir Thomas unquestioningly assumed that even a short visit by him to Jordan would be impossible. Thus, Jews were dismissed out of hand from consideration. It was taken for granted that the Jordanian government would be hostile to the presence of Jewish scholars in East Jerusalem while Jordan was at war with Israel.

Now, in speaking with Strugnell, I was not ready to allow scholarly apartheid—especially when the subject of the study is as important as the Dead Sea Scrolls—to be so easily rationalized. It might be just the wisdom of hindsight, but just as the Dome of the Rock in Jerusalem was left in the custodianship of Muslim authorities after 1967 (even if that relationship continues to be tense and based on an imbalance of power), there is something to be said for the right of Jewish scholars to have played some part in the study of the vast library of scrolls found in Qumran Cave 4. What would have happened, I asked Strugnell, if one of the scholars that Harding had contacted had insisted on appointing a Jewish scholar who happened to be unquestionably the world's greatest expert on a particular facet of scroll scholarship?

"Historians tend not to ask these 'what if' questions," Strugnell responded, "but it would have made no difference because it wouldn't have influenced the Jordanian army, which was in charge of frontier policy. It would have made an international incident, but a completely unproductive one."

And what of the different perspective that Jewish scholars might have brought to the study? Could Strugnell at least acknowledge that having scholars who were trained in Jewish law and early rabbinic literature might have made a difference in the early analysis of the ancient Jewish texts? Was the issue ever brought up? "I don't remember any discussion of the question," Strugnell told me, not quite understanding why I didn't simply drop this subject, "and I certainly don't remember any discussion of the . . . relevance or irrelevance of rabbinic literature. It's my subjective memory that I can't remember that as we sat down in the evening and chatted over our beer, or as we chatted as we did our work that this question of the Jewish scholars may well have been: 'You can't get them, so let's not waste our time.' "

Years later, that attitude would prove to be one of the causes of the team's sudden, jarring fall from power; by the 1980s, the political landscape of the Middle East had seismically shifted and at least lip service had to be accorded to the principal of equal opportunity. Of course, the prevailing official attitudes inside the Hashemite Kingdom back in the 1950s—the suspicion of Jews and the open hostility towards Israelis—were obviously beyond the power of the scroll scholars to change. Yet there is little evidence these attitudes were ever questioned. And it is a sign of how much the world took the Arab-Israeli conflict for granted that it never struck most observers as strange, or even exceptional, that a small group of scholars assigned to decipher the most important ancient Jewish manuscripts ever discovered, a group that proudly called itself "international and interconfessional," would have no Jewish members on their team.

The problem with the Inner Circle was not only in its restrictive composition, but how it went about its work. Here, too, any would-be critic has to be careful. The meticulous restoration, assembly, and study of the thousands of delicate ancient manuscript fragments would have taxed the resources of any museum in the world in the early 1950s—or, for that matter, today. As I've mentioned, the Palestine Archaeological Museum was then operating on a shoestring budget, and its relative geographical isolation, at a time when air travel from Europe was still measured in days, not hours, made consultation with preservation experts a luxury that was both expensive and relatively rare. Yet it is still somewhat shocking to learn how amateurish the treatment of the Cave 4 fragments was in the beginning. Whether anyone else at the time could have done much better is an open question, but it is a question that is at least worth raising in any discussion of the early history of the scrolls.

Several months before my first meeting with Strugnell, I had gone to interview Professor Frank Moore Cross, also of Harvard and also one of the members of the original team. Cross is a striking contrast to Strugnell; he is meticulous about his appearance (a bow tie and a neatly trimmed beard have become his recent trademarks); he is soft spoken and careful about his comments; and he has emerged from the Dead Sea Scroll experience with his very considerable reputation as a biblical scholar and epigrapher completely intact. Throughout all the years I have been involved in archaeology in one way or another, Cross has been a respected, even revered figure in American biblical scholarship. In his own quiet, reserved way, Cross had been a defender of the International Team throughout the recent upheavals, declaring that many of the protests and complaints against the Inner Circle of scholars were unjustified. Yet he also spoke openly and candidly about his early experiences in Jerusalem and about the way that the Cave 4 fragments were initially processed.

"I was the first of the team to arrive," Cross recalled of his initial work in Jerusalem in 1953. "I arrived in the summer and visited with Harding and De Vaux, and they decided that rather than bring out all of the new purchases, which were in a chaotic state, I should begin on all the excavated materials. So the first summer I cleaned and flattened and prepared and identified all the materials that were found in the excavation, which was a very fortunate enterprise because when we began to work on the purchased materials in September we knew that we were dealing with Cave 4 materials."

The "materials" were, of course, the fragments dug out of the earth less than a year before. Today manuscript finds in both Israel and Jordan are immediately entrusted to preservation specialists; if the find is unusual or its condition particularly delicate, foreign preservation experts are routinely called in. But, of course, that is today, not the Jordan of the 1950s. De Vaux and Harding were anxious to begin the project as soon as possible, so they assigned Cross to a small room at the museum, brought out the boxes of excavated manuscript fragments, gave him a bell jar and a pair of forceps, and put him to work.

"For the first summer I was entirely alone and worked away happily," Cross told me, noting that even though he had been trained as a linguist and historian and had never had any experience with archaeological preservation, he quickly established a routine of work. "The excavated material was not a huge amount, maybe fifteen boxes. I'd open a box and take out a fragment and put it in the bell jar and humidify it. That made possible placing it under glass plates and flattening it. But often I needed to clean the surface—there were a good number of urine crystals that obscured the script, probably from sheep."

I was amazed at the offhanded way Cross described his sudden immersion in such a delicate operation, but even now, almost forty years later, he did not seem to regard the work on the scroll fragments as particularly sensitive or delicate. "I learned about humidifying through experiment," he noted. "If the fragments were really bad, I cleaned them with castor oil." Apparently, De

Vaux had gained some experience working with Milik and Barthélemy on the earlier groups of fragments, and that is where the use of humidification and castor oil had begun. But now, in the case of Cave 4, there would be much more piecing together of fragments from individual documents. Cross had some regrets about one thing: "We made—I hate to confess it—some terrible blunders, which were a holdover from Cave 1. We used Scotch tape to make joins."

Several decades later, the Israel Antiquities Authority would devote thousands of hours to removing the gummy, destructive residue of Scotch tape from the backs of scroll fragments, and it is hard to believe that even in the early 1950s most museum curators would not have been horrified at the technique. But, as in so many facets of the early scroll study, this was an aspect of the work that De Vaux and Harding did not judge to be particularly important, and what was considered unimportant by them was simply dismissed. The international community of scholars was not as organized or as outspoken as it would later become. So in Jerusalem, the International Team worked on in virtual isolation, humidifying, flattening, castor-oiling, and Scotch-taping the most important collection of ancient Jewish manuscripts ever found.

What *was* considered to be most important was decipherment and identification, and during the first three years of the project there is no question that tremendous headway was made. From the beginning, Josef Milik seems to have been the leading spirit. Born in Poland and educated in Semitic languages in France, he had, according to Cross, "a very melancholy personality" and "a delightful sense of humor," but the quality that most colleagues remember from those days was his uncanny talent for reading even the most cramped or seemingly illegible handwriting and his instinctive knack for identifying the sense of previously unknown words in Hebrew and Aramaic. As the Scrollery developed, Cross recalled, and English became the main language of scholarly discussion, Milik tried his best to learn the language, to add to his fluent Polish, French, German, Latin, and Russian. He therefore became an avid reader "of ze American crime fiction," Cross remembered with a laugh, "and his early vocabulary was right out of Mickey Spillane."

Cross brought a talent more analytical than instinctive: as a protégé of the great American biblical scholar and orientalist W. F. Albright, he was a faithful believer in the precision of paleographical analysis for the study of ancient manuscripts. Albright, and naturally Cross, was convinced that in the regimented world of ancient scribes, handwriting styles changed uniformly and steadily, allowing modern scholars to date a certain manuscript by the characteristic letter forms it contained. Beginning in the 1930s, Albright had attempted to arrange all known ancient Hebrew manuscripts and inscriptions in a chronological sequence in which he pointed out how the shape of the Hebrew letters changed from the fifth century B.C.E. to the second century C.E. Cross would later become the champion of a refined version of this dating method, eventually isolating in the mass of Qumran fragments three successive handwriting styles: "Archaic" (c. 200–150 B.C.E.); "Hasmonean" (c. 150 B.C.E.–30 B.C.E.); and "Herodian" (30 B.C.E.–70 C.E).

Of course there was a greater significance to these categories than mere dating. Not only did the handwriting styles roughly correspond to the three major political periods in the history of Judea from the Seleucid conquest of the country to the Roman destruction of Jerusalem, but they offered seeming validation for the emerging consensus on the history of the sect that wrote the Dead Sea Scrolls. Sukenik, Albright, and Burrows all went along with the theory that the Dead Sea sect was none other than the ancient Jewish sect of the Essenes as described in the works of Philo, Josephus Flavius, and Pliny the Elder. According to these ancient accounts, the Essenes were an exceptionally pious religious group (perhaps ancient Shakers is the best modern way to describe them) who were separatist, especially in their exceptionally strict observance of the ritual code of purity. Apparently scorning the conventional worship at the Temple in Jerusalem, they pooled their private property and lived a communal existence, engaging in intense Bible study, performing a baptismal rite, and participating in common sacramental meals.

Long before the discovery of the Dead Sea Scrolls, Christian biblical scholars had valued the descriptions of Essenism as being, in some respects, a precursor of Christianity. In that sense, it was seen as spiritually more sophisticated than the rest of Judaism— on the way to becoming Christianity. Indeed, as I have already mentioned, there was an implicit evolutionary sequence in the common scholarly consensus about the religious developments within Judean society. An upheaval, so the consensus went, had occurred at the time of the Maccabean revolution, when the Judean state became independent again. While Maccabee (or more properly, Hasmonean) rulers became seduced with earthly power, more spiritual groups—the Pharisees and the Essenes among them—devalued political objectives and thereby represented the developments that heralded the way toward what the Christian scholars considered to be the sublime and unique faith that was Christianity.

What is important about this scheme of inevitable religious progression is that it tended to make each of the ascending stages simply a preparation for the preordained conclusion and not ultimately valuable in itself. That was certainly how the scholars saw Essenism: extremely interesting, but not as a legitimate way of life or philosophy that someone could really believe in. It, like the Dead Sea Scrolls themselves, was seen as valuable *background* material for understanding the spiritual world of Jesus, and as a source of literary parallels to understand better the idioms and allusions of the New Testament. And with the aid of paleographical analysis, the dating of the composition of the Dead Sea literature was pushed back to the time of Hasmoneans and thus made anterior to Christianity both in spirituality and in time.

Though there were inconsistencies and uncertainties in the ancient sources about various classes of married and unmarried Essenes living in town and cities as well as the Dead Sea region, the correspondences were close enough for the scholars to be drawn into something of a vicious circle: The descriptions of Josephus, Philo, and Pliny were used to explain obscure passages of the Dead Sea Community Rule and Damascus Document, and quotations from those scrolls were, in turn, used to shed new light on obscurities and inconsistencies in the surviving descriptions of the Essenes. What was striking was the way in which the customs and apparent beliefs of the Essenes were seen as rather static and completely detached from Judean political and social reality. If the paleographical analysis of the scrolls was correct, the formative period in the life of the sect took place around 150 B.C.E., and the authors of subsequent documents continued for more than two hundred years to pour out their scorn against the wicked Hasmonean priests and to praise a Teacher of Righteous who was apparently persecuted by them. Yet the monstrous rule of Herod the Great and the reign of blood, terror, and abomination of the Roman governors strangely passed without comment in the scrolls.

Of course there were always nay-sayers and dissidents to this evolutionary structure. Professor Solomon Zeitlin of Dropsie College in Philadelphia, certainly the most outspoken and stubborn curmudgeon of all the critics, dismissed the value of the Dead Sea Scrolls completely—and with it the schemes of religious evolution—declaring the manuscripts to be at first forgeries, and then, later, dating them to medieval times. As I mentioned before, Strugnell's teacher at Oxford, Godfrey Driver, considered paleography to be a pseudoscience and dated the scrolls to the post-Christian period on literary and historical grounds. In the end, however, faith in the elegantly simple logic of paleography, seemingly confirming the familiar spiritual progression, won out. Frank Cross recalled with a certain amount of bemused pride that "as I began to take part in this, I moved up from the status of 'dupe' in Zeitlin's categories to the status of 'liar,' which meant I had become recognized as a participant in the whole thing."

And so it was that the Maccabean origins of the Qumran sect became an unquestioned matter of faith. When documents like the Habakkuk Commentary were found to be written in a

"Herodian" style, and therefore datable to the first century C.E., the identification of the Wicked Priest with the long-dead Hasmoneans was never questioned. It was simply assumed that the sect remained fixated on the events of the Hasmonean period to the very end. It is hard to believe, though, that the authors of the scrolls were so cut off or so obsessive that they failed to record what was happening around them—until the morning that a Roman legion surrounded and burned down their community. The cultic missteps and lack of sensitivity shown by the Hasmoneans, after all, seem like the mildest of transgressions when placed beside the appointment of sycophants and stooges to the office of High Priest by Herod, the blasphemous provocations against the Temple by Pontius Pilate, and the unspeakable corruption and duplicity of the last High Priests of Jerusalem and the later Roman procurators. No one argued that the Dead Sea sect did not live through all these things—the date of the deposit was considered to be during the Revolt against Rome, probably in 68 C.E. Robert Eisenman would later describe the scholarly situation sarcastically but succinctly. The conventional dating of the historical allusions in the Dead Sea Scrolls were to him "as absurd as thinking that nowadays a preacher would interpret Biblical scripture in terms of the events surrounding the lives of George Washington, Napoleon, or the Duke of Wellington."

Yet during the first decades of Dead Sea Scroll study, any scholar or commentator who suggested that the historical references of the Dead Sea Scrolls might refer to a later period, or might even provide a running commentary on the ever-deepening evil of Roman rule, was declared to be eccentric or mistaken. Respectability in Qumran studies came to be judged not by innovative alternatives but by one's closeness to the hallowed consensual hypothesis. Paleography, ancient sources, and the internal references in the scrolls were not tested against each other skeptically but were all minced, diced, and mixed together to provide what to most religious scholars was a very satisfying stew. Two more ingredients would be added to make the recipe irresistible: potsherds and tumbled building stones from extensive archaeological excavations at the site of Khirbet Qumran.

The dozens of daily tour buses that rumble up the winding access road to the national park site of Qumran and let off their passengers in front of the snack bar and souvenir shop operated by the members of nearby Kibbutz Kalia continue to provide converts to the accepted story of the scrolls. The spectacular landscape of the looming, cave-filled cliffs on one side and the ruin-strewn plateau overlooking the Dead Sea on the other conspire to make a web of dubious archaeological assumptions seem like historical bedrock. Most visitors leave the site perhaps not remembering all the dates and the details. But I am convinced that most take away the feeling that the story of the scrolls and the Essenes is—to archaeologists and other scholars—above questioning or doubt.

After standing near the entrance to the ruins and hearing the story of the bedouin discoveries, the visitors are led past a ruined tower through a labyrinth of half-standing walls. There, with the help of the guide's dramatic monologue, they are told of the establishment and subsequent history of this isolated monastery, where Essene monks wrote their scrolls, had their sacred meals, performed their ritual baptisms, and dreamt of the great coming war between the forces of Light and Darkness—until, of course, the Roman legions arrived and slashed, smashed, and torched those dreams away. The terse informational signs placed here and there through the ruins by the Parks Authority act as subtitles for the story: here is the Scriptorium; there is the Dining Hall and the Kitchen; here is the Assembly Hall. It is all so neat and reminiscent of vivid images in our modern western consciousness—what else do monks do but live in isolation, silently taking their meals in common, and scrawling out sacred manuscripts?

Over the years, I faithfully repeated the story as I brought visiting friends or relatives down to walk through the site of Qumran. I remember one visit in particular—when I was working in the Department of Antiquities in the early 1970s—and my grandfather, toward the end of his life, was making his last trip to Israel. Our shared fascination with the Dead Sea Scrolls had continued from the time of his much earlier visits to Israel, when the seven scrolls in the Shrine of the Book were the main focus of attraction—and when he had brought that small souvenir scroll jar back to me. But now, in the aftermath of the 1967 Six Day War, Khirbet Qumran and the scroll caves themselves were no longer inaccessible, across the border in Jordan. In fact, they had become a highlight of sight-seeing trips to Israel.

We traveled around the country for several days together, and I suppose we could have posed for a photo in any of the other familiar Jewish-American tourist places: in front of the Western Wall or the Knesset, at the foot of Masada, outside the Hadassah Hospital, or along the lakefront at Tiberias. But Qumran had a special significance, and one of the last pictures I have of my grandfather and me together shows us there, squinting into the morning sunlight (me, with my long hair, moustache, Israeli shorts, and sandals, and him, with his Sansabelt slacks, sportshirt, sunglasses, and Miami Beach tan). The bleached white limestone and dark entrance of Cave 4 can be seen clearly in the background; nearby are the ruins of the excavated settlement. We both were fascinated by the history of the place and here we were in the middle of it. But what I didn't realize at the time, and I didn't start to realize until about twenty years later—when I began to listen seriously to the critics—is that the archaeological site of Khirbet Qumran, as it is now described and presented to the public, is not history but an interpretation. It is no less an artificial ideological construct than any other religious monument.

In my days as an uncritical admirer of the Qumran project, when I would occasionally—silently and respectfully—enter the storeroom at the Rockefeller Museum where the Qumran finds were deposited, I had no nagging postmodern doubts that archae-ological interpretation was *not* history. If an excavation was con-ducted carefully, if the finds were closely studied and accurately dated, it was possible, I believed and was taught, that an objective picture of the site could be obtained. The excavations at Qumran, conducted between 1951 and 1956 by Père De Vaux on behalf of the Jordan Department of Antiquities, the Palestine Archaeological Museum, and the Ecole Biblique, were respected as competent and thorough. In fact, as any archaeology student of the time knew, the excavated pottery from Qumran was used as a benchmark in Paul Lapp's pioneering monograph, *Palestinian Ceramic Chronology, 200 BC–AD 70*. And the layout of the Essene monastery at Qumran, as described and published by De Vaux in his 1959 lectures to the British Academy, became one of the few takens-for-granted in the archaeology of Hellenistic and Roman Palestine.

The colorful atmosphere of the De Vaux excavation camp there on the Dead Sea shore in the early 1950s has become almost legendary in the annals of Palestinian archaeology. Frank Cross, who participated as a staff member in the 1954 digging season, recalled that "De Vaux was a wonderful leader and the food was great," and he especially remembered the party held at the site to celebrate De Vaux's fiftieth birthday, with glasses of cognac raised high in toasts again and again. As usual, the workers were the Taamireh—the sometime allies, the sometime competitors of the archaeologists in the search for the scrolls. Muhammad "the Wolf," one of the three Taamireh who started this whole business by their discovery of Cave 1 eight years before, was now a married man and he was one of the workers. "He was small and delicate like a Yemenite," Cross remembered. "He had a very nice face, but he was not a celebrity within the tribe, and he certainly had no station of prestige. I believe he got a rifle and his first wife as his share in the sale of the scrolls."

Cross also recalled the daily dawn masses held in the ruins by De Vaux and the other Dominican scholars. Photographs from the period show Abbé Jean Starcky, a member of the International Team and a member of the staff of the Qumran expedition, celebrating mass with hands raised in the orans position next to an ancient wall that had been covered with an altar cloth. The image of white-robed Dominican friars directing bedouin diggers was unforgettable to all those who ever visited or wrote about the dig. But there was something more pervasive than mere background color in the phenomenon; every archaeologist approaches his or her site with some sort of preconception about the kind of things that they're likely to find there. It is impossible to approach a jumbled mound of rocks, dirt, and broken pottery without having some preconception of the kinds of buildings or artifacts those shattered fragments once were. By the time of the first Qumran excavations, the scholarly consensus about the authors of the scrolls was that they were pious, quietistic monks in the wilderness. And it is not hard to see where Père De Vaux got his store of mental images with which to reconstruct the finds.

I am not suggesting that in any sense De Vaux consciously manipulated the evidence. As far as can be determined from his regular excavation reports and other writings, the expedition team did the best they could to distinguish the stratigraphic levels accurately, to record the position of all pottery vessels, coins, and other artifacts, and to draw an accurate map of the site. And there is no question that the ancient settlement was communal in nature. But what kind of a community? It takes a leap of faith to deduce from the ruined furnishings of a room with benches, recessed cupboards, and a built-in basin that it "gives the appearance of having been designed for closed sessions in which those taking part did not wish to be disturbed." Or that a long room, identified as a dining hall (with an adjoining storeroom of identically shaped bowls) was the community's "refectory." There is also De Vaux's identification of a room with shattered plaster tables—and two inkwells—as a scriptorium. I could mention other turns-of-phrase and terminology used by De Vaux to describe the Qumran settlement; it should be enough to say that all this made perfect sense—it still makes perfect sense—so long as a simplistically conceived, Christian-style monastery was what you were looking for.

A more logical procedure would have been to view the archaeological material as an independent source of data. But by the time of De Vaux's excavations, the sources of data regarding the scrolls and the people who wrote them—paleography, Josephus, the internal evidence of the texts, and now archaeology and an idealized image of medieval European monasticism—had become so mixed together and so thoroughly mutually reinforcing that any contradiction or complication of the theory of the isolated monastery was quickly solved by the interplay of the images and the texts. A number of recent reviews of the archaeology of Qumran—those of Schiffman, Golb, Darceel, and Davies, for instance—have pointed out the religious preconceptions built into De Vaux's interpretations and have called for a reexamination of the evidence. But only Robert Eisenman has fully explored another dimension: De Vaux's explanations of the establishment, expansion, temporary abandonment, and reoccupation of Qumran are absurdly set apart from and unaffected by what we know of the tumultuous events of Judean history.

Here is the basic structure of De Vaux's story: Sometime around 125 B.C.E., a group of religious dissidents, angry and alienated from the Jerusalem establishment, left their former lives and homes to establish themselves in the wilderness in the ruins of a long-abandoned Iron Age fort. Where they got their financial resources or, for that matter, their skill in architecture and stonemasonry, De Vaux makes no comment, but he suggests that they constructed a place of asylum that included a large tower, spacious meeting rooms and workshops, and an elaborate system of water channels, storage cisterns, and ritual baths. According to the coin evidence, the dissident settlement expanded greatly during the reign of the Hasmonean king Alexander Jannaeus (103–76 B.C.E.), apparently the result of a new stream of anti-Hasmonean refugees. Never mind the fact that Jannaeus was particularly active in the Jordan Valley and the Dead Sea region and that he would be well aware of such a hotbed of sedition near the junction of roads running eastward across the Jordan and southward along the western coast of the Dead Sea. The isolation of the site in the Hashemite Kingdom of Jordan in the 1950s was unconsciously retrojected onto antiquity.

According to the evidence of a destruction of the settlement—an apparent lack of coins from the reign of Herod the Great (37–4 B.C.E.)—De Vaux postulated a period of abandonment. What was the cause of this sudden destruction? Did the destruction have anything to do with the twenty-five years of civil war, Roman invasion, and economic disruption that Judea experienced before the rise of the Roman client-king Herod? And did the abandonment have anything to do with the oppressiveness of Herod's reign? The real reason, De Vaux insisted—pulling a rabbit out of a hat, or perhaps the deus from the machina—was not politics but an earthquake that struck the region in 31 B.C.E. Why the religious dissidents did not immediately return to rebuild their scriptorium and refectory once the aftershocks had ended is not given an explanation, nor is the resumption of settlement at Qumran soon after the end of the reign of Herod and Archelaus, his incompetent, insensitive son. All these correspondences have great significance for understanding the connections of Qumran and the Dead Sea Scrolls with the history of Judea, Christianity, and Jewish nationalism.

But it was easier to tell the story of a monastery whose inhabitants lived in complete isolation, a religious oddity that in some ways was a pale precursor of Christianity. Beginning in the mid-1950s, a series of popular books by the members of the International Team and those associated with the Ecole Biblique poured forth, describing the discovery and history of the Essene monastery at Qumran. Even though there were minor divergences in the details of their stories, Cross's *The Ancient Library of Qumran,* Milik's *Dix ans de découvertes dans le désert de Juda,* and Van der Ploeg's *The Excavations at Qumran* were all singing from the same hymnal: that Qumran was an isolated, serenely apolitical settlement of monks away from the din of war and politics in Jerusalem. There was nothing here that would challenge the historical uniqueness of Christianity or suggest a connection with the characters of the gospels or, for that matter, of the Jewish Revolt against Rome.

Only a few voices attacked the consensus, and they were generally regarded as academic cranks or soreheads who did not understand what was going on. What was going on, in fact, was a neat compartmentalization of Judean society, robbing it of the overall coherence that would have made possible a new insight into the social conflicts and political reality that lay behind the rise of Pharisaic Judaism and Christianity. But everything, not only Qumran, was left in isolation. In Jerusalem and the Galilee were the Christian monuments of the life of Jesus, recording the pacific life of Jesus and his followers. At Masada, Yigael Yadin attracted worldwide attention with his large-scale excavations of the last stand of the Zealots. But when Qumran-type documents were found there, Yadin insisted that they had been brought by chance by individual Essene refugees fleeing for their lives: He was unable to envision an institutional or ideological link. The earlier opulent Herodian palaces at Masada and those at Herodium and Jericho were studied for their architecture and engineering, not their social significance. Caesarea, the seat of the Roman governors, was admired for its harbor, not for its oppressive influence. The villas of the Jerusalem aristocracy in the Upper City were seen as models of elegance, not corruption or decadence. And, of course, there was Qumran, with its splendid isolation and its pious monks.

There is good reason, as I mentioned, to believe that Qumran was neither as isolated nor as remote as the cloistered monastery theory would have us believe. But even more mistaken was the neat archaeological compartmentalization of social groups, economic classes, and varying lifestyles in first-century Judean society. In a living, dynamic society, rich people, radical people, stylish people, and pious people interact and react with one another. That is how history is made. But like Josephus Flavius, the Jewish turncoat and self-interested chronicler of the recent history of his people, the twentieth-century scholars made little effort to understand how all the pieces fit together. The familiar story of the isolated monastery in the desert was too facile an explanation to fulfill the real object of the exercise: to reconstruct or at least attempt to understand a complex, dynamic historical reality.

Sitting with Professor John Strugnell under the lacquered lanterns of a Chinese restaurant on Massachusetts Avenue in Cambridge, with the chatter and cigarette smoke of a busy lunch hour all around us, I listened intently to his detailed recollections of long years of faithful service on the International Team. His memories of his years in Jerusalem now seemed far off and tinged with sadness. He tried to explain to me how hard he had worked as editor-in-chief to distribute the texts to more scholars to speed their publication. He described his stormy relationship with *Biblical Archaeology Review* editor Hershel Shanks, and the circumstances behind the notorious newspaper interview that finally brought him down. Yet even now, Strugnell could not understand why he had been chosen as a target, why there had been such an intense public uproar over the behavior of what—to him—was the quite acceptable pace of work of the International Team. "Everyone should be as quick as we were," he insisted, citing, for instance, the scholarly publication of the well-preserved Gnostic manuscripts found at Nag Hammadi in Egypt. "It took ten years to do it, and they could have done it in a year."

As they say, he just didn't get it. The time spent by the International Team working on the Cave 4 fragments now stood at forty years and counting, and despite all claims to the contrary, the team members would never have completed their assignments if they had been left completely on their own. Strugnell, in public statements and television interviews, had always made it seem that the sudden death of John D. Rockefeller, Jr., in 1960 was the historical turning point in the project. Rockefeller money had enabled team members to spend extended periods of time in Jerusalem, and had the support continued just a bit longer, he implied, things would probably have worked themselves out. Yet there is absolutely no evidence in the Rockefeller files to suggest that Rockefeller would have poured more money into the project, which had already become, by the late 1950s, something of a pain in the neck.

It is often been said that academic conflicts are so bitter precisely because the stakes are so small. The entire Rockefeller funding for the Dead Sea Scrolls project from 1953 to 1960 was less than $100,000—at a time when Mr. Rockefeller was giving several million every year to Colonial Williamsburg. There were growing political problems in Jordan, which resulted in the termination of the services of Lankester Harding in the summer of 1956. Then, through the period of the Suez Crisis, there was constant agitation for the nationalization of the documents and the increasingly stringent restrictions on the future disposition of the texts. Add to that the continued procrastination of the scholars in getting out the texts as promised, and it becomes obvious why Mr. Rockefeller's advisors determined that the three-year grant given for the support of the scholars in 1957 would be the last Rockefeller contribution to the enterprise.

By 1960, in fact, the basic work had been completed, according to the memories of both Cross and Strugnell. Although the plates of unidentified fragments were still laid out on the long tables in the Scrollery, Cross recalled that only tiny pieces remained to be identified. Transcriptions and rough translations had been made for all of the assembled documents and a comprehensive concordance was compiled. "So at a certain point," Cross told me, "De Vaux came and said, look, you've gone as far as you can, you have to stop." But years passed and still none of the Cave 4 volumes appeared. In fact, the termination of the Rockefeller funding gave a new excuse for delay and deferral. According to Strugnell, "very few of us had any money to keep us alive while we worked on the scrolls." So the members of the International Team divided up publication rights to the material and went their separate ways.

Strugnell found a teaching position at Duke and, later, with Cross at Harvard; Allegro was back at Manchester; Skehan at Catholic University; Milik returned to Paris, left the priesthood, and worked for years at the Centre Nationale de la Recherche Scientifique. Now the team members worked mainly from photographs, only occasionally coming out to Jordan to examine the fragments themselves. The volumes of the official publication series came slowly, and the vast majority of the Cave 4 texts, though transcribed and offered for discussion in private seminars and occasional lectures, remained unavailable to the scholarly public at large. It was not a conspiracy to suppress things, but a closed club

of scholars who now had many other academic commitments besides publishing the Dead Sea Scrolls. Yet rather than give up their
exclusive publication rights or publish their texts in an unfinished
state, they held on.

The Israeli conquest of East Jerusalem made matters even
more tangled, and the status quo endured. To interested outsiders, not blessed with personal connections to the Inner Circle, the
situation eventually became intolerable. Hershel Shanks put it eloquently and succinctly in an op-ed piece in *The New York Times* on
September 7, 1991, at a moment when the scholarly monopoly
over the scrolls was about to be broken once and for all.

"I believe that under international law these editors are trustees, fiduciaries," Shanks wrote with both passion and conviction.
"The real beneficiaries of this trust are all the people whose heritage is illuminated by these precious texts—not an elite group of
scholars or even a single country, culture, or religion. In making
these transcripts, they were furthering their fiduciary assignment;
they were working for us. By keeping them secret for more than a
generation, they have breached this trust and violated their obligation. It is they who are the lawbreakers. It is they who are stealing from all of us, not we from them." And outside public
pressure eventually accomplished what quiet, respectful appeals
to the members of the International Team never could.

Strugnell's eventual removal as editor-in-chief and even the
publication of reconstructed transcripts and scroll photographs
did not mean that the struggle was over. Widened access to the
Qumran literature did not provoke a dramatic rethinking of historical and religious takens-for-granted. Some scholars will argue
that it is because the work of the original editors was so prescient
and precise that the conclusions they reached in the early 1950s
are still basically valid today. That would be unusual, maybe even
unique. Virtually every historical discipline has undergone astounding transformation in that same timespan. Cultural anthropology, social history, historical sociology, and a dozen other
" 'ologies" have dramatically transformed the way we think about
the past all over the world.

In the specific case of ancient Judaism and early Christianity, many biblical scholars have changed their focus dramatically in the last four decades, expanding scholarly horizons by incorporating an awareness of the role played by gender, social tensions, elite propaganda, protest and resistance movements, and thinly veiled political ideology in the creation of religious literature. We also know a great deal more about the material culture of Judea at the time of the writing of the scrolls. From nearly four decades of intensive archaeological excavation, we now have a wealth of data on the daily life, cultural interconnections, and economic conditions of Judea in the late Hellenistic and Roman periods that was unavailable at the time of the original Qumran dig.

Yet the tyranny of the paleographers and the philologists still endures in scroll studies, even though the names and nationalities of many of the participants have changed. The Dead Sea Scrolls and the people who wrote them are still seen in isolation. The religious literature of the scrolls is still seen as an interesting but ultimately sterile religious expression, of relevance only as background material in the study of Rabbinic Judaism and of Christianity. Thus the old scholarly consensus, based on arguable paleographical, historical, and archaeological assumptions, has survived the fall of the Inner Circle. Respectable scholars continue to show only disdain for alternative interpretations. And the strident modern conflicts for possession of the once-hidden scrolls are merely the surface ripples of a much deeper and profound theological struggle—between those who would faithfully serve the established institutions of religion and higher learning and those who would dare to challenge them.

4

SECRET MESSIAH

He would not be a humble carpenter or meek shepherd, preaching love and forgiveness in parables, nor would he be a divinely incarnated offering to atone for the sins of man. The last messiah (often messiahs) of Israel would be a triumphant warrior figure, a righteous judge, high priest, and wise ruler. In the literature of Qumran, the messianic figures appear in various guises and with varying descriptions, but the circumstances under which they would appear seem clear. At the end of an Age of Wickedness—characterized by the enslavement of the people of Israel to idolatrous foreign powers (itself a punishment for the Israelites' own faithlessness to the laws of the covenant)—divinely anointed leaders would arise to lead the righteous remnant to defeat their oppressors and preside over the establishment of a perfectly harmonious and egalitarian Kingdom of Heaven on earth.

There was nothing metaphorical or otherworldly about this brand of messianic fervor. The people of Qumran shared the common belief of the time that the Forces of Darkness were represented on earth by none other than the Romans and their Judean agents, and that the elimination of wickedness would be brought about by an almost unimaginably bloody Holy War. Then would come a period of Renewal, in which the meticulous observance of the divinely appointed festivals, temple sacrifices, and purity codes would make the land exceedingly fertile and, as a result, peace and harmony would prevail. This was the futurist vision of a people who knew only disorder, injustice, and the struggle to subsist in a poor country, where the rains were too often insufficient and where crops often failed. But what distinguished this messianic belief from a mere daydream was its balance of political and spiritual aspirations. The destruction of external oppression was only the first step toward spiritual redemption, which would only be achieved with the perfect fulfillment of the Mosaic law. In this apocalyptic drama, the people of Israel would play a direct role in their own redemption. Led by their long-awaited messiah and guided by a vision of righteousness, they would remake the world.

Messianic references run through the literature of Qumran and its people, yet their precise meaning is not always clear. Written on torn and deteriorated parchment of colors varying from bleached white to burnt umber by many scribes (whose skill varied widely), these references appear in a number of literary genres and individual documents, some of which are extremely fragmentary. In some of the most important texts, the pitch darkness of the leather, the wrinkling or the shrinking of the torn edges, or the cramped, hurried handwriting make it difficult to recognize unambiguously more than a word or two on every line. That is why studying the scrolls can be an intensely subjective experience, in which a scholar's hopes, fears, beliefs, and preconceptions might determine what he or she sees. In that sense, the Dead Sea Scrolls can be a spiritual Rorschach test as much as an exercise in epigraphic or historical research. The faithful Christian, the secular humanist, the cynic, and the iconoclast all see something very different in the wrinkled brown leaves of ancient leather with the Hebrew word *mashiach*, "Messiah," written all over them.

What that word *mashiach* means is, of course a problem, given its origins in ancient Israelite religious ideology and its later use as a central concept of the Christian faith. The Hebrew word *mashiach*, in its literal sense, means "anointed," that is, perfumed with precious oil as a sign of divine election to kingship or the priesthood in the ancient Near East. Throughout most of the books of the Old Testament, *mashiach* means exactly that: a powerful, divinely sanctioned leader. The term is used to describe earthly, political personalities like Saul, David, Solomon, and even Cyrus the Great. With the fall of the Israelite Kingdom to the Assyrians in 721 B.C.E., and more particularly with the destruction of the Judean monarchy by the Babylonians about 135 years later, a new concept of the *mashiach* arose. With the people of Israel stripped (temporarily?) of political independence and divine favor, they began to look forward to a time when a divinely appointed king like David—or perhaps even a distant descendant of the Davidic dynasty—would arise to defeat all of Israel's enemies and restore their nostalgically remembered political and economic independence. In other words, to establish, from a Judean perspective, the reign of God on earth.

In Jesus of Nazareth, however, the Jewish concept of the messiah underwent a far-reaching theological transformation. Though the term *christos* was a literal Greek translation of the Hebrew *mashiach,* and though many of the biblical prophecies were now interpreted as foretelling Jesus' earthly incarnation, little remained of the strictly national, political savior of the people of Israel in the otherwordly, apolitical Christ. Gentile Christians, of course, who would now share in the Kingdom, saw this transformation as a momentous spiritual turning point in human history. But in the last hundred years, as historians and biblical scholars have paid more attention to the ancient Jewish sources, this turning point is a lot less clear cut than it used to be. With the discovery of the Dead Sea Scrolls, it was seen that Jewish and early Christian conceptions of the messiah overlapped in many cases. And because the scroll texts were so cryptic and, in many cases, so fragmentary, any statements about the relationship between Jewish and Christian messianism—between Judaism and early Christianity—were less a matter of clear-cut documentary evidence than of the theological interpretations of a particular faith.

As the contents of the first scrolls were gradually made known to the scholarly public in the early 1950s, they were seen to contain some striking correspondences to terms and even concepts that appeared in the New Testament. Common to the Qumran Community Rule and the gospels were such terms as "the light of life," "sons of light," and "life eternal." There were numerous references in the Community Rule, the Damascus Document, and the War Scroll to the sect's messianic expectations, and some scholars even saw in the Damascus Document an indication that the members of the Qumran Community awaited the messianic return of their own Teacher of Righteousness. The Community Rule also revealed the centrality of the rite of baptism and the sacred communal meals of the faithful. The pooling of wealth and the adoption of celibacy also suggested similarities to early Christianity. The use of similar organizational terms by the Qumran Community and the early church was no less striking. Parallel Hebrew and Greek terms, both translated as "The Many," were used to designate the congregation of all the initiated members of the Dead Sea sect and groups of early followers of Jesus. Likewise, the Qumran Community was presided over by a Council of twelve lay members and three priests, which, some scholars have noted, corresponded uncannily to the Jerusalem Church's Council of the Twelve Apostles (with James, Cephas, and John as its three "pillars"). Furthermore, the chief administrator of the Qumran community was called the *mevakker* or "overseer," which, in the literal Greek translation, *episkopos,* became the title of the bishops of the early Christian communities. In fact, the connections between Qumran and early Christianity were so close that Frank Cross wrote in 1956 that he found it "extraordinary that the Essenes are not named in the New Testament. I know of no fully adequate explanation of this circumstance."

Others rather quickly came up with the explanations, stressing the differences rather than the similarities. The fear that the scrolls might somehow undermine the spiritual uniqueness of Christianity was real. In his 1955 book *The Dead Sea Scrolls,* Professor Burrows of Yale moved quickly to calm the faithful. "It has even been said that the discoveries will revolutionize New Testament scholarship," he wrote. "This may perhaps cause some alarm. There is no danger, however, that our understanding of the New Testament will be so revolutionized by the Dead Sea Scrolls as to require a revision of any basic article of Christian faith." More and more the established scholars placed as much stress on the differences between the doctrines of Qumran and the church as on the similarities.

The Community Rule and the Damascus Document, after all, spoke of hopes for the coming of *two* messiahs, one priestly and one royal, not a single Davidic one. And although it is certainly true that many of the terms and customs of Qumran were used by the Christians, they were—according to the scholars—given a completely different significance. The Christians preached love to all peoples, not merely fellow members of the community. For the Christians, the messiah had already come to inaugurate the Kingdom of God, while the Qumran texts spoke longingly of that event, which was yet to occur. In 1957, Abbé J. T. Milik put it definitively in a statement I have already quoted, insisting that, despite all parallels to the beliefs of the Qumran Community, Christianity "represents something completely new." More recently, in 1992, Professor James VanderKam of Notre Dame underlined the difference between the closed, elitist dogma of the Qumran Community and the universal message of Christianity. "The Qumran scrolls," he wrote, "also help to highlight Christianity's uniqueness: This lies not so much in its communal practices and eschatological expectations but in its confession that the son of a carpenter from Nazareth in Galilee was indeed the Messiah and Son of God who taught, healed, suffered, died, rose, ascended, and promised to return some day in glory to judge the living and the dead."

This is the language of religious belief, not an analytical, historical distinction. Indeed, most Dead Sea Scrolls scholars leave little doubt where their own religious sympathies lay. That is not to say that a Jewish or a Christian scholar would ever intentionally mistranslate, suppress, or destroy any scroll texts that he or she found to be a threat to the faith. Those who suspect complex conspiracies to cover up explosive religious secrets contained in the scrolls do not understand how subjective scroll study really is. The poetic language of the Qumran manuscripts is in many cases cryptic and highly metaphorical; the precise theological meaning of many messianic terms and allusions is extremely unclear. For an international conspiracy to work, its pious agents would have to be able to identify "explosive secrets" in order to suppress them. And the reality of Qumran study is that almost everything is subject to interpretation. A pious scholar, whether Jewish or Christian, is likely to see only what he or she believes is true. And he or she will likely come away from study of the Dead Sea Scrolls with only heightened appreciation for the historical basis of his or her particular faith.

For all the proud talk these days about openness and free access for all interested scholars, you still have to overcome a series of daunting roadblocks to get through the labyrinth of gatekeepers, doorways, padlocks, and inner chambers to arrive at the quiet, cramped room where you can examine the plates of assembled scroll fragments from Qumran Cave 4. There is still a protocol of recognitions, polite nods, and familiar codewords—conveyed by the right letters of recommendation and the right manner of speaking—that one must use to get to the inner sanctum where the hundreds of ancient Hebrew and Aramaic documents are stored.

Father Emile Puech of the Ecole Biblique et Archéologique in Jerusalem, one of the leaders in the field of scroll scholarship, agreed to take me to the Scrollery, to give me a glimpse at the work. Short, dark, with a square, jet-black beard and dark eyes, Puech is alternately patient, passionate, and irritable when it comes to discussing the scrolls. I had met him a year before at the Ecole, and he had taken me down to his small workspace in the school's famed library—though his place was hardly more than the cramped carrel of a normal American graduate student—and he showed me the collages on which he had made his reputation in the world of Dead Sea Scroll scholarship. Opening a large foldout, on which he had carefully pasted together cutout Xerox copies of scroll fragments, he proceeded with great excitement and with excited sweeping motions of his hand to show how he had rearranged the fragments from position to position. Proving the logic of his transpositions, he read out the new message contained in this rearranged document, identifying it as an angelic liturgy.

This was no agent of theological suppression, carefully going over secret documents and suppressing those which he did not like. Emile Puech is a priest who would find it very difficult to identify, much less search for, evidence in the Qumran texts that would challenge the messiahship or even essential uniqueness of Jesus Christ. "I am a peasant, you know," he later told me of his family background. "I was with the cows, and sheeps, and vineyards and so on, in the south of France, near Estaing, a very well-known village." It is, as Puech proudly informed me, the domain of the "very good family" of former President Valerie Giscard d'Estaing. But even at an early age, this farmer's son decided to devote his life to the church. Going off to study theology and Latin in a seminary near Lyon, Puech wanted more than most students. He recalled how, after discovering some old Hebrew books in the seminary attic, he resolved to learn the language by himself. Then after a period of army service with the French forces in West Germany in the mid-1960s (during which he was a radioman, expert in Morse code—which may or may not be significant for his later skill in scroll decipherment), he returned to the seminary. Receiving permission from his bishop to go to Paris to study ancient languages, he became the student of the famous orientalist André Dupont-Sommer and, later, the protégé of Abbé Jean Starcky, one of the members of the International Team. Dupont-Summer guided Puech's studies in ancient Semitic languages, and Starcky bequeathed to him some of the most important Dead Sea Scrolls Aramaic texts. Joining the Ecole Biblique et Archéologique in Jerusalem was just the final stage in Puech's lifelong preparation for bringing the message of the Dead Sea Scrolls to the world.

Years before, even just two years before, it would have been unthinkable for one of the scroll editors to casually bring a writer into the Scrollery and describe the details of important texts that were still unpublished, with the writer's tape recorder running and notebook open, lest he be reprimanded by his colleagues for a gross breach of scroll scholarly discipline. But now the team faced different problems and maintaining secrecy was not one of them. So on a morning in early June 1993, I drove from West Jerusalem to the Ecole Biblique on the eastern side of the city, picking Puech up outside the closed entrance on Nablus Road. In other times, I had known that road leading to the Damascus Gate of the Old City as a crowded, noisy, open-air bus station for the villagers and townsmen coming into the Old City of Jerusalem from the surrounding Arab towns and villages. But now on a general strike day in the midst of the Intifada, it was largely deserted, except for a checkpoint of the Israeli Border Patrol. Passing through the checkpoint, we turned left at the Damascus Gate plaza and drove to the Rockefeller Museum, on whose octagonal tower an Israeli flag flew, as it had since it became the headquarters of the Israel Department of Antiquities soon after the 1967 Six Day War.

The galleries, offices, and back corridors of the museum were my old stomping grounds—I had worked there twenty years before as an enthusiastic archaeological beginner—and somehow I didn't realize how much had changed. The first gatekeeper on the way to see the scrolls was chief curator Ruta Peled, a strong, no-nonsense professional, whom I had known since my days working as an assistant in the very same office she now occupied. Almost immediately, however, there was tension and unpleasantness in the confrontation between Ruta Peled and Emile Puech—a sudden bit of testiness that struck me as completely unnecessary. Peled, sitting behind her desk, was trying her best to follow the new access procedures, while Puech was showing how displeased he was to have to go through the humiliation of having to make a formal request for access to the scrolls. Until the recent uproar and change of policy, the scholars of the International Team had enjoyed direct and largely unsupervised access to the Scrollery.

Even after the large Scrollery was closed down sometime in the early 1970s and a small room in the basement storerooms had been put aside for scroll study, the plates of assembled fragments had been placed in flat file drawers for the scholars to browse among them as they pleased. But ever since the big uproar—and the widening of access to all interested and qualified scholars—the scroll fragments were more tightly guarded, and even International Team members now had to make a specific request for every document they wanted to see. The requirement that a visiting scholar fill out a form and wait for a museum official to bring the requested manuscript into a special study room did not seem to me to be too much of an imposition—and certainly would not ever be questioned at the British Library, the Smithsonian, or the Louvre. Yet Puech seemed to take it as an affront to his dignity. And he greeted each of the administrative innovations (I sensed the demonstrations were at least partially for my benefit) with a sullen, even petulant, grimace and shake of the head.

Riding down the ancient freight elevator to the basement level of the museum, I felt embarrassed to be part of this ritual, not wanting to appear to take the part of either side. In an outer room where we waited for the fragments to be delivered, two restorers were hard at work with surgical tools at a laboratory table, trying to peel away the gummy traces of 1950s Scotch tape from the now blackened surface of the skins. They explained—and I was to learn later—that this was a part of a large-scale preservation effort in which all the fragments would be cleaned and re-mounted. The traditional system of pressing the manuscripts between panes of glass had been judged to be damaging. They were hereafter to be mounted within artboard mattes, sewn between two sheets of fine polyester gauze. This would be another, even more disconcerting innovation for scholars set in their ways. Puech and I stood and waited. Next door in a cramped room, stuffy even now on a cool morning, two well-known scroll scholars were huddling over the plates that had been brought out, one-by-one, to them.

Grudgingly and irritably, Puech had written down a request for three manuscripts on a small lined yellow pad that I had handed him, in lieu of a more official request form. Though annoyed at having to translate the familiar designations (4Q521, 4Q525, and 4Q542, where "4Q" stood for Qumran Cave 4) into the new inventory numbers that the Israel Antiquity Authority used (330, 423, and 193), his whole demeanor changed as the documents themselves were finally brought into the study room. Now temporarily mounted between sheets of Plexiglass, each document formed a distinct pattern of fitted fragments, each of them more a mosaic than an unfinished jigsaw puzzle. The color of the wrinkled, pressed leather varied from pale yellow to rich golden brown; the tiny black Hebrew letters inscribed upon them were, in some cases, breathtakingly clear.

The texts suddenly become less of an abstraction when you examine them closely enough to see the ancient scribe's skill at forming the letters. A photograph of the same document, printed in a book and read in a library reference room, has none of the same impact. When you hold a Qumran text plate in your hands and tilt it slightly, you can see the subtle wrinkles and imperfections in the leather—and notice how the light plays off the ink. The boldness or ineptness of the penstrokes, the straightness of the lines or the sloppiness of the margins all create an indication that an *individual* had labored over this text. And rightly or wrongly, you almost cannot avoid forming an opinion about his intelligence and personality.

For Puech, the ragged pieces of inscribed ancient leather bearing the early messianic message were, first of all, a challenge to his ingenuity. Only secondarily were they a challenge to his faith. He explained that Starcky had only begun the process of putting the pieces together, and he had later been able to locate eight more of its pieces from "unidentified" fragment plates. Jabbing his finger toward various areas of the three reconstructed columns, Puech gave me a lesson in manuscript geography: "This was not so complicated here, but this is complicated and this small part was very complicated—and this was a problem . . . here you have a perfect join, but here, because it is curved, it doesn't fit any more; it shrunk, but you have the remains of letters here and here. When you put the whole thing together I put this one above this one, to get the same contour."

This was certainly not meant to be a systematic introduction to the Cave 4 collection; it was to be just an impression of the kinds of textual problems that Puech routinely faced. The first document we examined consisted of three fragmentary columns that Starcky had originally titled "On Resurrection," and which Puech had later renamed the "Messianic Apocalypse." Though its ancient title was unknown, its contents were extremely important, for it foretold of a real change beyond the Holy War and political revolution seen in most of the other messianic references: It envisioned a transformation in spiritual affairs and the well-being of humanity.

> [. . . The heav]ens and the earth will obey His Messiah,
> [The sea and all th]at is in them. He will not turn aside
>   from the commandment of the Holy Ones.
> Take strength in His mighty work, all ye who seek the
>   Lord.
> Will you not find the Lord in this, all ye who wait (for
>   Him) with hope in your hearts?
> Surely the Lord will seek out the pious and will call the
>   righteous by name.
> His spirit will hover over the poor; by his might he will
>   restore the faithful.
> He will glorify the pious on the throne of the eternal
>   kingdom.
> He will release the captives, make the blind see, raise up
>   the do[wntrodden.]

This elegantly written Hebrew poem went on to describe the future coming of a heaven-sent messiah who would heal the sick, resurrect the dead, and bring glad tidings to the poor. But was this just pious Sunday pew poetry, or did it represent a real expectation, a response to the conditions of this world? Despite the continuing attempts to separate Qumran messianism from Christianity, the acts of releasing captives, giving sight to the blind, and raising the downtrodden appeared in identical sequence in the Gospels of Matthew and Luke as the hallmarks of Jesus' ministry. Yet Puech was unwilling to exaggerate the importance of those mere literary connections. He took issue with the opinion that the poem referred to a single messiah (like Jesus) and preferred to believe that it referred to the more characteristic multiple messiahs, attested elsewhere at Qumran. And as for the references to healing, resurrection, and bringing good tidings, Puech preferred to ascribe them not to Qumran's messiah(s) but to God. And when we looked at the other documents that had been brought into the room for our examination, he went on to provide technical and textual explanations of the "Testament of Qahat" (with its fierce antiforeign polemic) and a "Wisdom Text with Beatitudes" (with its striking parallels to the Sermon on the Mount in the Gospel of Matthew) seeing each one as a possible literary model for the early Christian literature yet of little religious value in themselves.

So what did it all add up to, these ingeniously assembled leather mosaics of ancient Jewish poetry and prayer? When I asked Puech about the possible direct links between the Qumran sect and the early Christians, he was hesitant and cautious, suddenly bridling his enthusiasm. "I can't say too much because I still have to think it out for myself, but my opinion, my hypothesis of work," he answered in a pious speculation that mirrored his own theological preference, "is that I am sure that many Essenes converted to Christianity." Without reference to the complex social and political upheavals of Judea in the first century, he based his larger interpretation on faith. He suggested that they may simply have gotten tired of waiting for the return of their Teacher of Righteousness and joined the church of Jesus Christ. As for the possibility of influence in the other direction—that the Qumran sect could have shaped the ideas or message of Jesus—he was certain it could not have happened. "Jesus didn't know much about Qumran," Puech explained in an even more imaginative, yet still faithfilled assumption about the relation of Qumran beliefs and messianism to earliest Christianity. "To enter, you had to be a member of the sect. Maybe he knew that it existed, but he never went in."

This was a supposition utterly consistent with Puech's belief that the Qumran sect and Jesus' followers were separate. Where one was exclusive and isolationist, the other was open and unselfish in its brotherly love. The advantages of the gospel of Jesus Christ were, to him, self-evident. His interpretations, certainly based on skillful, learned, ingenious textual reconstruction, were nevertheless all aimed at illustrating a religious assertion, not a proven fact of history. The gospels proclaimed that Jesus Christ was the single true Messiah, the centerpoint of all human history. That is the faith of every Christian. But here is the problem for those who would also call themselves independent critical scholars: In dealing with a vast quantity of newly discovered religious literature from first-century Judea, doesn't a Dead Sea Scroll scholar have an obligation at least to consider that these ancient manuscripts might provide evidence that many of the gospel stories about Jesus are *not* true?

There is another historical possibility, perhaps a better explanation of the relationship between the people of Qumran and the followers of Jesus of Nazareth. The close similarities in organization and terminology may lie in the fact that both these groups were part of a vast popular movement in Judea—with many factions, leaders, and philosophies. By "movement" I do not mean to imply that these groups saw themselves as organizationally united. Far from it; there were undoubtedly fierce rivalries and bitter disputes between them. But in the sense that these groups all expressed a common passion for resistance to Rome and an anticipation of divinely aided liberation, their similarities (to outside, non-Judean observers) would have far outweighed their differences in details of terminology or even ritual. Like the popular movements that gave rise to the medieval peasant rebellions or to the French, Russian, and Iranian revolutions, the scattered yet widespread messianic groups in first-century Judea shared similar (if not always identical) political and social goals. And it should be noted that many of the messianic themes and terms that are common to the Qumran literature and the New Testament are also prominent in the ancient descriptions of the violent, anti-Roman activists in first-century Judea—people variously called zealots, bandits, and "knifemen," or Sicarii.

Josephus Flavius, the aristocratic Jewish turncoat-historian, who could never be accused of an excess of sympathy for revolutionary movements among his people, related regretfully after the Roman sack of Jerusalem that "what more than all else incited [the Jews] to the war was an ambiguous oracle, likewise found in their sacred scriptures, to the effect that at that time one from their country would become ruler of the world." The clearest scriptural basis for this belief was one of Balaam's oracles, quoted in Numbers 24:17, that someday "a star shall come out of Jacob and a scepter shall rise out of Israel" to conquer the world. The Roman historians Tacitus and Suetonius also mentioned the messianic prophecy as an important source of incitement for the Jewish Revolt.

The fact is that Jesus of Nazareth was but one of a long line of working-class prophets and would-be saviors who ended up in Roman custody. The pattern was similar in almost every case: A charismatic messianic prophet arose at a time of intensifying Roman political pressure, called the masses to leave their fields, their shops, their employers and accompany him to the wilderness. There great miracles were made manifest, clear omens that the Age of Redemption was about to begin. Almost inevitably, the Roman authorities responded to these mass gatherings and demonstrations as if they were hostile political actions—sending the cavalry to scatter the crowds and trample the confused and frightened men, women, and children who were desperate enough and poor enough really to believe in the Messianic Age.

A number of scholars have stressed how this intensifying messianism must be viewed both as a development of biblical tradition and a conscious response to the rise of the Cult of the Emperor. Until 27 B.C.E., the Romans were, for the Judeans, just another

Hellenistic kingdom with a powerful army that had brought Judea under its control. The installation of their protégé and client-king Herod in 37 B.C.E. was nothing new. But in 27 B.C.E., the Roman warlord Octavian renamed himself "Augustus" and declared himself son of god and world savior, creating a focus of civic worship that would preserve and promote the eternal power of Rome. For those people in all walks of life who benefitted from Roman civilization, the cult of the emperor was no more or no less important than reciting a pledge of allegiance. But for many of those who sincerely wanted the emperor dead and the empire in ruins, the Cult of the Emperor was an insult, a blasphemy.

King Herod, who was poised uncomfortably between Rome and the people of Judea, managed to keep the Cult of the Emperor out of Jewish territory (except for a symbolic eagle on the gate of the Jerusalem temple). His lavish devotion to the welfare of Augustus was made manifest elsewhere, with the establishment of two important cities, Caesarea and Sebaste, whose very names and whose elaborate temples to the Emperor made his ultimate political allegiance unmistakable. But after the death of Herod and the exile of his heir Archelaus in 6 C.E., Judea came under the direct rule of the Romans. Individual Judeans in all walks of life would now be required to pay homage to the emperor. A census was to be taken, an oath of allegiance administered, and daily sacrifices were henceforth to be offered in the Temple of Jerusalem for the health and well-being of Caesar in Rome.

One hundred and seventy-four years before this annexation of Judea to the Roman Empire, in 168 B.C.E., the Syrian Seleucid king Antiochus Epiphanes and his local supporters had similarly attempted to abolish the cultural autonomy of the Israelite religion and replace it with a Hellenistic king-cult. But the results of this experiment in compulsory patriotism were disastrous: rioting, guerilla war, and the rise of an independent Judean state under the Maccabees. At the time of the Roman annexation, there seems to have been widespread popular support for a replay of the Maccabean triumph, but this time—in 6 C.E.—the bloody national uprising, led by would-be national saviors in various parts of the country, was quickly and cruelly suppressed.

Thus the messianic movement went underground, and it developed not as a steady spiritual refinement, becoming ever more transcendent and moral—but as an up-and-down, rising-and-falling index of popular resentment to Rome. Through the first century C.E., in times of particularly intense repression or taxation, the messianic vision would flame brightly, focusing ever more sharply on the single, long-awaited messiah that would free the people of Israel. In times of relative calm and material prosperity, it would become more diffuse, perhaps more directed toward inner spiritual life. But whatever its form, it was a religious, political, and economic projection of the world of the *present*. The force of its message was revolutionary change.

That brings us to the most popular and influential book on the Dead Sea Scrolls ever written, a book that attempted to establish a direct link between the ideology of the scrolls and of Jesus, between an ancient Judean gospel of independence and the revolutionary movements of our own day. Its author was Edmund Wilson, a crusty, often acerbic American writer and literary critic who personified a chic, 1950s Manhattan-based intellectual iconoclasm that was *The New Yorker* magazine's stock in trade. Wilson's interest in the Bible, his liberal aversion to established religions, and his fascination with the Hebrew language (which he studied briefly in the early 1950s at Princeton) sharpened his interest in the recent scroll discoveries. And in the spring of 1954, in expectation of a intriguing feature story, *The New Yorker* sent him on assignment to Jordan and Israel.

Unlike other scroll books, past and present, Wilson's is not a deadpan dissertation but a fascinating stream-of-consciousness journey that wends its way from America to Paris; to the new State of Israel with its influx of immigrants and puzzling clash of modern ideals and unbending religious traditions; through the border checkpoint at Mandelbaum Gate amid the no-man's-land of "gashed and gutted houses" between Arab and Jewish Jerusalem; and finally to the Hashemite Kingdom of Jordan, to the Scrollery in the Rockefeller Museum, the Christian shrines of the Old City of Jerusalem, and the arid western shore of the Dead Sea.

Wilson had an eye for detail in his descriptions of the actors in the Dead Sea Scroll story. First he met Archbishop Samuel, now at home with his American congregants in Hackensack, New Jersey ("with his black and abundant beard, his large liquid brown eyes, in his onion-shaped black satin miter"); later the white-robed Dominican Father Roland de Vaux at the Qumran excavations ("he tells stories extremely well, continually smokes cigarettes and altogether has style, even dash"); and in Israel, the outrageously outspoken scholar David Flusser ("a short, stocky man, with sharp little cold green eyes that glint behind rimless glasses, under modestly Mephistophelian eyebrows, and red hair that stands straight up from his forehead"). In his vivid character descriptions, Wilson showed his readers that Dead Sea Scroll study was not a serene contemplation of scripture, but an ongoing, sometimes angry, theological debate.

Divine revelation had no attraction for Wilson; his was a humanist faith in the ability of mankind to improve itself. While the rest of America was being lulled to sleep in their suburbs by Norman Vincent Peale, Billy Graham, and Dwight D. Eisenhower, Wilson had already offered a powerful reshaping of biblical symbols in his 1953 piece in *The New Yorker,* "On First Reading Genesis," in which he applied his skill as a literary critic to the stories of the Israelite patriarchs—seeing them as epics of struggle and survival by determined individuals, not pious fairy tales. In the same way, he saw the literature of the Dead Sea Scrolls as more than liturgical or legal works of an obscure Jewish sect, but an important stage in the spiritual evolution of humanity.

He did not come to that realization without considerable input from scholars. For Wilson, the most influential among them was Professor André Dupont-Sommer of the Sorbonne (a tutor of several generations of would-be scroll scholars) who was not a member of the International Team, but who nonetheless sent shockwaves through the academic establishment. On May 26, 1950, Dupont-Sommer presented a paper to the august Académie des Inscriptions et Belles-Lettres in Paris on the text of the Habakkuk Commentary found in Cave 1 and whose complete text had been published only a short time before in New Haven by the American Schools of Oriental Research.

As I mentioned in an earlier chapter, the Habakkuk Commentary is a document of twelve damaged columns which intersperses quotations from the Book of Habakkuk with descriptions of later events that seemingly fulfilled the ancient prophecies. Thus, where the biblical text prophesies the fearsome rampage of "Chaldeans," the author of the Habakkuk commentary sees its fulfillment in the "dominion of the Kittim." Where the ancient prophet speaks abstractly of the fate of "the Righteous and "the Wicked," the commentator speaks of the careers of the sect's own Teacher of Righteousness and of someone known as the Wicked Priest. Scholars had long attempted to connect these characters with historical figures known from other sources, and the consensus was that the Teacher of Righteousness was a dissident priest from the Jerusalem Temple who established the Qumran sect around 150 B.C.E. The Teacher's arch-enemy was believed to be one of the early Hasmonean rulers, perhaps Jonathan (160–143 B.C.E.) or Simon (142–134). There were hints in the Habakkuk Commentary—as well as in the Damascus Document and perhaps even in the Thanksgivings Hymns—that the Teacher of Righteousness was pursued and killed by the Wicked Priest. And the Teacher was thereafter remembered and venerated as a righteous martyr by the Qumran community.

There was a chronological problem with this interpretation, since the mention of the "dominion of the Kittim" (almost unanimously identified with the Romans who invaded Judea in 63 B.C.E.) seemed to refer to events almost a century later than the deadly encounter between the Teacher of Righteousness and the Wicked Priest. The usual explanation was that the Habakkuk Commentary was indeed composed at the time of the Romans but referred to an event in the distant past that was of unique spiritual significance to the sect. André Dupont-Somer disputed the conventional dating of the events, placing all the characters at the time of the Roman invasion. But he saw in the events and descriptions a shockingly familiar pattern: This Dead Sea Scroll told of a spiritual Teacher who preached penitence, poverty, humility, chastity, and love of one's brother; who received direct revelations from God; was persecuted and put to death by the priestly establishment; and—at least according to Dupont-Sommer's interpretation of a cryptic passage in the Damascus Document—was expected to return to earth as a messianic figure at the End of Days. Dupont-Sommer's conclusion was shocking to a world that dated its years from the birth of a supposedly divine and unique messiah. Yet that "Galilean Master, as he is presented to us in the writings of the New Testament," Dupont-Sommer asserted, "appears in many respects as an astonishing reincarnation of the Teacher of Righteousness."

Though a number of Dupont-Sommer's assumptions were based on dubious readings of several of the broken lines in the original manuscript, his theory of a hidden predecessor to Jesus—when transfigured by Wilson and published first in *The New Yorker*, and later in book form as *The Scrolls from the Dead Sea*—posed a direct challenge to the historical (and implicitly spiritual) uniqueness of Christianity. For Wilson, the Qumran New Covenant was a revolutionary spiritual development: In its adherents' resistance to the ossified religious establishment of Jerusalem and to the wicked, earthly greed of the Romans, and in their expectation of imminent, divine deliverance from sin and injustice lay the foundations of the New Testament. "We can see how the movement represented by the Essenes," Wilson wrote, "stood up for perhaps two centuries to the coercion of the Greeks and the Romans, and how it resisted not only the methods of Rome but also the Roman ideals."

This, Wilson believed, was the true birth of a spirit of conscious resistance to political and cultural domination, the revolutionary spirit of Russia he saw and admired in Lenin in his bestseller *To the Finland Station*. As the world's first genuine revolutionaries, unbounded by temple worship or political subservience, the Qumran sect had, according to Wilson, "made itself free to range through the whole ancient world, touching souls with the gospel of purity and light to which the brotherhood had consecrated itself, and teaching the contempt of those eagles which they had noted—with evident astonishment—that the army of their enemy worshipped."

Wilson went far beyond what the scholars told him, far beyond anything that they could have imagined themselves. His call for a reawakening of a lost spirit of resistance and fierce pride in freedom—political and religious—obviously struck a sympathetic chord in the public consciousness, as the *Scrolls from the Dead Sea* remained near the top of the bestseller lists from the time of its publication in the fall of 1955 until the summer of 1956. Wilson wrote at a time when Mr. Levitt was building little boxes in meadows soon to be suburbs, and America's idea of religion was a crusade against the Red Menace, Billy Graham's shouted sermons, the Power of Positive Thinking, and a numbing conformity. But here was a gospel of liberation that was based more on the will to freedom than metaphysical doctrine.

"The monastery," Wilson wrote of the excavated ruins at Khirbet Qumran that he had so recently visited, and which for him now served as an archaeological object for spiritual contemplation, "this structure of stone that endures, between the bitter waters and the precipitous cliffs, with its oven and its inkwells, its mill and its cesspool, its constellation of sacred fonts and the unadorned graves of its dead is, perhaps, more than Bethlehem or Nazareth, the cradle of Christianity."

Few Dead Sea Scroll scholars that I have ever talked to have dared to speculate on the possibility that the scrolls might provide evidence for a thorough revision of New Testament history. To venture into these dangerous realms of historical speculation is to risk being called a maverick or an eccentric—or, worse yet, an enemy of the church. Most still prefer to remain in the safer and more familiar pastures of paleography and close textual analysis, leaving ultimate historical conclusions for the future—which is another way of evading them. And while most scholars speak on the subject with only great circumspection, one of the chief characters of Edmund Wilson's book, Professor David Flusser of the Hebrew University of Jerusalem, has always had a lot to say about Wilson, his theories, the religious significance of the Dead Sea Scrolls, and their connection to Christianity.

Flusser, born in Czechoslovakia and settled permanently in Israel since 1950, made an indelible impression on Wilson. One of the most memorable passages in Wilson's book is his colorful description of a conversation with Flusser in the lobby lounge of the King David Hotel on the evening of March 31, 1954. "I have rarely known a scholar," wrote Wilson, "who expressed himself—with all the material at his fingertips—so brilliantly and so much to the point. He would give me, to each of my questions, a full and closely reasoned answer, and stop when he had covered the ground." But there was more to Flusser's personality than brilliant scholarship. "Such were the pressure and tempo of Mr. Flusser's talk," Wilson continued, "that he was carried at one point to lengths that had no parallel in my experience of even the most enthusiastic talkers. Not only did he raise his voice when some insight had taken possession of him, quite oblivious of the people sitting near us and as if he were lecturing in a classroom, but when—at the climax of one of his arguments—though we tried to get away from the orchestra by going to the farthest corner—the music impinged on our conversation, my companion, caught up by a familiar tune, actually sang a few bars of his exposition, as if it were part of an opera."

The libretto of that Flusserian opera was that the Dead Sea Scrolls—in their apocalyptic message that God had preordained redemption and renewal as the climax of human history and that he had designated the Sons of Light to help bring it about—was the beginning of a tradition of revolutionary arrogance that led from the Teacher of Righteousness through Paul, to Spinoza, Calvin, Hegel, and Marx. This concept was, according to Flusser's characteristically sardonic overstatement, "one of the most disastrous of human ideas!"

When I went to the quiet, respectable neighborhood of Talbieh in West Jerusalem to interview David Flusser, I found that he still had a powerful message to convey. More than forty years have passed since that memorable evening with Edmund Wilson, yet I found that Flusser still enjoys the notoriety that Wilson bestowed upon him in the mid-1950s, and he is ready to be called upon by visitors and offer more of his provocative epigrams.

Our meeting took place around a large table in the book-lined study of his ground-floor apartment, late on a Friday morning, with the aroma of that evening's Sabbath dinner already filling the air. Though now in his mid-seventies and paunchy and gray, Flusser can still show flashes of the old passion, wheezing out witty asides in a steady stream of heavily accented commentary and pontification—working his way through my questions at his own pace and ending what amounted to a series of monologues only when he was satisfied that he was done. By the end of our conversation I discovered, or at least suspected, that Flusser's fabled cynicism was and always had been just a protective mask for an idealism that has been bruised too often by reality.

The Wilson book was almost our first subject of conversation, and Flusser has no illusions about how he was portrayed by Wilson. "In that book is the famous talk about the Dead Sea Scrolls where he described me as a kind of humoristic Pickwick, and I had with this a strange story as he said about me that I am not obliged to any religion, and it is not true." Flusser was referring to what amounted to Wilson's offhanded and certainly admiring statement that while the theological implications of the scrolls might be unsettling to both Christian clerics and Orthodox Jews, "an independent scholar like Flusser, not committed to any religion, had no reason for being upset."

He was, even now, upset at the comment. "I don't know if I changed my opinion very much since that time," Flusser admitted, "but surely I am obliged to the Jewish faith—the Jewish religion. At first I decided that I didn't want to protest because he portrayed me so stupidly, as if Hamlet would protest against Shakespeare. My description is a description of a personality who he needed, so he strained reality. I didn't want to protest, but my friends said, 'How can you allow it?' and I decided to write to him because of those friends. But the gods of art and poetry saved me. I have written a letter to him saying that I am surely obliged to the Jewish religion. But as I said, Apollo has saved me. I addressed the letter to Edmund Wilson at New Yorker and not 'The New Yorker,' and several months later I received the letter back stamped 'Not at Hotel New Yorker.' So I am until now in his book and not obliged to any religion, and he was from this point of view right, yes? Because men don't know how to read, even though he was wrong he was right. Because I am surely not obliged to any revealed religion." Wilson's description, Flusser admitted, was "not bad, but not completely me . . ."

Flusser would never claim to be a revolutionary, but neither has he ever been a member of the Inner Circle. Despite his reputation as a scholar of early Christianity and his long association with the scrolls, he was never given access, even as a professional courtesy, to texts that were of direct relevance to his work. He now told me another story,—or should I say parable?—this one about a Qumran text known as 4Q246. Despite the assurances of the International Team over the years that they had published most of the really important documents from Cave 4, now and then news leaked out of some intriguing new discoveries.

Such was the case in December 1972, when J. T. Milik, invited to Harvard for a series of lectures, revealed *some* of the contents of a two-column fragment in Aramaic in which a seer (possibly the prophet Daniel) interprets the dream of a king. The truly remarkable part of this fragment, dated by Milik to the first century B.C.E., was that the dream interpretation centered on the future appearance of an individual who will be called "Son of God" and "Son of the Most High." Since these were precisely the titles the angel Gabriel used in the Gospel of Luke to describe the coming of Jesus at the time of his annunciation to the Virgin Mary, their occurrence in a Qumran document was of the highest significance. The more common messianic titles used at Qumran were the dual "messiahs of Aaron and Israel" mentioned in the Community Rule and the Damascus Document. But since Milik had not officially published the document, its full contents and context remained secret—except for the few crumbs that Milik was willing to toss to the scholarly world. Who knew what other messianic secrets were contained in the hundreds of still unpublished documents from Cave 4?

Father Joseph Fitzmyer, a junior member of the International Team, was in the audience at Milik's Harvard lecture, and he took the (then) daring step of mentioning this striking parallel between Qumran and the New Testament in an article and, later, in his commentary on Luke. But here was the heart of the matter: Milik believed that the titles had nothing to do with a messiah but were a mocking reference to the Syrian king Alexander Balas (150–145 B.C.E.) who, like a number of Hellenistic despots, proclaimed his own divinity. Fitzmyer, on the other hand, saw the terms as more likely referring to a future heir of the Davidic throne, though he was reluctant to ascribe them to a messianic figure. When Flusser saw published reports about this document, he had a third, typically heretical, theory: that "Son of God" and "Son of the Most High" were the derisive titles to be used by an *evil* figure like the Antichrist of later Christian literature.

Flusser published his theory in a 1983 article entitled "The Hubris of Antichrist in a Fragment from Qumran," reproducing and translating the lines that Fitzmyer had published:

. . . he will be great on earth
. . . [all] will worship and all will serve [him]
. . . great he shall be called and by his name he shall be
    designated.
He shall be named son of God and they shall call him son
    of the Most High. Like a shooting star
of a vision, so shall be their kingdom. They shall reign for
    some years on
the earth and trample everything. One nation shall

> trample on another nation and one province on
> another province
> until the people of God shall rise and all will desist from
> the sword.

Flusser stressed that the absolute duality of light and darkness, of righteousness and wickedness, in the Qumran sect's apocalyptic worldview made it possible that the text referred to the "wars and rumors of wars" brought on by the forces of Evil that would plague the earth in the Last Days. Thus he argued (though there were a number of scholars who would later contest this interpretation) that "Son of God" and "Son of the Most High" were the arrogant and mistaken appellation of the leader of the Sons of Darkness in the World. But because Flusser did not have access to the remaining lines, he could not tell if the end of the text mentioned the rise of a God-sent messiah or contained any other evidence that would explain how the titles found their way into the Gospel of Luke.

Here was an intriguing question about the relationship of Qumran to Christianity, of Jewish messianism to the role of Jesus, but the rules of the Dead Sea Scroll game did not permit such questions to be pursued. By 1972, Milik had kept the fragment for two decades without permitting outside scholars to see it. By the time Flusser wrote his article about it, another decade had passed. "It was permitted to publish such lines as were already published," Flusser told me, "and it was permitted to see those parts of the scrolls that were already published, as already Milik and Fitzmyer read it, until the line I mentioned but not beyond. So I wanted to see the original, the non-published part of this fragment. I wanted to see what was written there to see if it didn't contradict what I had seen." He was permitted to examine the original, "and then I did a thing which is surely not criminal, but it was not then permitted. I had taken with me an expert in paleography and he read with me quickly the unpublished lines. This was the absurd situation that I was permitted to read only up to the line which was published by these scholars, but I read what was forbidden to me to publish. Now you can see a part of a difficult situation," he concluded, "that is not completely finished today."

Flusser now adopted the cynical conviction that the study of the scrolls' possible connection to Jesus and early Christianity ultimately did not matter much at all. "It is some days ago that a group of men of industry from Stuttgart came here and wanted to hear about the Dead Sea Scrolls," he told me. "It was impossible to say to them anything because they wanted to believe, and they said to me that the evidence is so strong that nothing could calm them. But I said that even if it would be written in some document that the mother of Jesus was a harlot and that Jesus was homosexual, even if it would be true, it wouldn't change Christianity, because some experts could say it was not true. Many years ago a man from BBC came to me," Flusser continued, "and he asked me if the Dead Sea Scrolls will harm Christianity. I said to him that nothing can harm Christianity. The only thing which could be dangerous to Christianity would be to find a tomb with the sarcophagus or ossuary of Jesus—still containing his bones. And then I said I surely hope that it will not be found in the territory of the State of Israel."

These anecdotes were amusing, yet there was something entirely unconvincing in Flusser's cynical assertion that the quest for the historical Jesus was pointless. Flusser had spent his career studying the historical relationship of Judaism to Christianity and had on occasion written powerfully and movingly about the legacy of hatred and bloodshed that sprang from Christian anti-Semitism. As a Jewish refugee from Eastern Europe, he didn't have to learn that lesson from graduate school seminars; his genuine world-weary skepticism had attracted Edmund Wilson's fascination and even sympathy. But he wanted to convey to me the larger point about the revolutionary nature of Jewish messianism.

"There is a short story written by Anatole France," he told me. "He was a French writer whose name you maybe don't know—very good for the education of children. You see, France has written a short story with the title 'The Procurator of Judea.' Of course he didn't know that this was not the correct title of Pilate, who was not a procurator but a *praefectus,* as we know from the Caesarea inscription." But Flusser's main point was not archaeological. He conveyed to me the main outlines of France's story with obvious relish, describing how the fictional Roman nobleman L. Aelius Lamia happened to meet and spend an evening with the aged, bloated, and gout-plagued Pontius Pilate, now enjoying a quiet retirement in Sicily after his stormy ten years as governor of Judea.

Pilate sadly recounted to Lamia how his public career was cut short by backbiting rivals in the imperial service and the whispers of a powerful Jewish lobby in the capital, even though he had always tried his best to further the majestic ideals of the Pax Romana and was always unselfishly committed to honoring the divinity of the emperor. The people of Judea, Pilate grumbled, had rejected all the blessings of technology and prosperity that Rome had to offer. For some reason they stubbornly, inexplicably, maintained their adherence to primitive ancestral customs and to a peculiarly jealous national God. Pilate was convinced that the Jews posed a mortal danger to the serenity of Roman rule and a war of extermination would, someday, be inevitable. For if the Jews were permitted to challenge the divine right of Romans to come, to conquer, and rule all the world's peoples, the consequences for Roman power would be dire. If the Jews were not taught a lesson, would-be rebels might be emboldened to rise in other parts of the empire. Because of the unbending rebelliousness of the Judean people—Pilate insisted from bitter personal experience—Jerusalem must some day be levelled and its Temple put to the torch.

Lamia, who had visited Judea many years before in the course of a youthful period of exile, now spoke up in defense of this stiff-necked people, expressing some admiration for their men's devotion to national ideals and national religion, and, no less significant for this Roman patrician, admiring their women's exotic Semitic sensuality. Lamia nostalgically, wistfully, recalled his steamy encounters many years before with a seductive, red-haired Jewish dancing girl (apparently Mary Magdalene, from the details of the description) whom he had once ardently pursued in the taverns and back alleys of Jerusalem. But Lamia also recalled that this dancer had suddenly disappeared from her usual haunts to join—so he heard—the ragtag band of followers of a young Galilean miracle worker, someone named Jesus, from Nazareth.

In idle curiosity Lamia casually asked Pilate if he remembered anything about that miracle worker, who was later crucified for some crime or another. But the aged Pilate, despite all his knowledge of the political affairs of Judea and all his awareness of its looming dangers to the Roman Empire, drew a complete blank on the name. "Jesus?" Pilate murmured, wracking his brain to recall this obscure person, "Jesus—of Nazareth? I cannot call him to mind."

David Flusser leaned back in satisfaction when he reached the punchline of Anatole France's story. This time his usual mocking and cynical style did not conceal the important point he wanted to make. The biographical details of an incarnated messiah were irrelevant to Judaism's timeless revolutionary message. Flusser chuckled again at Pontius Pilate's inability to remember an obscure Galilean named Jesus. "It is so . . ." Flusser said, nodding toward me. "It is so . . ."

It is because of John Marco Allegro that most Dead Sea Scroll scholars have always reacted to serious discussions of Jesus and early Christianity with suspicion and nervous hostility. The memories of John Marco Allegro by those who knew him and worked with him most closely are invariably bitter. Words like "dishonest" and "amoral" slip easily off the tongues of those who refuse to be pinned down to almost any definite statement on the nature of the scrolls. In fact, it was Allegro, far more than Dupont-Sommer or Edmund Wilson, who fostered a perception in the minds of the general public that the scrolls contained some explosive information about the character and life of Jesus—and that the pious members of the International Team, knowingly or unknowingly, were suppressing the historical implications of the discovery.

Allegro appears as prominently as De Vaux or Harding in the memories of the members of the International Team. Frank Cross remembered his first meeting Allegro and recalled him as "a very cocky character with sometimes wry wit and sometimes mordant wit. Very quickly I discovered that he could not tell the truth about anything, and as the years passed it was clear that he created his own world." John Strugnell knew him from Oxford in the early 1950s, when they had been students together at Godfrey Driver's seminar. Strugnell knew him then as "Gunner" Allegro, for he was a World War II navy veteran, considerably older than his classmates, and with a far more cynical view of the world. Immediately after the war, Allegro had intended to become a Methodist minister and had studied theology, but later he turned away from the church. His talent for languages and knowledge of biblical literature would in time be used as weapons to attack what he considered to be superstition and outmoded mythologies. And it is a testimony to Allegro's intelligence and personal presence that he ever managed to get as far as he did in the world of the Dead Sea Scrolls.

"He always teased me for my religious interest," John Strugnell remembered, suggesting that Allegro always had a secret religious vendetta. "Later on when he wrote these things about me, that 'in a couple of years the Church will be destroyed,' it had just become a little more specific." It was clear from the start to Strugnell that Allegro's scholarship on the scrolls was inspired and motivated by his atheism. In the first division of fragments in the Scrollery, Allegro had been given the biblical commentaries. Unlike the biblical books given to Cross and Skehan, where the big discoveries were tiny textual variations, obvious only to specialists, or in the Community's mystical, apocalyptic texts that had been given to Milik, the biblical commentaries from Qumran dealt with the description of historical events.

Quoting, line by line, from the words of the ancient prophets, the Qumran commentators showed how the misfortunes they were now suffering were actually fulfillments of prophecy. The Commentary on Habakkuk, with its reference to the Wicked Priest, the Kittim, and the fateful confrontation on the Day of

Atonement led to the kind of speculations about the history of the Qumran Community that had filled Edmund Wilson's book. Allegro, however, now studying other commentaries, like the Commentary on Nahum, with an explicit reference to crucifixion, went far beyond what Edmund Wilson had done. Instead of seeing the Qumran sect as the moral foundation from which Christianity later refined its message, Allegro suggested that Qumran's vision of a Teacher of Righteousness who would return as the messiah represented a common (if benighted) first-century Judean superstition. Jesus Christ was just a latter-day variation of a rather tired religious hallucination. And John Allegro, never one to keep his religious opinions to himself when there was an opportunity to broadcast them widely, first presented his heretical Dead Sea Scroll theories to the general public in a series of BBC programs in 1956.

The broadcasts were made on Allegro's own initiative, without consulting or even informing the other members of the International Team. And for the International Team in Jerusalem, Allegro's broadcasts, with their imaginative speculations about myth and messianism in first-century Judea, were a cause for outrage and immediate action. It is a measure of how deeply concerned the scroll scholars were with authority, orthodoxy, and discipline that they immediately clubbed together with an "official" statement to the London *Times,* rather than responding one by one in an ongoing scholarly debate.

"I think we got the news of the Allegro broadcast from the English newspapers," John Strugnell remembered, "and we had a little meeting and decided that we really should suggest that there was a certain measure of hypothesis in this and it wasn't all as solid as he might pretend. So I wrote the draft of a letter to the *Times,* in the style of letters to the *Times*—your humble servant, and things like this." Over the signatures of De Vaux, Milik, Skehan, Starcky, and Strugnell, the letter denied that there was any "close connection between the supposed crucifixion of the 'teacher of righteousness' of the Essene sect and the crucifixion and resurrection of Jesus Christ." It was the scholars' conclusion that Allegro had "misread the texts, or he has built up a chain of conjectures which the materials do not support."

Although Allegro at first responded to the accusations of the other team members coolly and politely, his antagonism to his colleagues grew with time. Perhaps his theories were mistaken in some of their details, but he was determined to make the larger questions about the scrolls and their relationship to the origins of Christianity the center of the debate. For Allegro, as for other would-be rebels in the Dead Sea Scroll story, details were not as important as ideas. Through the 1950s and 1960s, he became ever more firmly convinced that early Christianity was a fraudulent mimic of the faith of the Qumran Community—and it should therefore be abandoned as an outmoded myth by right-thinking people everywhere. In letters to De Vaux, he mocked what he believed to be the dilemma of a faithful Christian scholar confronted with the evidence of the scrolls. "Your religious convictions seem to me to warp your judgment slightly on any matter remotely connected with Christianity," he noted with a tone of modernist condescension. "This I can expect fully, and expect nothing else."

And so the battle was joined in the coming years, with Allegro devoting his career to what amounted to a humanist crusade to prove the emptiness of the idea of the unique revelation of the gospel of Jesus Christ. For him, however, the messianic belief of the Qumran Community was no more attractive than Christianity; it was useful primarily to show the modern Christian public that they had been lied to for two thousand years about the historical uniqueness of their faith. The goal of Allegro's work had always been a kind of anti-evangelism. "Clearing away the deadwood is the first condition of intellectual progress," Allegro wrote in 1964, "but whether this generation has courage or vision to grasp the opportunities of reassessment offered by these miraculous discoveries in the Judean wilderness, remains to be seen."

Unlike Edmund Wilson, with his elegant prose, or even David Flusser, with his humorously cynical anecdotes that challenged the conventional wisdom, Allegro grew more militant and more strident as time went on. After 1968—when he finished the publication of his assigned texts (one of the very few team members ever to do so)—he confirmed his reputation as an enemy of organized religion with a series of books, attacking what he called "the Myth of the Chosen People," and characterizing all divine worship as a hindrance to human progress in a book he titled ominously *The End of the Road.* But the topper came in 1970, with his book *The Sacred Mushroom and the Cross.* In it, he claimed that the scrolls and other ancient Near Eastern religious writings revealed that early Christianity was nothing more, nothing less, than a drug-addled, orgiastic fertility cult. Needless to say the scholarly ridicule was vicious, eventually forcing him to leave his faculty position at the University of Manchester. And when Allegro died in 1980, he was regarded by most as an eccentric gadfly whose theories had been thoroughly disproved.

Yet there is something that cannot be so easily dismissed in the idea that the scrolls—being contemporary, unrevised religious literature of first-century Judea—provide evidence about the beliefs of Jesus and his followers that were later transformed and concealed by later generations of Christian scribes and theologians. Belief in the imminent advent of Israel's messiah or messiahs was the secret hope, faith, and shared secret reaction of every Judean and Galilean who did not benefit directly from participation in the Roman provincial regime. And in times of famine, expropriation, and intensifying urbanization of the rural population, it was an image that would come to mind every time a Roman soldier or official exercised his power, every time a Roman governor attempted to alter the religious status quo. The messiah would not be a metaphysical savior but a down-to-earth leader. And the hope for national salvation—and its eventual translation into violent political action—grew more desperate as the Roman administration of the province grew more and more determined to pacify the Judeans once and for all.

Judean society in the first century of the Common Era was badly fragmented, with many religious sects, leaders, and theological possibilities. And while it can be argued that each of the groups was quite different, the general similarities also force us to recognize that they all shared a single overall ideology of resistance, often elaborated down to the tiniest details. This was the story of how the Righteous Remnant of Israel would recognize its sins through the appearance and preaching of a prophet, who spoke of the advent of the Messianic Age. The historical Jesus of Nazareth, born about the time of the death of the tyrant King Herod and growing to manhood at the time of Pontius Pilate, shared with his Judean contemporaries a fairly standard set of symbols and expectations. The followers of Jesus, of John the Baptist, and the Teacher of Righteousness were all part of the same movement, or, if the word "movement" has too many organizational implications, they shared a rage against empire. And when the time came for unified action, they all would rise against Rome.

The people of Qumran and the early Christians could not avoid that inevitable political reality. In the War Scroll, the importance of the political action is made explicit. After a detailed description of the timetable, equipment, weapons, and tactics to be used by the Sons of Light in their final, cataclysmic battle against the Forces of Darkness, the officers of the Sons of Light are instructed to encourage the troops with a series of prayers to God and martial exhortations, including the familiar oracle:

> Our strength and the power of our hands accomplish no mighty deeds except by Thy power and by the might of Thy great valor. This Thou has taught us from ancient times, saying: "A star shall come out of Jacob and a sceptre shall rise out of Israel. He shall smite the temples of Moab and destroy all the children of Seth. He shall rule out of Jacob and shall cause the survivors of the city to perish. The enemy shall be his possession and Israel shall accomplish mighty deeds."

In later times, Christians would abandon the Law of Moses, turning to faith in an incarnated messiah's atonement for the sins of all mankind. But for the people of Judea in the first century—as seen in the scrolls and in the secondhand reports of Josephus Flavius, such a concept would have seemed alien and blasphemous. At a time of political and economic subjugation by an empire led by a deified Caesar, the destiny of Israel was rather to remain true to the traditions of family, farm, and Temple, and to make the Sons of Darkness, both Roman and Judean, die for *their* sins. The redemption and renewal of Israel would not come through abandonment of the covenant but through the strict observance of all its laws. The Temple, not the Tomb, was be the focus of liberation. And as time went on and many of the long unpublished Qumran texts were released and made available to scholars, evidence mounted that the original faith of Jesus and his followers in the imminent arrival of political and spiritual liberation may have been—in many respects—uncannily close to the angry, righteous gospel of the Dead Sea Scrolls.

5

THE TREASURE

The Copper Scroll is dying. Its twenty-three curved, corroded sections—the narrow lengthwise strips into which the brittle scroll was cut when unrolling seemed impossible—are slowly crumbling to dust. For more than thirty years, the strips lay side-by-side in special velvet-lined cradles in an exhibit case in Amman at the Jordan Archaeological Museum. But by the late 1980s, curators and visiting scholars grew concerned about the signs of deterioration. The edges of some of the sections had receded nearly half an inch along the line where they were cut by a small circular saw in 1955 and 1956 in England at the Manchester College of Technology. So in 1993, in response to this situation, the Department of Antiquities of Jordan initiated an ambitious project of photography and restoration. At the same time, after years of relative neglect by scholars, the Copper Scroll suddenly provoked a flurry of new studies and new theories, many of them directly challenging earlier interpretations of the scroll.

The Copper Scroll has always been a fascinating oddity among the Qumran documents—and not only because it is the only major find from the scroll caves that remains in Jordanian hands. From the beginning, it was considered peculiar. Its material, its script, and its contents are so different from those of the other Dead Sea Scrolls that scholars have been hard pressed to explain how it came to be deposited at Cave 3 at Qumran. Found by a team of archaeologists from the Ecole Biblique in the spring of 1952, it consisted of two rolled pieces placed on a ledge at the back of a small cave, where fragments of the usual Qumran type documents were found. The rolled, riveted copper sheets were eventually identified as parts of a single text (called 3Q15 in the technical designation) containing a list of sixty-four cryptic descriptions of hiding places around Jerusalem and throughout Judea where an almost unimaginable treasure of gold and silver bullion, precious unguents, sacred vestments, sacred vessels, and sacred scrolls had been deposited in antiquity.

Here was something you could really sink your teeth into: not fragmentary scripture or apocalyptic poetry, or tenuous and vague historical connections to early Christianity, but a detailed treasure map—enough to set the heads of even the most sober and conservative biblical scholars reeling with the possibilities. In twelve columns of writing were the names and descriptions of pools, tombs, subterranean tunnels, and ruins throughout Judea where the treasure was said to be buried, with precise measurements of each hoard's position and depth. The quantities of precious goods were so massive (with the *lowest* estimates being almost sixty tons of gold and silver, and the highest around two hundred) that questions arose in the minds of the scholars as to where the Qumran sect could have collected so much bullion. Or whether, in light of the frequent mention of ritual vessels and consecrated offerings, the Qumran Community with its many priestly associations had anything to do with the Temple of Jerusalem.

The Copper Scroll had nothing whatever to do with the rise of Christianity—no messianism, no baptism, no communal ideal. It had everything to do with the Temple of Jerusalem and its worship and the complex of ritual offerings. In that sense, it struck the early scholars as culturally primitive—an impression that was not helped by the copyist's many spelling errors and the clumsy way he formed the letters as he punched them into the copper with a hammer and a chisel-edged tool. But he was not a mere lunatic, a lonely dreamer, as many scholars would later say. The author was well acquainted with the villages and towns in Judea, with the tombs and complex system of watercourses that ran through them that had long been the province of Jerusalem priests. More than that, the author used the technical terminology of tithes, consecrated vessels, and offerings that were part of the complex balance of national obligations and economic independence that the Temple stood for.

Whatever might have been the glories of the First Jerusalem Temple under David and Solomon and subsequent kings of Judea, its symbolic function was completely changed when the armies of the Neo-Babylonian king Nebuchadnezzar sacked the city, tore down the Temple, and sent most of its priests into exile in 586 B.C.E. Yet unlike the central shrines of so many other peoples, the Temple of Jerusalem would not merely be given over to the cult of its conquerors as a sign that the victorious god of the Babylonians was clearly the strongest one. For among the communities of expatriate Judeans, exiled by force to the waters of Babylon, a new conception arose—that Jerusalem and the Temple had been destroyed not by the earthly might of the Babylonians but by God himself as punishment for the sins of the Israelites. If they were to return to the perfect observance of the law, however, their national well-being would be assured. So after a few decades, when the Babylonian empire crumbled, and a small delegation of Judean priests and civic leaders was allowed to return to Jerusalem by the newly victorious Persian Empire, the proper observance of the cult of the rebuilt Jerusalem Temple became a mechanism for national survival. Not unexpectedly, its regulations became stricter, more exclusive, and more complex than ever before.

As an odd little temple-state ruled by High Priests in the out-of-the-way hilltop town of Jerusalem, Judea was a poor candidate for modernization in the days of Pericles, Sophocles, and Pythagoras. Although the inhabitants of the port cities of the eastern Mediterranean (proud descendants of Philistines and Phoenicians whose national histories intertwined with those of the

Greeks) began to look westward for commerce and culture, the people of Judea clung stubbornly to their hillside olive groves and vineyards, to their patchwork grain fields and pastures in the valleys below. The Temple of Jerusalem—with its regulation of agricultural production in sabbatical year cycles, and with its meticulous collection of tithes, offerings, and sacrifices of first fruits and unblemished farm animals—served to maintain a balance of simple piety and modest agricultural prosperity.

The Judeans—the "Jews"—must have seemed quaintly rustic and a bit old-fashioned when the Macedonian armies of Alexander the Great and his successors stormed through the land. For they brought not only idols, painted vases, and iambic pentameter to Judea, they brought a shockingly new way of life. Vast royal estates were created in which single commodities like olive oil, wine, or balsam were produced in huge quantities as sources of profit, to be shipped to foreign cities and to be sold again. It was a mentality of ever-greater concentration of effort—and ever-wider links to other parts of the world. No one in Judea could stop progress, but the Temple of Jerusalem, with its symbols of the old order and antique ways of doing things, became a replacement symbol for all that had been lost with the coming of the Hellenistic Age.

By the second century B.C.E., no one would ever have thought that Judeans could turn the clock back, but that is exactly what happened around the time of the Maccabean Revolt. We tend to get misled by modern Hanukkah songs and Hanukkah menorahs—that the war against Antiochus Epiphanes, king of the Seleucid Empire, was just a matter of freedom of worship and the maximum miles-per-gallon that could be obtained from consecrated Temple oil. But the revolt was really about returning to a way of life of one's choosing, a return to the age of independent smallholders, whose membership in the independent People of Israel was reinforced, not merely symbolized, by the cult of the Temple at Jerusalem. And so the revolt that began in the village of Modi'in under the leadership of the priest Mattathias of the House of Hasmon—and which achieved astounding victories at first in ambushes and then on the battlefield against the professional Hellenistic armies—led to political independence and the rededication of the Temple. And that last act was not merely one of certifying that the idols had all been removed and the swines' grease had been completely scoured from the altar. It marked the establishment of a strange, religiously fundamentalist priestly kingdom—not a bucolic return to a biblical Eden, but a temple-state of Judean ayatollahs and zealous revolutionary guards.

There were, naturally, bitter disagreements over the proper rituals for worship in this born-again Temple. There were some within the priesthood who were outraged when, after the death of the saintly holy warrior Judah the Maccabee (who never apparently aspired to overt political power), his brothers Jonathan and Simon named themselves High Priests in the Temple, dispossessing the traditional holders of that office who claimed to be scions of the Zadokite line. The resentment of even the slightest impiety, by at least some factions in the Judean population, could flare up at almost any time. Later, when the Hasmonean king Alexander Janneus (103–76 B.C.E.) appeared in the Temple to officiate as High Priest at the celebration of the Feast of Tabernacles, he was greeted with catcalls and pelted with ethrogs. After the fall of the Hasmoneans and the appointment of Herod's yes-men as High Priests in the Temple, popular feeling for the need for a purification of the Temple grew. By the Roman period, the regard for ritual strictness in the Temple of Jerusalem served as a kind of national psychic transference, in which demands for reforms in the way sacrifices were offered and priests appointed was about the only type of independent political activity left to the people of Judea and Jerusalem.

But the Essenes, according to Josephus, were almost entirely out of the mainstream in their decided lack of fervor for the Temple cult. "They send votive offerings to the Temple," he noted, "but perform their sacrifices employing a different ritual of purification. For this reason they are barred from those precincts of the Temple that are frequented by all the people and perform their rites by themselves." This odd rejection of the Temple in the interest of higher spirituality proved appealing to Christian scholars, who saw in it a precocious precursor of Christianity's own rejection of the traditional burnt sacrifices and purity laws. With the discovery of the Dead Sea Scrolls, there seemed to be a direct reference to this "Essene" rejection of empty Temple ritual, as seen in this telling passage from the Community Rule:

> They shall atone for guilty rebellion and for sins of unfaithfulness that they may obtain lovingkindness for the Land without the flesh of holocausts and the fat of sacrifice. And prayer rightly offered shall be as an acceptable fragrance of righteousness, and perfection of the way as a delectable free-will offering.

Thus, for many scholars, the report of Josephus, combined with this passage, was conclusive evidence that the people of Qumran were Essenes who had made a fateful theological decision to substitute prayer and clean living for expensive incense and unblemished lambs. More than that: The discovery of buried pottery vessels with animal bones throughout the courtyards and open places in the Qumran settlement persuaded scholars that the Essenes' private sacrifices were made as symbolic offerings—almost an act of communion—in the secret ceremonies of the sect's communal meals. Thus, in this evolutionary perspective, which saw spiritual life as gradually moving toward Christianity, the Essenes may have been very imperfect messianists, but they nonetheless proved themselves (regarding their rejection of the Temple) to be very advanced Jews. And that is what made the Copper Scroll in Qumran Cave 3 so puzzling. How could a detailed, coded description of the Temple treasure, with its list of heave offerings, second tithes, and sacred vessels have anything to do with people who had rejected the cult of the Temple?

In his first published article on the Copper Scroll, Father Josef Milik, who was entrusted with the text for the "official" publication on behalf of the International Team, devalued its historical significance bluntly and arrogantly, in the same way he might have frowned at an excited story told to him by one of the Palestine Archaeological Museum janitors or guards. "It almost goes without saying," wrote Milik in an article in the *Biblical Archaeologist* in 1956, "that the document is not an historical record of actual treasures buried in antiquity. The characteristics of the document itself, not to mention the fabulous quantity of precious metals and treasures recorded in it, place it firmly in the genre of folklore. The Copper Document is thus best understood as a summary of popular traditions circulating among the folk of Judea, put down by a semiliterate scribe."

And what an odd, compulsive behavior it must have been: An anonymous and clearly obsessed individual, according to Milik, had sat down someplace with a sheet of copper and punched out 3,000 or so Hebrew characters to express a base, materialistic fantasy. In Milik's opinion, the Copper Scroll was little more than an Aladdinlike vision of caves overflowing with treasure; the kind of semicomic Thousand-and-One-Nights hallucination that he disdainfully believed Middle Easterners were prone to. His early comparison of the Copper Scroll to a completely modern work (Ahmed Bey Kamil's *Book of Buried Pearls and Hidden Treasures,* published in Egypt in 1907), revealed much about how readily and unconsciously Milik applied the same orientalist stereotypes to the peoples of both the ancient and modern Middle East.

In recent years, some scholars have begun to take the Copper Scroll far more seriously than mere folklore, because of its exacting technical Temple terminology, and—no less important—because of the political atmosphere in the Middle East at the time. At the time of the first public announcement of the scroll's contents in June 1956, the first wave of modern pan-Arab nationalism was sweeping through the Middle East. Gamal Abdel Nasser's potent message of nonalignment and anti-imperialism made the position of western advisors and officials in Jordan (as in much of the Arab Middle East) increasingly uncomfortable. On March 1, 1956, General John Bagot Glubb and his fellow British officers at the head of the Arab Legion were dismissed and exiled from the country, and an ambitious young Jordanian officer, Ali Abu Nuwwar, was installed in his place. The forced resignation of Gerald Lankester Harding as director of the Department of Antiquities was made public in mid-summer. He left Jordan in the fall.

So through 1956, as Radio Cairo stirred up a feeling of pan-Arab solidarity throughout the region—and as international tensions rose over Egypt's nationalization of the Suez Canal Zone—the position of Westerners in the Middle East became a highly sensitive one. It is little wonder that the members of the International Team in Jerusalem, all of them foreign nationals, were reluctant to speak too enthusiastically or too loudly about ancient treasure supposedly buried in Jordanian territory. In fact, through the summer and early fall, Harding, De Vaux, and Milik all ridiculed the idea that the Copper Scroll had anything to do with real treasure. It was just an oriental—oops—maybe just a specifically *Jewish* kind of fairytale. In his 1962 publication, Milik produced two oddly chosen supporting examples, diplomatically dropping his earlier reference to the Egyptian *Book of Buried Pearls*. His examples were now a modern marble plaque found some years before (by Father Jean Starcky) in a Beirut synagogue, and a medieval rabbinic midrash about the legendary treasures of Solomon's Temple called *Masseket Kelim*. Thus Milik's "crank" theory, with its unspoken anti-Semitic implications passed into the conventional wisdom, into the scholarly literature, into the textbooks, and into the brains of college students like me.

Yet the crank theory lingered long after the Suez Crisis was over, not necessarily because it was in any way confirmed by subsequent study but because it was safe. It had to do with the larger historical picture and the tendency (I stress it is a tendency, not a preconceived strategy) to *separate*, rather than link, the Qumran material from other elements in Judean history. Having demonstrated to their own satisfaction that the members of the Qumran sect were Essenes and that the Essenes were implacably hostile to Temple worship, they simply ignored the Copper Scroll. Noting the peculiarities of its language (a style of Hebrew that was closer to that of rabbinic literature than most of the Qumran manuscripts), Milik came to the conclusion that the Copper Scroll was nothing more than a harmless, foolish collection of folktales deposited in the cave around 100 C.E. (according to the script and the language) by some sort of a lunatic, or disturbed person, who happened to be wandering around the long-abandoned ruins of Qumran.

There was another very good reason to insist that the Copper Scroll was mere legend: John Marco Allegro, now regarded by the Inner Circle as an Angel of Darkness, was insisting that the scroll was not the work of a crank. Allegro had been deeply involved in the Copper Scroll story from the beginning, though it had never been among the documents assigned to him. Because of the fragile state of the scroll, no attempt had been made to open it until 1955, when Allegro conferred—on his own initiative—with metallurgists at his home institution, the University of Manchester. Allegro soon persuaded Harding and De Vaux that the Manchester experts would be able to open the document without doing it any damage; and from the perspective of far-off Jerusalem, the image of eager and competent English technicians in white lab coats must have convinced De Vaux and Harding to sanction the delicate operation at once.

I want to be fair and keep things in perspective, but on reading Allegro's description of the opening of the Copper Scroll at the Manchester College of Technology and looking at the photos he took to record the process, it is hard not to laugh. With all due respect to the dedication of Professor H. Wright-Baker—with his kindly gaze, safety glasses, and lab coat as he appears in Allegro's photos—it is hard to believe that a more sophisticated approach to opening the scroll could not have been found somewhere else. Professor Wright-Baker had devised a Rube Goldberg machine ("constructed almost entirely from ex-Service equipment, obtained at the end of the war," Allegro noted with some admiration) consisting of a tiny wheeled trolley (on which the scroll, covered with airplane glue and then baked to seal its surface, would be mounted), which would roll back and forth beneath a stationary circular saw. A narrow lengthwise segment would be cut

off, and the scroll would be rotated slowly until the entire document was cut up into lengthwise strips. Through the fall and winter of 1956–57, as Allegro stood by the side of Dr. Wright-Baker
with his whizzing saw and loaded trolley, the scroll was gradually
cut up into twenty-three slices, and Allegro became the first
scholar in the world to transcribe and translate the text.

In agreeing to supervise the work of unrolling, Allegro had
promised to respect the publication rights of J. T. Milik, who was
the authorized editor of the scroll. Yet Allegro became so intrigued by the Copper Scroll's treasure list that he undertook his
own transcription, translation, and even commentary. By that
time, he had come to believe the treasure was indeed genuine,
and he gradually developed the idea that it was an accurate record
of the Temple treasure and other sacred booty amassed and hidden by radical Jewish rebels during the Great Revolt against
Rome. Why exactly the Zealots would have deposited their copper
treasure map at Qumran was uncertain, but Allegro insisted that
"it seems only reasonable to give its author the benefit of any
doubt on his sanity, and not to dismiss the whole exciting text as
the work of a fanatic, as some have done."

Ever eager to play devil's advocate, Allegro was anxious to
challenge Milik's fairytale theory, and this push for reinterpretation, for the possibility of more than one viewpoint, led to some
far-reaching political infighting as well. Allegro loudly urged that
the full text be published at once so the scholarly public could
make up its mind whether the Copper Scroll was the work of a
crank or of an otherwise well-informed, intelligent priestly official
who had never written a document on copper before. After his
public dispute over the question of crucifixion and other suggestive messianic references, Allegro was more eager than ever for
battle against the power of De Vaux and the International Team.
In the following year, 1957, after convincing the newly appointed
Jordanian director of antiquities, Dr. Abdul Karim al-Gharaybeh,
that the treasure mentioned in the Copper Scroll was not only real
but could be uncovered, Allegro gained the director's express permission to publish his own unauthorized translation of the scroll

text—even before Milik's "official" publication had appeared. As far as the International Team was concerned, this was an act of scholarly thievery. But even worse was yet to come.

Beginning in the spring of 1960, Allegro began a series of highly publicized archaeological expeditions to Jordan to search for the bars of gold and silver mentioned in the Copper Scroll. These expeditions infuriated and unsettled Père De Vaux and the other International Team members, but there was little that they could do. Over the previous few years, while the International Team was busy trying to discredit Allegro in western newspapers and scholarly journals, Allegro had been carefully cultivating the friendship of various Jordanian officials, taking them into his confidence in a plan of action that was breathtaking in its ambitiousness, if not in its practicality. In a 1959 letter to Awni Dajani, the newly appointed director of antiquities, Allegro sketched out his master plan to raise money to buy the scrolls and scroll fragments still believed to be in the hands of the bedouin, and create a second, much larger and diverse team of scholars to edit and publish them.

The plan he envisioned was for the government of Jordan to issue invitations to academic institutions all over the world, creating in Jordan an advanced institute for Near Eastern studies, entirely free from political and religious pressures, dedicated to publishing a steady stream of transcriptions, translations, and commentaries of the hundreds of still unpublished documents from Qumran. Here, all of Allegro's ideas about the scrolls, about religion, about the future of the Middle East—past and present— began to merge. He was convinced that the Dead Sea Scrolls contained conclusive proof of the utter unoriginality of Christian doctrine, which had stolen virtually all of its messianic ideas, beliefs, and rituals from the Qumran Community. And for him, full and quick publication would be a blow struck against the tyranny of organized Christianity, for he naively believed that the public would immediately see in the scrolls powerful proof that the church was founded on a stolen and rewritten gospel of Jewish messianism.

The only way to "free" the scrolls, he believed, was to rip them out of the grasp of the International Team. To that end, he found some important allies among the officials of the Jordanian government and its Department of Antiquities. Thus, even though his treasure hunts in the Judean Desert failed to come up with even a single bar of gold or silver, they did bring considerable positive publicity. While the International Team members poured scorn on Allegro's theories and actions in scholarly journals, his quest for lost treasure (and his reputation as a colorful maverick) ensured him the status of a hero in the tabloids and on T.V. Even King Hussein was intrigued by reports of the adventure; he helicoptered down from Amman in the spring of 1960 to make a personal visit to the expedition base camp. Even though Allegro was now completely ostracized by De Vaux and the other International Team members, he remained a player in the Dead Sea Scroll story. His political connections in Jordan provided him with an independent power base.

It is hard to gauge how much influence Allegro exercised in Jordan. Yet whether due to his efforts or to a resurgence of nationalistic feeling, events were pushing the Jordanian government toward tighter control over the scrolls. Since 1953, the government had permitted a few foreign institutions (each of them with close connections to International Team members) to contribute toward the purchase of the scroll fragments with the expectation that they would eventually obtain the Dead Sea Scroll fragments for themselves. By 1960, despite the fact that the vast majority of the Cave 4 material was still unpublished, preparations were being made to send off large numbers of Cave 4 manuscripts to McGill, Manchester, and Heidelberg universities; to the McCormick Theological Seminary in Chicago; and to the Vatican Library. Yet even as the inventories were being assembled and submitted to the Department of Antiquities for export permits, reports of the imminent shipment of the Dead Sea Scrolls out of the country was grist for the radical anti-Hashemite mill.

Opposition politicians and editorial writers in Jordan, who had never before paid much attention to the patriotic value of an-

cient Hebrew and Aramaic manuscripts, suddenly became outraged. "The Scrolls at the Jerusalem Museum are the Property of
the Government and Should Not Be Allowed to Leave the Country" read the headline in the hardline Jerusalem daily *ad-Difa'a*,
on May 30, 1960. Minister of Foreign Affairs Said Mussa Nasser
quickly signaled a sudden change in policy when he announced
that "the Jordan Government consider these scrolls as valuable
treasure which should not be parted with or exposed to danger by
sending it abroad for any reason whatever." And by mid-July, the
new policy position on the scrolls was made official. The Council
of Ministers passed a resolution declaring that all scrolls found in
the Dead Sea region were the unalienable property of the Hashemite Kingdom, and that any foreign institutions that had contributed funds for their purchase from the bedouin would be
reimbursed from the royal treasury.

In 1961, John Allegro was appointed to the honorary position
of "Scroll Advisor to His Majesty's Government," and he seemed
determined to do whatever he could to hasten the disbanding of
the International Team. An opportunity to strike a blow in that
direction arose in 1966, when the Council of Ministers voted to
nationalize the Palestine Archaeological Museum and dissolve its
international board of trustees. From the tone of his letters in this
period, it is clear that Allegro greeted the news of the impending
nationalization with unembarrassed glee. Soon the International
Team would be subject to the direct supervision of the Jordanian
Department of Antiquities, whose director, Awni Dajani, was a
longtime friend and political ally. In a letter in September 1966 to
Dajani, Allegro promised to "prepare a paper on the whole subject of the future care of the Jordan scrolls, and the steps which
need taking forthwith to oblige the scholars concerned to publish
their documents." He also had in mind a worldwide appeal to
raise funds for the physical preservation of the fragments ("I am
by no means certain that binding them tightly between glass is correct," he noted), as well as the construction of a special wing of
the museum where scholars from all over the world could have
easy and free access to the texts.

On November 28, 1966, the collections, equipment, and buildings of the Palestine Archaeological Museum were officially handed over to the Government of Jordan, and in the months that followed, Awni Dajani and Aref al-Aref, a veteran Jerusalem politician who was named Director General of the Museum, proposed some far-reaching changes—among them, a reassessment of the handling of the Dead Sea Scrolls. That issue, in fact, was listed on the proposed agenda of the first scheduled meeting of the museum's new advisory board.

It is impossible to know if Allegro, Dajani, and al-Aref could really have succeeded in breaking the monopoly of the International Team. Certainly De Vaux, Cross, and the other International Team members had their own powerful connections, and a fight for control of the unpublished manuscripts in 1967 would probably have been just as bloody as the fight that erupted in 1991. Yet these speculations are pointless, since the first meeting of the newly constituted advisory board of the Palestine Archaeological Museum was scheduled for July 3, 1967—and by that time the tides of modern Middle Eastern history were about to rob John Allegro of what might have been his greatest victory.

On June 5, 1967—after nearly a month of military and rhetorical threats from Egypt and Syria—Israel launched a massive preemptive strike against Egypt. On the following day, sporadic fighting broke out on the border between Israel and Jordan. In the predawn hours of June 7, the Battle for Jerusalem began. Sixty miles away in Amman, the Copper Scroll remained safely in its velvet and wooden display case, but the majority of the precious collection—the hundreds of plates and larger manuscripts from Qumran Caves 4 and 11—remained in the Scrollery at the Palestine Archaeological Museum in Jerusalem. Since 1956, at the time of the Suez Crisis, preparations had been made to ensure their safe removal from Jerusalem in the event of a military emergency. (At that time, Harding had ordered that special wooden cases be constructed, as the Museum trustees were informed at the time, "into which sheets of glass with the actual fragments of the scrolls would be shipped in the event of emergency and sent out of Jerusalem.'') But now, due to a missed or misunderstood instruction, the truck driver dispatched from Amman to pick up the scroll crates at the Palestine Archaeological Museum never arrived.

By late morning on June 7, a detachment of Israeli paratroopers, advancing slowly toward the northern walls of the Old City, captured the strategic museum building after a brief exchange of fire with Jordanian troops. At about the same time, Israeli armored columns swept eastward toward the Jordan Valley to drive the Jordanian forces from Jericho and the northwestern coast of the Dead Sea. The site of Khirbet Qumran and the hundreds of plates of Dead Sea manuscript fragments had now fallen under Israeli control. Yet there was to be no revolution. In yet another bitter irony of the long Dead Sea Scrolls story, the power of the International Team to maintain its implicit control over the scrolls and their interpretation was to be miraculously *preserved*—not challenged—by the sudden Israeli victory.

The first three Israeli archaeological representatives who entered the Palestine Archaeological Museum on the morning of June 7, 1967, in the midst of the Battle for Jerusalem, did not really know what they were looking for. Dr. Avraham Biran, then director of the Department of Antiquities, Professor Nahman Avigad of the Hebrew University, and Joseph Aviram of the Israel Exploration Society had all been roused from their sleep by a predawn phone call from Yigael Yadin's wife, Carmella, instructing them to report to the headquarters of the paratrooper brigade and get an armed escort to the recently conquered museum. With a pitched battle still underway between the Israeli troops occupying the museum and the Jordanian forces defending the nearby battlements of the ancient city wall of Jerusalem, Biran, Avigad, and Aviram searched quickly through the galleries, corridors, and offices that they had all once known well—before the 1948 partition of Jerusalem—but had not seen for nineteen years.

Exhausted Israeli paratroopers rested in the shaded walkways around the museum's elegant reflecting pool where, in more peaceful days, the International Team once had enjoyed their lunches and good company al fresco, before returning to the painstaking work in the Scrollery. Biran and the others had all seen the famous news pictures of that room with its long tables spread with hundreds of glass plates of Dead Sea Scroll fragments, with the International Team members huddling closely over them. From their memories of the museum—the "Rockefeller Museum" as so many people called it back then—they could even identify the Scrollery as a room once used as the museum archive in the building's northern wing. They therefore knew where they were going, but now the long tables were empty. Only later would they discover that just before the outbreak of the fighting, the scroll plates had been hastily gathered together and packed in their wooden crates.

Eventually, two Israeli scholars—Magen Broshi, the curator of the Shrine of the Book, and Joseph Naveh of the Department of Antiquities—were sent to the Rockefeller Museum to make a complete and detailed inventory of the captured scrolls. Broshi recalled that neither he nor Naveh had ever seen anything like it: hundreds of bound glass plates containing flattened, ragged groupings of fitted fragments, painstakingly pieced together by the International Team members over the previous fourteen years. Each plate bore a sticker with a provisional title or identification of the document's contents and a letter-and-number code, which Broshi and Naveh duly copied onto their inventory lists. This was the Holy of Holies of Dead Sea Scroll study. No one except the members of the International Team had ever had such free access to the plates before. John Strugnell later derisively described this post-war inventory to me as a "reading party," reflecting his still possessive feeling toward the documents. And there was good reason to feel possessive. Broshi recalled his mystification at the letter codes *M, C, Sn, Sy,* and *Sl* that appeared at the start of each plate's serial number. Only later did he learn that they were the identifying marks for the exclusive intellectual property of Milik, Cross, Skehan, Starcky, and Strugnell.

In the immediate aftermath of the 1967 War, the members of the International Team who had been scheduled to come to Jerusalem quickly canceled their airplane reservations to await word from De Vaux. De Vaux himself remained within the Ecole Biblique compound, biding his time and waiting for the dust to settle, and before long informal discussions got underway between De Vaux and Avraham Biran, director of the Israel Department of Antiquities, and Professor Yigael Yadin, representing Hebrew University and the Shrine of the Book. The irony is that had the Palestine Archaeological Museum—the Rockefeller—still been run by an International Board of Trustees, the fate of the scrolls might be much different today. For through the summer and fall of 1967, the Israeli government was careful not to infringe the rights of foreign or international organizations operating in Jerusalem.

Had the Jordanian government not nationalized the museum the previous November, the Cave 4 scrolls (all purchased on behalf of the museum) would have been as secure from direct Israeli control as the Latin Patriarch's vestments or the confidential account books of the American Schools of Oriental Research. Yet the International Board of Trustees *had* been disbanded. And because the legal experts of the Israeli Foreign and Education ministries were unanimous in their opinion that the Rockefeller and all the antiquities it contained were Jordanian national property—read: captured enemy property—it was determined that they should now come under the jurisdiction of the Israel Department of Antiquities.

The matter of the Dead Sea Scrolls Publication Project was more complex than the question of physical administration. And it was here that the Shrine of the Book became more directly involved. As usual in the Middle East, even the most semantic of distinctions can serve as political assertions (the name of the "Rockefeller" or "Palestine Archaeological Museum" was an obvious one). In that regard, the long-time title of the official scroll publication series was to be a serious stumbling block. In a spirit of scholarly courtesy, and in light of previous contractual arrangements with Oxford, both Yadin and Biran were prepared to allow Père De Vaux, as editor-in-chief, to continue to make editorial assignments, and they agreed not to question any of the assignments already made. But since the publication series had always been called *Discoveries in the Judaean Desert of Jordan,* it was clear to the Israelis that some changes, at least on the title page, had to be made.

Biran later recalled to me the ingenious negotiations over the future title of the Dead Sea Scroll volumes by which he, Yadin, and De Vaux each got something for themselves. The official sponsoring organizations for the scrolls project were the Ecole Biblique, the Palestine Archaeological Museum, and the Jordanian Department of Antiquities. De Vaux was adamant in refusing to substitute "Israel Department of Antiquities and Museums" on the title page for the "Department of Antiquities of the Hashemite Kingdom of Jordan." Who knew how long the Israelis would control East Jerusalem? Who knew what the costs of collaborating with the Israelis would be? Yet he agreed to the participation of the nongovernmental Shrine of the Book. The agreement between Yadin, De Vaux, and Biran was never put in writing, and the responsibilities of the three groups they represented were never formally defined. So the Israel Department of Antiquities, the Shrine of the Book, and the International Team became gentlemanly partners. "We always honored the assignments of the scholars," Biran recalled, "the critique against us is not fair in what we did do to honor the allocations, distribution, and assignments by the committee. Where we were probably at fault was in not insisting on dates."

With all his charm and natural charisma, Père De Vaux emerged as the clear winner, as far as his relationship with both Israelis and Jordanians was concerned. His challenge was now to bide his time and keep all his options open, neither appearing to get too close to the Israelis (lest the Jordanians return to Jerusalem) nor acting too militantly pro-Jordanian (should the Israelis be here to stay). The best course, he decided, was to put the whole enterprise into something like suspended animation, keeping a low profile but at the same time maintaining a visible presence at the museum. This strategy might not have been entirely ethical, and it certainly did not aid the cause of scholarship (much less the publication of the remaining plates of Qumran material), but the political situation in Jerusalem was complex and delicate. Père De Vaux, in his white habit and with his disarming Gallic charm, was more than a match for his new Israeli colleagues. And despite the fact that the assembling of the scroll fragments had been largely completed by 1960 and that the time had come for publication, De Vaux insisted that the old Scrollery be set up in the museum again.

You have to smile at thought of John Strugnell slumped in the seat of an airliner circling Ben-Gurion airport in the summer of 1968. In the seats and rows all around him were excited tourists to Israel clapping their hands to the lilting strains of "Heveinu Shalom Aleichem," craning their necks toward the windows to get their first glimpse of the Promised Land. "When I landed there, you know," he told me, "I first saw the strange habit of the Israelis clapping their hands when the plane landed, as if it were a major problem of some sort." Strugnell was coming to Israel for the first time in his life, but he quickly parted company with his tour group traveling companions after passing through passport control.

"I meant to come out two years before, on a sabbatical," he noted, mentioning that in the meantime his own academic career had advanced with his move from Duke to Harvard Divinity School. "I had been planning to come out with my wife and children, but we decided that things looked as if they were tricky, so I went and stayed at the Ecole Biblique. They sent Benoit down to the airport to guide me through the customs, to show me the 'new' half of the country that I had never seen. Benoit was a first-rate Palestinian topographer, and that ride back to Jerusalem took about five hours and we stopped at every little tell and point of significance."

As I talked with Strugnell about that first trip to Jerusalem through Israel rather than Jordan, I wanted to get more of a sense of how it felt to be—after fourteen years of personal experience in Jordan—suddenly on the other side. I know I experienced a frightening exhilaration the first time I traveled to Jordan after

years of living in Israel. There is an accumulated deposit of fear
from years of newspaper articles, TV broadcasts, and casual conversation that paints the Other Side as a dangerous, inaccessible
realm, which does not dissipate easily even after you've had a good
meal and checked into your hotel. There is the continuing fear of
exposure, a vulnerability that Strugnell expressed hesitantly to
me. "I think—how shall I put it—if you've lived fourteen years in
one country and become fairly attached to it, you stay attached
even when the political circumstance has changed."

Strugnell was the only one of the International Team with either the interest or the courage to see how the Six Day War would
affect the continuing study of the scrolls. While others team members were remaining far away and sending detailed advice and
suggestions to De Vaux on how he might best defend their interests in light of the new political situation, Strugnell had written to
De Vaux with a simple request. "All I needed to know from him
was if he judged it worthwhile to come out for a year now," Strugnell recalled, "and if I would have reasonable access. His answer
to that was that I can't give you an answer right now, but I judge if
you come out and are there on the doorstep, no one would refuse
you." In fact, it would be Strugnell's *job* to sit on the doorstep.
After settling in at the Ecole Biblique, De Vaux gave him instructions: "Go see Biran and see the people he wants you to negotiate
with and get as much of the free access to the manuscripts as you
can."

Things had begun to change dramatically over at the Rockefeller Museum; a year before, in July 1967, the headquarters of the
Israel Department of Antiquities and Museums had been formally
moved there and office space—any kind of space—was at a pre-
mium. That is why Strugnell's request to reopen the Scrollery was
such a problem for both Biran and then Broshi at the Shrine of
the Book. The coolness of their initial meeting still made Strugnell sputter when I spoke to him twenty-five years after the fact:
"They had no idea about how you work with six hundred plates of
manuscripts, which you want to have all out for simultaneous view-
ing. They thought a small little office and a locked cabinet would

be enough." In fact, the ease of identifying additional fragments was not the main scholarly challenge. The plates had been complete enough in 1960 to be prepared for shipment to Rome, Chicago, Montreal, and Heidelberg—and at that time Père De Vaux had been hopeful that the time had come for the various scholars to publish what they had. But now, suddenly, Strugnell acted as if the assembling phase was still very much in progress. And whatever the logic or the advantage to the larger project, Strugnell's demand for the restoration of the *status quo ante*—of obtaining precisely the same conditions and courtesies enjoyed under Jordanian rule—was the standard request of all the foreign institutions and organizations in East Jerusalem that had come under Israeli jurisdiction as a result of the war.

Amir Drori, the director of the reorganized Israel Antiquities Authority since 1988, who would eventually have to deal with the tangled legal legacy of this period of transition, described to me how hard it is to understand exactly what agreements were reached at this period. Nothing was ever officially put down in writing; it was more of a gentlemen's agreement between Yadin, Biran, and De Vaux that Israel would protect the rights of all those involved in the project as it was before. This agreement, Drori speculated, "was connected with the general policy that Israel followed in 1967. All kinds of foreign organizations, religious institutions in Jerusalem among them, were uncertain about what would happen under Israeli administration, what Israel would do to them. So the policy of the government of Levi Eshkol and Yigal Allon, who was Minister of Education, was to calm them down. They said don't be afraid—just continue with what you are doing."

The Dead Sea Scrolls were certainly not the most important issue on the negotiating table at a time when the nation of Israel was exhilarated by its sudden rule over all of the territory west of the Jordan, the Palestinians were in a state of shock, and the defeated Arab states were licking their wounds. As far as the scrolls were concerned, all sides were satisfied for the time being. "They didn't get down to the details, and I don't imagine that anyone

considered that this would be a project that would take forever,"
Drori added. "They probably thought that in a reasonable time
these things would eventually come out."

The truth was that at no time in the history of the project was
the prospect for complete publication more remote. The scattered team members in Paris, Washington, and Cambridge were
happy to take advantage of the uncertain political situation in Jerusalem for putting an indefinite hold on their work. Yet few of
them were ready yet to give up their exclusive rights to their allotted texts. As a result, John Strugnell became the symbolic
scholar—a lonely presence assigned to preserve at least the appearance that something was going on. Thus the hundreds of
plates were spread out on the long tables, and Strugnell spent his
sabbatical year in 1968–69 in blissful isolation, working on his
manuscripts and preparing a slashing, scathing 113-page review of
John Allegro's recently published volume of Cave 4 texts in the
Discoveries in the Judaean Desert series—bidding him a disdainful
scholarly good-riddance from the team once and for all.

"De Vaux came in and was often in the basement," Strugnell
recalled of this period, noting that by this time the editor-in-chief
of the scrolls project had turned his attention to completing two
major works on the early biblical period—his *Institutions of Ancient
Israel* and *The Early History of Israel*—that had nothing directly to do
with Qumran. But the slowdown in the work on Cave 4 was hardly
noticed. An important new Dead Sea Scroll had come to light in
the meantime, and its surprising contents of a detailed law code of
piety, purity, and kingship was soon to change the direction of
scroll studies, bringing up once again the mystery of the Qumran
Community's apparent obsession with the Temple of Jerusalem.

In 1967, two Dead Sea Scroll worlds were suddenly thrust together. After nearly twenty years of almost total segregation, two
quite different perspectives were brought face-to-face. I do not
think the point is stressed often enough that during the 1950s and
early 1960s, when Christian scholars spoke of the Dead Sea Scrolls
and when Israeli or Jewish scholars spoke of the Dead Sea Scrolls,

160 THE HIDDEN SCROLLS

they were usually talking about two different things. For Christians—as I have tried to show—the scrolls were seen as the missing evolutionary link between Judaism and Christianity. The recurring themes of Christian scholarship were baptism, messianism, monasticism, and ecclesiastical administration—all of them implicitly having to do with the rise of Christianity. There might be free-thinking troublemakers like John Allegro who would try to show that Christianity was just a stolen Essene gospel, but very few denied that the scrolls were valuable as background for New Testament history. Thus, in 1966, John Strugnell, with thirteen years of work on the scrolls as his main professional undertaking, was appointed to the faculty of the Harvard Divinity School as professor of Christian Origins.

Israeli and Jewish interest in the scrolls through the 1950s and early 1960s naturally veered off in very different directions. For Israelis, there was never any interest in the Dead Sea Scrolls as a weapon for overturning organized religions or as a source of mystical secrets. The Dead Sea Scrolls had a much more basic nationalistic significance. Like the Western Wall, the Solomonic Gate at Megiddo, or the burnt palaces at Masada, they were tangible relics—touchable, feelable proof that Jews had once lived, fought, and prospered in this land. The romantic juxtaposition of Sukenik's purchase of the scrolls on the day of the United Nations decision to partition Palestine—and thereby create the State of Israel—gave the ancient documents a miraculous, almost heaven-sent, quality in the modern Israeli consciousness. When the Shrine of the Book was opened in 1964 and the original seven scrolls were placed on display, the emotional impact of modern Israelis—adults and children—reading aloud even a word or two from the boldly penned two-thousand-year-old Hebrew manuscripts offered a powerful demonstration of cultural survival and continuity. The image of pacifist, proto-Christian Essenes was a problematic one in the 1950s for Israeli self-definition (even though there was some interest in the communal lifestyle of the Essenes among members of the kibbutz movement, and the martial furies of the War Scroll attracted some interest), but the new treasures that came to the Shrine of the Book in the early 1960s clearly showed the militant, passionately nationalistic side of ancient Jewish history.

In 1960 and 1961, Israeli archaeological teams combed the ravines of the southwestern Dead Sea shore close to the border with Jordan, in response to reports that bedouin scroll hunters had been looting caves within Israeli territory. Yigael Yadin's announcement of the discovery of letters and other papers of participants in the Bar Kokhba Revolt (132–135 C.E.) moved and exhilarated the nation. The personal military dispatches of Simeon bar Kosiba, the fabled Jewish rebel leader known by his messianic codename "Bar Kokhba"—signed with the same title used by the modern presidents of Israel—were tangible tokens of the continuity of Jewish past and Jewish present, even if the revolt was, in its time, a lost cause. In fact, so closely were the Bar Kokhba letters associated in the international press with the modern State of Israel that the Jordanian director of Antiquities, Dr. Abdel Karim al-Gharaybeh, issued an order to remove all Bar Kokhba manuscripts from display at the Palestine Archaeological Museum because they only served as "obvious propaganda for the Zionists." The symbolic value of archaeological discoveries in the Dead Sea region soared even higher with Yadin's spectacular dig at the mountain fortress of Masada, where more ancient manuscripts were found.

In 1956, the last of the major Qumran caves—Cave 11—had been discovered by the Taamireh; like Cave 1, it contained both fragments and complete scrolls. At the time, Lankester Harding still had his exclusive agreement with the bedouins' middleman Kando, and the Rockefeller Museum records show that Kando left "eight cardboard boxes and one package on deposit for safe keeping" on March 2. The standard, gentlemanly procedure that Kando and Harding had established was that the members of the International Team would examine the documents and identify them as far as possible, and determine fairly—as gentleman—the fair market value of the new material. By the middle of May, the team had decided that Kando's new cache, consisting of an ancient scroll of psalms, a small scroll of Leviticus, and fragments of several other manuscripts, was worth 32,000 Jordanian dinars, then about $75,000, and Kando agreed to the deal. Yet in light of the civil unrest in Jordan and the beginning of pressure against foreign-born officials in the government, Kando had apparently already begun to consider outlets for his merchandise besides the Palestine Archaeological Museum. There are those that will swear to this day (John Strugnell is one of them) that they were shown by bedouin a complete manuscript of the Book of Enoch and perhaps another that is now owned by a private investor somewhere in the Arab world. It is impossible to know if that is accurate. But what is certain is that Kando kept for himself at least *one* well-preserved scroll.

Across the border in Israel, Professor Yigael Yadin had continued to publish articles on the Qumran literature, but, except for occasional correspondence with Père De Vaux, conducted through mutual acquaintances in Europe, he had no personal contact with the world of scroll study and scroll acquisition in Jordanian Jerusalem. But in the summer of 1960, he received the first of what would be many strange letters from the Reverend Joseph Uhrig of Lynchburg, Virginia, an ordained Baptist minister and would-be TV evangelist, who claimed to be the exclusive international agent for Kando, who was offering for sale ten scrolls of gazelle and goatskin, one of bronze, and one of gold.

Yadin was understandably wary of both the minister and his story, but he became a sudden believer when, several months later, Uhrig sent him a large, authentic scroll fragment—through the mail. Yadin purchased that fragment and began a tedious and often infuriating correspondence with Uhrig, in which agreed-upon sale terms and purchase prices unexpectedly skyrocketed at the last moment and in which there was considerable uncertainty on exactly the number and size of the scrolls that were for sale. Yadin eventually lost a $10,000 deposit in the course of the negotiations, yet before he cut off all contact with Uhrig, Yadin received another small scroll fragment—this one apparently from the complete document for sale—and the text that it bore men-

tioned a specific Temple sacrifice and the proper role of the High
Priest.

By the spring of 1967, there were other eager potential buyers. Frank Cross and Dr. James Swauger of the Carnegie Museum
in Pittsburgh recalled a secret trip they took to Beirut to negotiate
for the purchase of what were reportedly twenty or more Dead Sea
Scrolls. As things turned out, their expedition was a fiasco. They
spent most of their time waiting in their hotel rooms for phone
calls from a shadowy intermediary, and Cross eventually met
Kando himself, who stubbornly refused to show him more than a
few scroll fragments unless he unconditionally agreed—ahead of
time—to what Kando hoped would be a multimillion-dollar deal.

That was March 1967, and then came the June 1967 War.
With Israeli forces now in control of all of the West Bank, Yadin, a
former army chief-of-staff and special security advisor to Prime
Minister Eshkol, was now in a position to apply direct pressure on
Kando and make him see things his way. Dispatching a special unit
of intelligence officers to find Kando, they brought him from his
home in Bethlehem to his shop in Jerusalem. By 1967, Kando,
who was already wealthy, had invested in a large souvenir and antiquities store next to the St. George Hotel and had become a familiar figure—sunning himself in a chair outside the main
doorway, wearing his trademark red fez.

As evasive and as garrulous as ever, Kando denied that he
knew what the Israeli officers were talking about. It was only after
two days of confinement and interrogation in a Tel Aviv safe house
that Kando finally broke. He took the officers back to his home in
Bethlehem and led them into one of the bedrooms. There, alone,
and resigned to surrender, he pushed a heavy bureau slightly to
the side, paced off a certain number of floor tiles from the room's
corner, and used a toilet plunger to remove one of them. Below
was a specially constructed concrete compartment. And inside
that, wrapped in a towel and enclosed in a plastic bag, was a spec-
tacularly beautiful twenty-six-foot-long manuscript—soon to
become famous as the Temple Scroll.

The legal ramifications of this confiscation and the opening and preservation do not really need to detain us; Kando was eventually reimbursed about $135,000 for the document, and the scroll was opened under the supervision of Joseph Shenhav, the chief conservation officer at the Israel Museum. The important thing to keep in mind here is that Yadin operated by his own standard of conduct. For him, fortune belonged to the daring, and he was thoughtlessly, if not arrogantly, the most daring scholar around. Yadin was in many respects a larger-than-life character; every major archaeological project he attempted grabbed headlines, and so it was to be with the Temple Scroll. After keeping its contents and even its existence secret from all but a few of his closest associates, he presented it to the world for the first time at a festive public meeting of the Israel Exploration Society. And the scroll he presented was not in the least messianic, otherworldly, or in any sense proto-Christian. It was a code of detailed, almost *halakhic*, regulations for the observance of cultic festivals, the architecture and layout of the ideal Temple, the proper conduct of its sacrifices, the rules of conduct for a righteous king of Israel—and exceptionally strict laws of purity to preserve the sanctity of the Temple and the Holy City of Jerusalem.

Visionary descriptions of a perfect Temple to the God of Israel were for centuries a familiar Hebrew literary genre—perhaps because the reality of the earthly Temple of Jerusalem diverged so radically and so painfully from the ideal. In the mid-sixth century B.C.E., at a time when Solomon's Temple lay in ruins, the Prophet Ezekiel was transported in one of his visions from Babylon to the Land of Israel, where God "set me down on a very high mountain, on which was a structure, like a city, opposite me." Before his eyes in this trance rose a massive square platform on which stood the Sanctuary of God. In tedious detail—more in the manner of master builder than of a wild-eyed prophet—Ezekiel described the courts, the gates, doorposts, vestibules, inner chambers, and Holy of Holies of this Temple, to provide the people of Israel with a glimpse at the place of God's presence on earth, so that the people of Israel "may be ashamed at their iniquities."

There was obvious symbolism in this ideal vision. The hidden meaning of the numbers, orientations, and dimensions of the walls, gates, and windows in Ezekiel's vision would become the obsession of mystics and numerologists for centuries, intent on unlocking God's secret code of sanctity. Just as the ritual calendar was meant to represent the divine division of time, this ideal temple, with its symmetries and mirror images, was meant both to represent and embody the divinely decreed articulation of sacred space. Yet there was also a subtle polemic in this kind of utopian writing. The Temple reerected by the Judean exiles returning from Babylon seems to have been blessed with a large and zealous priesthood, but it seems also to have been a fairly rough-hewn affair. Poised on the summit of Mount Moriah, it was constructed of roughly quarried limestone blocks. Around its sanctuary and altar were storerooms, priestly chambers, and outer courtyards in which pilgrims and penitents gathered on important festival days. Human nature being what it was—and what it is—squabbles must have continually arisen among competing priestly factions over precedence and cultic participation. And their opposing positions might have been expressed most clearly in the composition of utopian visions of the Holy City that combined traditional, otherworldly symmetries with a few specific, down-to-earth suggestions about "how things ought to be."

Among the Qumran texts are some fragmentary compositions that are apparently part of this priestly literature. They describe the perfect, gridlike city plan of an ideal Jerusalem, whose Temple and uniform blocks of houses are surrounded by an enormous, rectangular turreted wall. We have no way of knowing how far back these traditions go—or what crisis or complaint inspired their composition. For even after the Maccabean rebellion, with its renewed religious fervor, the earthly Temple was still just so much limestone, cement, and cedarwood fitted together by the calloused hands of workmen—just a poor version of the sanctuary that would be built in messianic times. Purists' complaints about the conduct of the Temple worship seem to have centered on the qualifications of the High Priest for his office—rather than on the

Temple's architecture. Thus the Hasmonean High Priest-King Alexander Janneus, whose family was seen by some as having usurped the rightful legacy of the Zadokite line, was once booed, hissed, and pelted with ethrogs by the pilgrims during his officiation of the ceremonies of the Festival of Tabernacles.

So long as the Jerusalem Temple remained the old hand-me-down structure—with at least physical continuity with the first small shrine put up by the returning Babylonian exiles—it embodied the faith of the people, despite all its obvious flaws. You might say it had the same relationship to the ideal temple that the boisterous, bustling commerce of Jerusalem's markets had to the serene order and sanctity that would prevail among the Holy City's sedate inhabitants in the World to Come. Even if, from time to time, foreign rulers had attempted to violate the Temple—like Antiochus Epiphanes, who set up idols, or the Roman general Pompey, who stole some of its treasure and entered the Holy of Holies to satisfy his curiosity—these were all passing abominations that could be redressed with appropriate priestly lamentations and a dedicated maintenance crew. But in 20 B.C.E., the history of the Jerusalem Temple was changed forever, when King Herod, the half-Idumean, Rome-imposed despot undertook an enormous reconstruction project on Mount Moriah. Its effects have still not been reversed.

Every modern visitor to Jerusalem marvels at the gigantic dimensions of the Herodian Temple platform, the vast, raised foundation on which the Dome of the Rock and the al-Aqsa mosque now stand. Even with modern cranes, winches, and earth-moving equipment, the idea of filling in a major valley, creating what amounted to constructing an artificial mountain, in which millions of tons of fill are kept in place by walls of gigantic ashlar stones, would cause an international sensation even today. Herod the Great wanted to make the Temple of Jerusalem his showplace, a sign of his devotion to the Israelite religion (no matter what the purists would say about his family background) and a monument of his greatness to be bequeathed to posterity. While retaining the original core of the Temple sanctuary and altar, Herod's ar-

chitects planned and directed the construction of vast new courtyards, impressive public entrances, and a breathtakingly ornate
portico running along all sides of the new Temple enclosure, with
a ceiling of carved cedar and supported by marble columns forty
feet high. In its sheer scale and sumptuous splendor, Herod's
Temple was regarded as one of the most spectacular structures in
the entire Roman Empire.

Josephus Flavius and the later rabbis lavished praise on this
magnificent architectural achievement. Growing numbers of pilgrims now came from the Jewish communities all over the Mediterranean and from Mesopotamia and Persia to participate in the
great festivals and offer sacrifices to restore ritual purity or atone
for their sins. Yet even as tourist revenues skyrocketed, there must
have been some priestly dissidents who saw the rebuilding of the
Temple as a blasphemous pretension, no less damning than
Herod's tacit acknowledgment of the divinity of the Roman Emperor. And the two were indeed linked, for Herod had installed a
golden eagle, the symbol of Rome, above the main gate to the
inner chambers of the new Temple, as a not-so-subtle reminder of
where the *real* power lay.

Today, Dead Sea Scrolls scholars disagree widely on the date
when the Temple Scroll was composed or when the various traditions it embodies were woven together. Yadin, who published it in
1977 in Hebrew, argued that it was written in the second century
B.C.E. in opposition to Hasmonean practices, perhaps even as a
founding document of the Qumran Community, and composed
by the Teacher of Righteousness. Other scholars have insisted that
it is the product of a much earlier and wider visionary tradition.
Because it lacks the familiar apocalyptic distinctions between
Light and Darkness and Qumran sectarian terminology, they believe it was written long before the establishment of the Community, placing it in the context of priestly politics and dating it to the
Hellenistic period in Jerusalem.

Whatever its date of composition, or date of its final redac-
tion, the Temple Scroll contains an amazingly comprehensive vision of the order of time, space, and leadership. Although only

scattered fragments remain of its first thirteen columns, the fifty-three that follow contain detailed descriptions of the proper sequence of festivals and sacrifices to be performed in the Temple; the design of the Temple structures (strikingly different from Ezekiel); the strict purity regulations to be observed in the Holy City; uncompromising injunctions against idolatry; and exacting rules of marriage and personal conduct to be adhered to by the Israelites' king. And the Temple Scroll was explicit in noting that "it is from among your brothers that you shall appoint a king over you. You shall not appoint over you a foreigner."

Read as a polemic—as well as a vision—the Temple Scroll evokes a situation in which the rituals, design, and purity of the earthly Temple were regarded as faulty; in which fornication, idolatry, impurity, and treason were rampant in Jerusalem; and in which, among other offenses to God's ideal order, there was a non-Israelite king. The scroll's metaphorical recommendations were for a completely redesigned and rebuilt temple and an ever-more stringent separation between pure and impure, holy and profane.

Now it may well be that the Temple Scroll or its sources were compiled during the time of the Hasmoneans, yet the beautifully penned copy of the text that was preserved and recovered from under the ceramic tiles in Kando's bedroom has been confidently dated by most scholars to the late first century B.C.E. This was precisely the time when Herod's opulent, ungodly structures suddenly dominated the Jerusalem skyline, hardly different in megalomaniac conception and cultural inspiration from the tyrant's spectacular pleasure palaces in Jerusalem, Masada, and Herodium. At what point would the impiety of Herod and his successors render the Temple unfit for proper Israelite devotions? If Herod's Roman, rather than biblical, architectural plan were tolerable, what of the eagle over the gate? And if the eagle were accepted, should a sacrifice be offered every morning for the health and well-being of the emperor, as the Roman governors insisted after the annexation of Judea in 6 C.E.? How long would the Temple continue to be violated and Roman governors have the power to order their troops in Jerusalem to break up festival crowds whose behavior seemed threatening—and to confiscate sacred tithes and Temple treasure to defray the costs of administering this rebellious occupied territory?

Anyone reading the Temple Scroll in this period would have understood the subtext. The people of Qumran, and all readers of texts like the Temple Scroll throughout Judea, had good reason to believe that the Temple had been taken from them—and that they would get it back some day. The latter-day scholarly idea that Essenes of Qumran rejected the Temple worship because they had perfected a more spiritual ritual is nonsense. Visions of the Temple were dreams of Judean independence. And many believed that the messianic age would come only when righteous priests reformed and purified Temple observance—and had deposed the clique of soulless empty suits who called themselves High Priests.

By the early 1970s, even if the International Team members would have wished it, the likelihood of a Jordanian return to Jerusalem grew more remote and eventually vanished with King Hussein's renouncement of all claims to Palestine at the Arab League Conference in Rabat in 1974. The members of the International Team now had no one but the Israelis to deal with, and some members, like J. T. Milik in Paris, preferred not to deal at all. His plates of fragments at the Rockefeller Museum remained unexamined; repeated letters sent to him in Paris by the Israel Department of Antiquities went without any response. Maurice Baillet came out to work on his fragments in 1970, but other than that there was little activity at the museum. The Scrollery (whose continued existence had become such a point of honor to some of the team members) was locked and deserted most of the time.

It was also the period, Strugnell recalled, that "the incursions on our territory began." In the unspoken partition of responsibilities over the scrolls between the Israel Department of Antiquities and the Shrine of the Book, physical conservation was the responsibility of the Shrine of the Book. And the truth was that the conditions under which the Cave 4 fragments were being kept in the Scrollery—in a drafty room with large windows that flooded it with morning sunlight—were disgraceful. Common sense said that something had to be done. So after consulting with Joseph Shenhav at the Israel Museum, who had worked on the Temple Scroll and finds from Masada, Magen Broshi decided to take all the fragments to a room where light, temperature, and humidity could be controlled. The room, down in the cold, damp Rockefeller basement, was about a quarter of the size of the Scrollery. He brought in flat file drawers for the storage of the plates and installed an air conditioner to keep the air as dry as possible. Baillet was horrified at the "dark little chamber," but there was nothing he could do. These bare-minimum conservation measures would have been judged too lax by most of the world's large museums if they had had a collection of manuscripts as valuable as the Dead Sea Scrolls. It was a response, in some small measure, to the complaints of John Allegro in the early 1960s, yet to some of the members of the International Team the changes were viewed as "incursions" on their right to do with the scrolls whatever they pleased.

Death also played a role in the team's gradual weakening. The 1971 passing of Père Roland De Vaux, at age sixty-eight, left the publication project suddenly without the editor-in-chief who had guided it from its beginnings in 1952. Word of his death came to Harvard by a cable from Father Jerome Murphy-O'Connor, a member of the Ecole Biblique faculty. "Cross and I realized that there was a terrible vacuum," Strugnell recalled, "so we telephoned the rest of the team and said that it seems to us that the successor should be from the team, available in Jerusalem, and respected. So this was Benoit." Père Pierre Benoit was only three years younger than De Vaux, and although he was soft spoken where De Vaux was dramatic, he was accorded great respect in Jerusalem. Cross and Strugnell acted quickly. "We then telephoned Benoit and asked if he would accept, and after we got his OK, we called the rest of the team." At the same time, the Israel Department of Antiquities remained committed to its noninterventionist policy. "It was our feeling that we should honor the wishes of the committee," Antiquities Director Biran remembered, "and when De Vaux died we honored their request for Père Benoit to continue as the editor-in-chief."

Yet Benoit's contemplative management style eventually created a problem. Where De Vaux was in complete control of the political situation, if not of the pace of the team members' publications, Benoit gradually lost control of both. By the early 1980s his health was clearly failing, and he was anxious to find a successor to take over the scrolls project from him. The leadership of the team was being determined by a process of elimination. Milik was in Paris and had no intention of leaving. "Who else was there?" Strugnell recalled. "Skehan was dead. Cross said he wasn't interested. I was the only possible candidate." Thus John Strugnell, no longer a boy wonder but a fiftyish Harvard professor, was designated Benoit's deputy and successor-to-be.

It is ironic that John Strugnell was later widely depicted in the press as an anti-Semite, because by the early 1980s he had developed some important new contacts among a new generation of Israeli scroll scholars. "I found myself moving more easily among Israelis," he told me. "I went up to the university to Michael Stone's seminar. The Israelis wanted to entertain, to invite you over to dinner." Yet more than ever he felt like an outsider. "The Israelis were a friendlier world, and yet you had a tremendous sympathy for the Arabs, who were underdogs." He continued to live at the Ecole Biblique, sharing the fellowship in the refectory yet left all alone to battle mounting bouts of manic depression and a growing problem with alcohol.

His work on the scrolls continued fitfully on some texts, more intensely on others. In conversations with Yadin during the course of his work on the Temple Scroll, Strugnell became aware of the new emphasis and scholarly interest in the history of the *halakhah*, or Jewish religious law. This was a rather marginal interest for a professor of Christian Origins and, besides, Strugnell was skeptical about the evidence for pre-70 C.E. rabbinic-type legal disputation. In his understanding, *halakhah* was a code of regulations for all the

people of Israel under everyday conditions. And neither the utopian laws of the Temple Scroll, nor the fraternity regulations of
the Community Rule or the Damascus Document, could be considered real *halakhah*. That is not to say that real *halakhah* could
not be found somewhere in the Qumran material. There was, in
fact, a fragmentary legal text he had been working on since 1955
that now drew his attention. "It was very difficult to make headway
because the law was so strange," Strugnell remembered, "but
when I started to work with Qimron, things began to fall into
place."

And thus we come to the story of the Qumran document that
became one of the focal points of the final battle to free the
scrolls. It certainly is not much to look at. Preserved in six copies
(all of which are highly fragmentary), the reconstructed text now
amounts to something like 120 lines. Back in the early 1950s,
Strugnell and Milik had worked closely together in identifying the
fragments, arranging them in several manuscripts, and then trying
to make some sense of the text itself. This document, 4Q394-399,
contained a long list of regulations about sacrifices, purity, Temple administration, and intermarriage, written in an idiosyncratic
style of Hebrew, closer in a number of respects to the language of
the Mishnah (and, strangely enough, of the Copper Scroll) than
the biblical Hebrew of the vast majority of the Qumran texts. For
that reason, Milik called the text 4Qmishn(ique). At first the two
scholars believed that the list was not of earthly legislation but of
angelic laws, as in the Book of Jubilees. Strugnell had put it to the
side, never considering it particularly important. And that was
about all that was done on the text until a rainy afternoon in 1979,
when a young Israeli scholar named Elisha Qimron came to the
Ecole Biblique to pay a courtesy call on Strugnell. Qimron, a Hebrew linguist, had completed a dissertation on the peculiarities of
Qumran Hebrew and was clearly intrigued when Strugnell showed
him some photographs of the legal document—and he readily
agreed to make a study of its distinctive vocabulary and grammar,
in the hope that they might figure out the significance of its text.

By no stretch of the imagination can I pretend to understand the nature of Strugnell's scholarly relationships. He has a wide circle of faithful former students and many Israeli friends and colleagues who still admire his scholarship, even after all that he has said and the way he has been described in the press. Yet it is undeniable that by 1981 the association between Strugnell and Qimron deepened, and by working together the two were eventually able to use the six fragmentary copies of the document to reconstruct, if only roughly, the contents of the original text. On one of the copies, the document began with the detailed description of the festivals and holy days of a distinctive 364-day solar calendar (identical to that used by the Temple Scroll and the Book of Jubilees). Following that was a public proclamation, or an open letter, setting forth a list of laws of purity and Temple observance that the authors felt especially strongly about. At the top of the list was the demand that no Gentile offerings or sacrifices be accepted in the Temple; farther down were recommendations for making priestly standards of behavior considerably stricter, for enforcing personal purity laws to the letter, and for safeguarding the sanctity of Jerusalem.

The ancient authors concluded this text with the defiant statement that they had separated themselves from the rest of the people of Israel because these imperatives were not being observed, causing the Temple to be profaned. Appealing directly to someone who was apparently the leader of the nation, they appealed to him to remember the earlier kings of Israel, who prospered when they remained faithful to the law and were punished when they did not. Hoping that this leader might see the light and adopt their suggestions, they wrote that

> you will rejoice in the end when you find some of our
> words correct. And let it be considered right for you, and
> lead you to do righteousness and good, and may it be for
> your benefit and for that of Israel.

Qimron and Strugnell adapted a new title for the document from the beginning of the legal section: *Miqsat Ma'asei ha-Torah*—

"Some Works of the Torah." It would soon become famous as MMT.

After his 1981–82 sabbatical in Jerusalem, Strugnell went back to Harvard and Qimron continued working on this document, refining his transcription and translation and beginning to seek the advice and opinions of a small circle of colleagues. And even though the text's complaints about lax Temple worship were strinkingly similar to those known from Herodian and post-Herodian times, the few scholars who were consulted went along with Qimron and Strugnell's assumption that the text was composed at the time of the supposed founding of the Qumran sect, in the second century B.C.E. Compounding this theory, there was a truly astounding leap of imagination: Since the list of disputed laws was contained in something like a public broadside, or open letter, Strugnell and Qimron came to the conclusion that it was written as a party manifesto by no less a figure than the Teacher of Righteousness—still unidentified—who sent it to the figure otherwise known as the Wicked Priest.

When Elisha Qimron stepped to the podium of the International Congress on Biblical Archaeology, held in Jerusalem in 1984, and presented this important new document, with its long list of laws, and his assertion that it was a personal letter of the Teacher of Righteousness, the scrolls scholars in the audience who were unaware of MMT's existance were both elated and shocked. Here, after all, was what seemed to be the Declaration of Independence of the Qumran Community, explaining that the sect's objection to certain marriage, sacrificial, and purity practices—apparently condoned by the current priesthood—were the reason that they had "separated themselves from the majority of the people." Here was the convincing proof of the purely *halakhic* origin of the Community—not in messianism, baptism, or proto-Christian spirituality, but in the rigorous observance of Temple worship and ritual purity. It also placed the very identification of the Qumran sect with the Essenes into serious jeopardy. The specific legal rulings advocated in MMT, as in the Temple Scroll, were identified as *Sadducean* in later rabbinic literature. The value of

MMT was indeed incalculable for the future of Qumran studies. If a document of this importance had remained virtually unknown since the early 1950s, who knew what other treasures lay among the unpublished texts from Cave 4?

Yet in mid-1984, the long-term prospects of the Dead Sea Scrolls Publication Project were more uncertain than ever. Père Benoit was sick, and John Strugnell was doing the best he could to juggle his research and his teaching responsibilities, but his own scroll work, which was now about twenty years behind schedule, was further impeded by his new role as deputy editor-in-chief. And at this time, also, a new voice arose to question the International Team's continuing monopoly: Writing in the *Biblical Archaeology Review* in the summer of 1984, editor Hershel Shanks reported on Qimron's presentation of MMT at the Jerusalem congress but expressed astonishment that Qimron had made public only a few passages from the obviously important historical document. He was surprised that MMT was not now freely available to all interested scholars. This was just a passing editorial comment that showed a decided lack of familiarity with the longtime operating procedures of the Qumran Publication Project. Yet in its tone of criticism for scholarly selfishness, it was an omen of things to come.

The irony of all of this was that MMT expressed a message of priestly protest that fit far better in the first century than in the second B.C.E. The concern with the purity of the Temple, the gifts of Gentiles, and the behavior of the Temple priesthood formed the constellation of abominations that would eventually lead the nation to war. The links of MMT with the Temple Scroll and its purity concerns were obvious. Obvious, too, were the similarities with the religious ideology of the Jewish revolutionary movement that grew more and more obsessed with the purity of the Temple during the course of the first century C.E.

Last of all was MMT's link to the mysterious Copper Scroll, which had been for so long considered just a curiosity. The connections between the two documents went far beyond the linguistic peculiarities that MMT and the enigmatic copper treasure map shared. For even after the suppression of the Great Revolt and the Roman sack of Jerusalem, militant faith in the observance of the Law was not completely extinguished. Though King Herod's once magnificent showplace was now charred, desecrated, and largely demolished, the *ideal* of the Temple endured. Secretly and surreptitiously, Jewish priests continued to collect offerings and tithes from coreligionists who had somehow survived the reign of terror, assuring them that if they remained faithful to the Covenant, God's Day of Judgment would soon come and the House of the Lord in Jerusalem would be gloriously restored.

Those offerings naturally had to be ingeniously hidden from the Roman occupation forces, who were intent on rooting out the last vestiges of Judean independence wherever they were found. As we will see later, it was most probably a determined survivor of Roman persecution—not a mere crackpot or lunatic—who hid the Copper Scroll in a cave near the ruins of Qumran. In its careful accounting of the dispersed Temple treasure, the Copper Scroll was a document of faith as well as of earthly riches. Though quite different from the visionary Temple Scroll or the legal argumentation of MMT, it was, nevertheless, part of the same tradition. It was—and still is—eloquent testimony that even *after* the Revolt, some Judeans were willing to risk slavery or crucifixion to keep the dream of the Temple alive.

6

Sons of Light, Sons of Darkness

From his office in a turn-of-the-century brownstone building on the south side of Washington Square Park in Greenwich Village, Professor Lawrence Schiffman of New York University has become a major player in the world of the Dead Sea Scrolls. As a scholar, he is one of the leaders in the study of the Qumran literature from a rabbinic perspective—utilizing his knowledge of Talmudic sources to provide a deeper and richer context for the legalistic faith of the scrolls. As an orthodox Jew, he is unashamedly, joyfully, observant—finding an obvious personal connection to the *halakhic* debates and messianic expectation of these ancient Jewish texts. Now in his late forties, Schiffman is immediately recognizable at academic conferences. Lanky, animated, and—in contrast to the terminal tweediness of most university professors—he wears a full beard, a black skullcap, and a dark, sedate suit. But Schiffman is certainly not a sedate personality. He delights in spicing his conversations with rabbinic parables, colorful Catskill jokes, and good-hearted self-deprecation. And in recent years, he has become a much sought after speaker for religious and academic groups all over the country, who appreciate his message about the importance of the Dead Sea Scrolls for understanding the history of Judaism.

For Schiffman, the group that produced the Dead Sea Scrolls does not represent an evolutionary stage of religious development or an inspiring example of national resistance, but a disturbing example of religious pathology. Despite his obvious professional fascination, Larry Schiffman has no romantic illusions about the obsessive, rigidly dogmatic nature of the Dead Sea sect. Though there are many purity concerns and biblical interpretations shared by the Qumran literature and the rabbinic tradition, Schiffman believes that the feverish visions of Sons of Light battling Sons of Darkness, of the presence of angels in the Council of the Community, and of the imminent arrival of the messiah are all the result of the dangerous radicalization of priestly purists, not signs of spiritual enlightenment.

More than twenty years ago, when Schiffman was a graduate student in Judaic Studies at Brandeis University, he began his involvement with the scrolls as a complete outsider. In those days, Qumran literature was not something you studied on a doctoral level unless you had access to the vast collection of unpublished Cave 4 manuscripts. And the cruel fact of the matter was that if you were not a student of Frank Cross, John Strugnell, or any other International Team member, there was no realistic possibility of access. Back in the days when the International Team had gone into a form of suspended animation, Strugnell, Cross, Skehan, and Starcky began to treat their allotments of Cave 4 texts as private intellectual property—regularly using photographs of unpublished texts as teaching materials in advanced seminars and, on occasion, bestowing them as prestigious dissertation topics to their most cherished scholarly protégés.

Although Schiffman lived and studied at Brandeis University in Waltham, only a few miles away from the Harvard campus in Cambridge, he might have lived on another planet as far as the Dead Sea Scrolls was concerned. All that he really knew of the Qumran Community's sectarian literature were the texts that had been published: the Damascus Document, the Community Rule, the War Scroll, the Thanksgiving Hymns, the Habakkuk Commentary, and the other documents that had trickled out into the scholarly literature since the mid-1950s or were contained in the first five volumes of the *Discoveries in the Judean Desert* series. When Yigael Yadin came to the United States for a sabbatical in the 1969–70 academic year to lecture on the Temple Scroll, with its complex law codes about Jerusalem, the Temple, and the ideal king of Israel, Schiffman decided to write a doctoral dissertation about the role and function of ritual law at Qumran. He remembers how his faculty advisors tried their best to dissuade him from wasting his time with such fragmentary material. "They told me, 'You can make a much better mark—you're much better off with substantive scholarship and not this puzzle-putting-together stuff.' "

Schiffman persisted. He has never lacked energy and enthusiasm in his studies. His Ph.D. dissertation, published in 1975 as *The Halakhah at Qumran*, is not what you might consider poolside reading, but it made an important contribution in examining Qumran purity laws, festival observances, and ritual regulations, and their striking similarities in form, if not incontent, to the later rabbinic discussion and codification of Jewish religious law. There was in the Qumran literature, he believed, clear evidence that Talmudic-style legal debate had already emerged in the days of the Temple, not just in the aftermath of its destruction, when a new kind of Jewish devotion was required. Yet few serious scholars of Rabbinic Judaism seemed to pay any attention. "I realized that I had to convince people of the importance of this," Schiffman told me, "because I would go to a conference and there would be seven people talking about the Mishnah and they didn't know anything about these texts. I'd get up and talk about the laws of Shabbat at Qumran and nobody cared."

A year after the now-famous 1984 conference in Jerusalem, when MMT was presented for the first time to the scholarly public, Schiffman was one of the organizers of a Dead Sea Scrolls conference at N.Y.U. that proved to be the next landmark along the road to open rebellion against the power of the International Team.

That is only evident in retrospect, however, for the assembled scholars were then quite respectful and grateful to be given a detailed briefing by John Strugnell himself about various interesting texts on which the International Team members and their assistants were now working, and how the vast majority of the Cave 4 materials would soon become generally available.

"The atmosphere was very nice, very pleasant," Schiffman remembered. "John gave his report on where things stood at that time, which everybody believed like suckers. That's the other thing: We always believed that it was coming out next year. You know, it's like the messiah. There's a story about someone who sees two signs in the mountains going up to the Catskills. One says 'Come to the new Grossingers Opening Soon,' and the other says "The Mashiach's on the Way.' So that person says, 'I see. When Grossingers finally opens the *Mashiach* will come.' It was the same thing at the conference," Schiffman recalled in amusement at his own naivete. "He said it and we believed it."

Yet in the years that followed the 1985 N.Y.U. Conference, Larry Schiffman slowly began to be accepted into the leadership of a new generation of scroll scholars. Since he was increasingly recognized even among the members of the International Team as a specialist in Qumran's rabbinic connections, he was eventually asked to offer his opinion on the still-secret 120-line text of MMT. The level of secrecy was stringent. On a summer research trip to Israel, he spent several weeks reading the commentary that Strugnell and Qimron had prepared with the help of Professor Yaacov Sussmann of the Hebrew University.

Strugnell, Qimron, and Sussmann had all recognized some of the striking connections between the Temple Scroll and MMT. In both, the authority was Scripture: the one-time revelation by God to Moses on Mount Sinai, as expressed in the Torah. Whether the issue was one of royal polygamy, Temple architecture, or the acceptability of Gentile offerings, the authors of MMT and the Temple Scroll arrived at their positions through a careful study of the Law. And even though Strugnell, Qimron, and Sussmann were convinced that MMT was written by the Teacher of Righteousness (Yadin had believed that the Temple Scroll was also his composition), Schiffman found that the tone of MMT was far too mild-mannered and level-headed to have been written by the Teacher. It contained no hint of the sudden, stunning divine revelations, newly revealed apocalyptic secrets, or ancient mysteries now made clear only to the initiated members of the Community that characterized the intense, sectarian frame of mind of the War Scroll, the Thanksgiving Hymns, the Damascus Document, and the Community Rule.

Those documents starkly separated the world into Light and Darkness. They commanded the members of the sect, the Sons of Zadok, to love their brothers and to cut off all contact with God's enemies. In the Qumran sect's fully developed apocalyptic vision, the lots of Light and Darkness had been determined by God at the Creation, and events on earth, paralleling the struggle in heaven between the forces of Light and Darkness, were moving inevitably, inexorably, toward their cataclysmic end. In the Thanksgiving Hymns, the author (the Teacher of Righteousness?) offered his praise to God for selecting him to be a vessel of revelation through which he could communicate news of the coming Day of Judgment to the Elect of Israel. This was a very different conception of divine revelation; it was one that did not end at Mount Sinai but continued in times of crisis to the author's own day. It was as if MMT and the Temple Scroll were written by a completely different group of people. And although the traditional tendency in Qumran studies was to treat ancient sects like the "Pharisees," "Sadducees," and "Essenes" as archetypal groupings that could be rearranged and moved around like chessmen in varying historical perspectives, Schiffman did not try to reconcile the polite argumentation of MMT with the apocalyptic rage of the other documents. He saw in the contrast between them potent evidence for the internal history and increasing radicalization of the sect.

In a way, the Damascus Document—the first of the Qumran texts to be discovered—told the story of the early days of the sect in poetic language. It related that in an Age of Wrath, three hundred ninety years after the destruction of Jerusalem by Nebuchadnezzar, God

> visited them, and He caused a plant root to spring from Aaron and Israel to inherit his land and to prosper on the good things of His earth. And they perceived their iniquity and recognized that they were guilty men, yet for twenty years they were blind men groping for the way.

This is precisely the period, Schiffman believes, when MMT was written, when a dissident group within the Jerusalem priesthood took serious objection to the way that certain cultic practices were observed. The figure of 390 years after the Exile (which would date the sect's moment of first inspiration to 196 B.C.E.) has been seen by many scholars as a purely symbolic figure—echoing the Prophet Ezekiel oracle of 390 "days" of penance that must be suffered by the righteous remnant of Israel. Yet whatever the date, the initial period was apparently one of religious uncertainty for a particularly conservative priestly group.

"They don't start with violent fantasies," Schiffman explained. "They start very calm. They write a letter apparently and say, look, we don't agree with this, this, and this, and you should know that if you don't repent, you're going to suffer in the way our previous kings did. But when you follow Torah, everything is fine." But the problem was, according to Schiffman, that this mild-mannered and well-reasoned appeal by the priestly group that considered themselves the true heirs of the Zadokite priesthood simply did not work.

Indeed, the Damascus Document went on to describe the rise of a leader, after the first twenty years of spiritual unease and uncertainty, among the Sons of Zadok:

> And God observed their deeds, and they sought Him with a whole heart, and He raised for them a Teacher of Righteousness to guide them in the way of His heart. And he

made known to the latter generations that which God had
done to the latter generation, the congregation of traitors
who had departed from the way.

This is the point at which Schiffman believes the group is transformed from a movement of priestly protest into a radicalized, isolationist sect. From that time forth, legal argumentation began to
take a backseat to direct, divine communications, and the revelations accorded to the Teacher became central to the theology of
the sect. God-sent inspiration, not just earnest study, became the
key to understanding the deeper meaning of the Scriptures—
what the group came to identify as mysteries and "hidden law."
And drawing on a rich tradition of apocalyptic speculation, this
group envisioned itself as the head of the worldly forces of Light at
a turning point in the history of creation. They lived in the company of angels and required of themselves the highest standards
of purity. And that is the reason for the difference between MMT,
the Temple Scroll, and the specifically sectarian documents, according to Schiffman. In the Dead Sea Scrolls we can gain a
unique glimpse at the genesis of what the newsmagazines and TV
tabloid shows might call a cult if such a group arose today.

But what happens when a cult's teaching appeals to a far wider
public than the inner circle of fervent believers who are willing to
leave their hometowns, jobs, and families to follow the way into
the Wilderness that leads to oblivion at places like Waco or Jones-
town? The process Schiffman described was one of the dangerous
radicalization of alienated believers, who failed at persuading
their coreligionists that their vision of the world was identical to
God's. Yet there is some evidence in Josephus's histories that
teachings very similar to those contained in the Qumran literature
spurred ever-wider segments of the Judean population to action
during the first century c.e. Though occasional dissenters and rivals are mentioned in Josephus's account of King Herod's reign,
the violent attempt—while Herod lay on his deathbed—by some
religious purists to tear down the golden eagle that adorned the

main gate to the Temple and the widespread outbreaks of messianic enthusiasm and even open rebellion in the reign of Archelaus, transformed the calm discussion of legal matters into the lighting-bolt recognition by many that the messianic era had actually arrived.

There were undoubtedly those who ceased regarding the present as politics as usual and began to see even everyday events as the fulfillment of a divine plan for history. While the public was undoubtedly listening to many different groups, each with their own teachers and their own standards of righteousness, the extent to which the general phenomenon was spreading as a conscious movement is betrayed by Josephus himself. By the time of Pontius Pilate (26–36 C.E.), who was more energetic than his predecessors in trying to make Judea a normal province, the religious protests of individual zealots began to give way to religious demonstrations by the population at large. The issues at stake in the time of Pilate were his confiscation of funds from the Temple treasury and his order that his troops' gilded battle standards (bearing the image of Emperor Tiberius) be set up in the fortress overlooking the Temple. Both acts aggravated the already sensitive issues of the purity of the Holy City and the inviolability of the Temple that had been the main concern of the authors of MMT and the Temple Scroll.

There is no question that the sudden public response to Pontius Pilate's actions was remembered for decades. In Josephus's earliest work, *The Jewish War*, the incident of the standards is the first time that resistance to a Roman governor's action is ascribed to "the populace" in general, not to a particular sect. According to his description of the events, Pilate ordered that the standards be brought into Jerusalem and set up under cover of darkness. On the next morning, a mass protest erupted, with a large multitude of both city and country people making their way to the port city of Caesarea, where Pilate maintained his official residence. In earlier times, during the reign of Herod, individual zealots would rise up to take action against violations of the sanctity of the Temple—

as in the case of Herod's golden eagle—but this was a far more serious threat.

From Pilate's standpoint, this was merely a matter of exercising legitimate Roman power. The battle standards, to which Roman troops offered sacrifices to the goddesses of Victory and Fortune, were the symbols of the empire's prestige. To allow a mob to prevent the troops' free movement—anywhere in the empire—would be to surrender to lawlessness. But to the Judeans, Pilate's act was an insult—a double cross of the Judeans' sufferance of Roman rule, permissable as long as at least lip service was paid to their religious autonomy. But now with Tiberius's grim-faced head being prayed to and sacrificed to within a stone's throw of the Inner Court of the Temple, there was no longer even a charade of respectfulness. And for someone like the author of the Qumran Commentary on Habakkuk, the issue of the standards in Jerusalem was not just a religious misunderstanding to be solved by negotiation but was one of the God-given signs that conclusively identified the Romans as the Kittim, the Sons of Darkness: for according to their interpretation of the ancient oracle, they would be a brutal people who "sacrifice to their standards and worship their weapons of war."

Massing outside Pilate's residence, the protesters refused to disperse when the governor rejected their demand that he remove the graven images from the Holy City at once. Finally, Pilate summoned them to the city's amphitheater on the pretext that he was willing to talk. According to Josephus, he ordered his soldiers to surround the protesters in the arena, and, "after threatening to cut them down if they refused to admit Caesar's images, signaled to the soldiers to draw their swords. Thereupon, the Jews, as a concerted action, flung themselves in a body on the ground, extended their necks, and exclaimed that they were ready rather to die than transgress the Law. Overcome with astonishment at such religious zeal, Pilate gave orders for the immediate removal of the standards from Jerusalem."

These people were willing to give up their lives for the Law, because by the first century many Judeans had come to believe that while the fate after death of most people was uncertain, the righteous dead would surely be brought to life again on Judgment Day. This powerful belief in the immortality of any Jews who willingly chose to be religious martyrs seems first to have arisen in the wars and religious revivals of the Maccabean period. The Prophet Daniel's promise of everlasting life for the righteous "who sleep in the dust" and the ideal of sacred martyrdom expressed again and again in the Books of the Maccabees seems to have been especially useful at times when heavy casualties were suffered—by the soldiers and border settlers of the expanding Hasmonean state.

More victims and martyrs were to be created in the ten-year term of Pilate. After he confiscated funds from the Temple to fund an ambitious public works project, he slipped plainclothes thugs, armed with cudgels, into the crowds who gathered for protest and, according to Josephus, Pilate "from his tribunal gave the agreed signal. Large numbers of Jews perished, some from the blows which they received, others trodden to death." Here was an activist governor, not one likely to wash his hands of the responsibility to keep order. And it is not at all unlikely that among the thousands of resisters-turned-martyrs who arose in the time of Pontius Pilate was a charismatic religious leader named Jesus, who was arrested for subversive teaching, put to death by the Romans, and was, like all the other holy warriors and pious victims, assured bodily resurrection from the grave.

Through the country, in fact, the idea of resurrection spread widely, and was adopted even by those who lived lives of quiet accommodation. This belief is evidenced in the spread of the curiously elaborate Jewish burial practice around Jerusalem of secondary burial in bone boxes, or ossuaries. After a year of entombment (and decay of the flesh from the body), the deceased's bones would be gathered together by family members and placed together in a neat limestone box, often inscribed with the deceased's private name. The vast cemetery at Qumran, with its row upon row of identical individual interments, has been seen by some scholars as evidence of a similar belief in bodily resurrection. But the belief seems to be evident in the Thanksgiving Hymns with its hope of assurance that "bodies gnawed by worms may be raised from the dust"; in the War Scroll that God would raise the fallen; and, most explicitly, in the text that Emile Puech called the "Messianic Apocalypse," in which God's anointed would "heal the sick and resurrect the dead." Thus, whether by martyrdom, righteousness, or individual interment, many Judeans began to look longingly to beyond the thousand year Reich of the Romans, to a time when their current indignities and exploitations would be exchanged for a much better life after death.

Needless to say, a prospect like this was particularly attractive. It offered bodily healing and a youthfulness more perfect than that offered by any modern spa or miracle drug; prosperity and happiness for every man, woman, and child who had previously suffered; and offered psychic revenge against bullies and oppressors by imagining their own redemption compared to their enemies' sufferings. The belief was part of what must certainly be understood as a national revulsion against the conditions of its own existence, in which those Judeans who dared to challenge the Romans directly were considered martyrs and saints, whose resurrection was assured and whose sins were fully forgiven, even if some of them would otherwise be considered malcontents, troublemakers, or common criminals.

The Romans were determined to do everything they could to discourage Judean resistance, though they did not understand that strong-arm measures would only mobilize more and more candidates for martyrdom. At the time of the Emperor Caligula's mad attempt to erect a statue of himself in the Jerusalem Temple, the whole nation—not just a stadium full of zealots—abandoned their fields and daily routines for several weeks of continuous mass protests, vowing to the Roman governor of Syria that if he pressed on with the plan to set up Caligula's image in the Temple, "he must first sacrifice the entire Jewish nation." Caligula's welcome assassination and replacement by the more reasonable Claudius averted the ultimate confrontation—but only for a while. For the result of the repeated clashes between Roman imperialism and

Jewish piety was the radicalization of both. And through the thirties and forties of the first century, during times of an especially intense drought and economic hardship, and through the short-lived reign of Herod's grandson Agrippa (40–44 C.E.), more and more of the population became convinced that the messianic age was nearing and that righteousness—expressed by strict observance of the Law and by personal resistance to the encroachments of their enemies—would earn them a place in the world to come.

The many coins and distinctive first-century pottery forms recovered from the Qumran excavations show that this was one of the most active periods in the life of the Community. Yet most scroll scholars insist that the Community's creative literary period was over. During the days when Pilate raged, Caligula plotted desecration, and drought and famine caused massive economic dislocation, the members of the Community—according to the mainline scroll experts—were concerned only with the ritual peccadilloes of a long-dead Teacher of Righteousness and long-dead Hasmonean kings. But there was something more to Judean religious life in the first century than its fragmentation into countless insulated religious sects. A shared national feeling of resistance was mounting, even if leaders' egos and local group allegiances sometimes stood in the way. In that sense, the literature of Qumran reflects the growing radicalization of the nation at the same time that it embodies the developing ideology of the Dead Sea sect. The outbreak of the Revolt against Rome in 66 C.E. would show how widespread this belief was among the people of Judea. There was a vast shared national treasury of religious poems, oracles, testimonies, and commentaries on the themes of messiah, holy war, resurrection, and redemption. The members of the Qumran community were avid collectors and apparently authors of this esoteric literature. And if the texts' terminology is not always consistent, or their descriptions of the events contradictory, they were not necessarily meant to express a single codified theology. The hundreds of manuscripts recovered from the caves of Qumran are a palimpsest of decades of protest and revolutionary speculation. They were the creative expressions of a shared tradition that projected ancient biblical dreams onto a glorious national future. And there is good reason to believe that the early followers of Jesus were—despite the later, anti-Semitic insinuations of Church Fathers—active participants in this movement as well.

Professor Robert Eisenman of California State University at Long Beach speaks with the fervor of a true believer who has been shown a revelation of such stunning splendor that he is driven to preach it, to spread it, and to elaborate upon it at every opportunity, rarely considering the cost to his professional career or to himself. Eisenman's words, his theories, and even his sometimes abrasive personal style have all made a deep impression on me. He is convinced that there *is* a point to using the evidence of the scrolls as a challenge to, not an illustration of, the conventional historical wisdom. And he is convinced that once his message is given a fair hearing by a wider audience (without the ridicule and disdain usually heaped upon it by Qumran insiders), no one will ever think of Qumran, Christianity, or Jesus in quite the same way again.

As I have mentioned, I first got to know Eisenman at the stormy 1992 New York scrolls conference, and during the months that followed I began to learn about his theories in a series of lengthy conversations and in a close reading of his two books, *Maccabees, Zadokites, Christians, and Qumran* (1983) and *James the Just in the Habakkuk Pesher* (1986). These books do not make for easy reading. They are highly technical discussions of Qumran, apocryphal, and New Testament literature, in which the footnotes are dense, complex, and extensive. And despite everything the established Qumran scholars continue to say about his books, I found them to be provocative and insightful, offering a radically new approach to understanding not only the Dead Sea Scrolls but also the early history of Christianity. There may be mistakes and overstatements. Certainly many of Eisenman's proposed connections are based on intuitive leaps rather than on demonstrated textual evidence, but I maintain that they offer an intriguing challenge to conventional wisdom—seeing Qumran not as an isolated, non-political monastery in the wilderness but as a center of a movement of Jewish national resistance to the Roman imperial administration in Judea—and to the self-serving Jewish aristocracy of Jerusalem who made fortunes for themselves as willing agents of that exploitative regime.

What Eisenman suggests is that the original angry gospel of Jewish messianism, expressed clearly in the Qumran literature, is typical of the idealistic, fundamentalist, even revolutionary faith of many first-century Judeans—in spite of the fact that Josephus, the New Testament, and rabbinic literature, each for their own reasons, wanted either to minimize the popularity of this distinctive brand of popular biblical religion (liberation theology, you might call it) or disavow their own participation in it. For Eisenman, the Qumran Teacher of Righteousness was not an evolutionary ancestor of Jesus. He and the other apocalyptic teachers of the era were activists in a single powerful movement, unmovably faithful to the idea that the one True God would lead the Jews to victory over the Romans and their despicable Judean collaborators—no matter how incomparably powerful the forces of Darkness presently seemed.

This, he insists, was the context for the activities not only of the "Teacher of Righteousness" but also of John the Baptist, Jesus, and James the Just, the brother of Jesus, who later headed the Council of the Jerusalem Church. All these religious figures, Eisenman explains, were "the fomenters among the masses, they were the ayatollahs of their day. They taught among the disenfranchised. They were recognized as saints, sheikhs, tzaddiks, and holy men." And he insists that all of them were part of a national underground dedicated to the strict observance of the Law and the overthrow of Rome. "When the Christians call them 'early Christians,' " Eisenman points out, "we tend to see them as little people walking around with halos around their heads and monks' robes. That's nothing of what they were."

Of course many New Testament scholars and ancient historians have long been interested in the political and social dimensions of Jewish resistance to the Roman Empire. In the most recent developments in the continuing quest for the historical Jesus (which began with the then-heretical investigations of the German freethinker Gotthold Ephraim Lessing in the eighteenth century and continued with the writings of Ernest Renan in the nineteenth and Albert Schweitzer in the early twentieth centuries), modern scholars like Richard Horsley and John Dominic Crossan have eloquently sketched out the revolutionary implications of Jesus' teaching as, at least partly, a political response to the class tensions and relentless Roman imperialism in Judea and Galilee in the first century C.E. Martin Goodman of Oxford has provided a searing indictment of what he calls the "ruling class of Judea" (whose homes have been excavated and turned into tourist attractions in Jerusalem's Jewish Quarter), and he has placed the blame for the disintegration and ultimate destruction of Jewish independence squarely on them.

Yet none of these scholars has recognized the potential of the Dead Sea Scrolls as an important source for reconstructing Judea's *political* history. All of them take at face value the consensus position that the Qumran sect was entirely marginal to Judean society and cut off from the intense revolutionary agitation in the cities and towns of the country. But is it likely that the walls of Qumran kept out whispers of the horrors and the outrages taking place in former hometowns and villages? Was the members' inner discipline so unmovable that at least some of them would not turn their apocalyptic speculations toward action? At what point would the leading sages of the Community not see that their words could rouse their people to action against the Sons of Darkness—and thereby fulfill the ancient prophecies?

The footnotes and endnotes of the standard Qumran literature are littered with passing, dismissive notices of scholars who have rejected the usual Essene monastery theory and have tried to link the scrolls and the Community that wrote or collected them with well-known groups of the first century C.E. In the 1960s, Cecil Roth and Godfrey Driver insisted that the Dead Sea Scrolls were the literature of the radical Zealot faction headed by a charismatic leader named Menachem, son of an earlier rebel, Judah the Galilean. According to Roth and Driver, Menachem was the mysterious Teacher of Righteousness. There were others, like Joel Teicher at Cambridge in the 1950s and Barbara Thiering in Australia in the 1980s, who connected the scrolls and their messianic allusions to early Christianity. In Teicher's view, the Teacher of Righteousness was none other than Jesus; Thiering preferred John the Baptist for that role. But no one before Robert Eisenman, as far as I am aware, has so decisively closed the equilateral triangle connecting the community at Qumran, the Zealots, and early Christianity. For him, they were all part of the same movement, and the boundaries between them may have been entirely unclear. Their messianic expectations were all firmly fixed on the future, and they posed a direct threat not only to the Roman administration of Judea but to the continuing political ambitions of the Herodian dynasty as well.

What is so intriguing about placing the Qumran community and its literature in the first century C.E., not the second and first B.C.E., is that the main concerns of the sect—the "three nets of Belial" designed to ensnare the wicked, namely Riches, Fornication, and the Pollution of the Sanctuary—were precisely issues that were the focus of such bitter first-century conflict. There is little evidence beyond pure speculation—as Eisenman points out repeatedly—that the matter of Gentile gifts to the Temple or the practice of older men marrying their nieces (part of the charge of "fornication," which both the Damascus Document and the Temple Scroll condemn) were matters of particular concern in the Hasmonean period. But Josephus's accounts of the events of the first century contain abundant examples of Roman interference with the cult of the Temple and, even more tellingly, the kinds of uncle-niece marriage condemned in the scrolls were increasingly common among the many Herodian princesses and princelings jostling each other for power through trysts with other Near Eastern dynasties and strategic marriages among themselves.

For the pietists and religious fundamentalists of the nation who used the Torah, the Temple Scroll and similar visionary literature to set their standards of behavior, the Herodians were part of the problem, not legitimate national leaders. With the exception of the brief reign of King Agrippa, who was the last royal pretender who could trace his maternal lineage to the Hasmonean dynasty, the Herodian family had been seen by most as more Roman or Idumean than Jewish—and therefore completely disqualified for rule over the people of Israel.

But the interest of the Herodian House was not merely to rule Jerusalem and the hilltop towns and villages of Judea; its more important political interests were to promote integration—commercial or otherwise—between Jews, Idumeans, Ammonites, Moabites, Philistines, and Samaritans and the more distant peoples of the Greco-Roman world. At huge cost, Herod the Great had built a glittering kingdom that straddled the boundary between Jew and Gentile. For while he spared no expense in the construction of his stupendous Temple in Jerusalem, he also underwrote the construction of impressive pagan temples in Caesarea and Samaria, and as far away as Beirut and Delos. And he saw only doubled, not diminished, honor in serving as the protector of world Jewry and as the president of the Olympic Games.

Could this Herodian political strategy have actually stimulated a trend in theological speculation? Could there have been an ideological *reaction* by the supporters of the Herodians against the unrelenting attacks of the religious puritans? Eisenman suggests that after the death of Herod the Great, when the various Herodian princesses and princelings were given or married into scattered petty kingdoms throughout Syria and Asia Minor, a syncretistic new version of the biblical religion was born that mixed (rather than separated) Jew and Gentile, an ideological admixture that would be a perfect boost for their dynastic fortunes. In one of Eisenman's most daring papers (one that, he later proudly recalled, brought an outraged audience walk-out at the meeting of the Society of Biblical Literature where it was delivered), he identified the Apostle Paul as a kinsman of King Agrippa, who saw in the Jewish messianic movement and one of its many martyred leaders the raw material for a very different faith.

Eisenman expressed it more directly to me when we talked about the passage in the Book of Acts where the former Saul of Tarsus was dispatched by the Herodian-appointed High Priest to Damascus "so that if he found any belonging to the Way, men or women, he may bring them bound to Jerusalem." The "Way," of course, was a frequently used term in the Qumran literature to describe the Community. And it was on the road to execute this manhunt against subversives that Saul was struck blind with his vision of Jesus, thereby becoming a born-again Paul. But was the light from heaven on the road to Damascus a direct revelation or a breathtakingly brilliant transformation of radical Jewish messianism into something quite different? "When Paul comes into the movement as a Herodian satrap, lackey, he may even be a visionary, maybe even a sincere person," Eisenman told me, "But he's still a Herodian stooge. He comes into the movement; he doesn't know its individuals, but he opposes them and starts getting visionary experiences of an otherworldly kind of Christ Jesus in heaven who is more or less his alter-ego, who just reflects his own persona, whom he exteriorizes into an actual supernatural being. And from that moment on becomes Jesus Christ Superstar. But that has nothing to do with the historical events in Palestine."

We might be inclined to dismiss such a heretical version of the birth of Christianity and its complete mythologization of a person named Jesus were it not for the fact that there is precious little external corroborating evidence for the version conveyed in the New Testament and the historical works of the Church Fathers. Rabbinic references to Jesus are cryptic and largely polemical; a single paragraph about Jesus in Book XVIII of Josephus Flavius's *Jewish Antiquities* has been heavily edited by Christian scribes and has long been suspected of being entirely contrived. Archaeological evidence is enlightening as background, but largely circumstantial. While excavations have provided much new information on life in Judea and the Galilee in the Hellenistic and Roman periods, definitive contemporary evidence of only two people who played a significant role in the life of Jesus has ever been found: In

1961, at the ancient port of Caesarea, an Italian team discovered a Latin inscription bearing the name of Pontius Pilatus, Praefect of Judea, and in 1990, a staff archaeologist for the Israel Antiquities Authority discovered a tomb in southern Jerusalem used by the family of the notorious High Priest Caiaphas. Beyond that, all reconstructions of the life of Jesus are based on later Christian literature and a speculative interpretation of Judean history.

Since the beginning of Dead Sea Scroll studies, scholars have been fascinated with the question of the identity of three vivid personalities repeatedly mentioned in the Qumran texts: the "Teacher of Righteousness," the "Wicked Priest," and the "Scoffer," or "Man of Lies." While the vast majority of scholars, as I have said, place these historical figures somewhere in the Hasmonean period, Eisenman sees them as the personifications and the leaders of factions that were in a bitter three-way battle for the hearts and minds of the Judean population in this period: the Messianic movement, the traditional high priesthood, and the Hellenized aristocracy. Eisenman believes that Paul is the Man of Lies, mentioned with such disdain in the Commentary of Habakkuk, who together with the "unfaithful of the New Covenant . . . have not believed in the Covenant of God and have profaned his Holy Name."

In his close, line by-line exegesis of the Qumran Commentary on Habakkuk, Eisenman suggests that the polemic between the Man of Lies and the Teacher of Righteousness centered on the strict observance of all the laws of purity and Temple cult. And indeed he points out the tense confrontation over similar issues in the fateful Apostolic Council held in Jerusalem around 50 c.e. At issue was whether Gentile converts to belief in the messiah needed to undergo circumcision and strictly observe Jewish law. Needless to say, Paul emphasized the centrality of faith in Christ and James emphasized the necessity that all converts observe at least some of the basic tenets of the Law of Moses regarding idolatry, unchastity, and impurity. Elsewhere, for example, in the Letter of James preserved in the New Testament, there is angry condemnation of those who turn their back on the Covenant, even in its strictest regulations: "For whoever keeps the whole law but fails in one point has become guilty of all of it." These were the kinds of words the Teacher of Righteousness might have preached in his own Council, and indeed Eisenman suggests that even the traditional sobriquet of James, "the Just," substantiates his hypothesis that *he* was the movement's Teacher of Righteousness. James was killed in 62 C.E. on orders of the High Priest Ananus, and Eisenman identifies *him* as the "Wicked Priest" of the scrolls.

Thus Eisenman has come to believe that Christianity was born as a conscious, intentional ideological inversion of radical Jewish messianism that occurred only after the death of Jesus. While the Jerusalem community apparently continued to insist on full observance of Jewish ritual and custom, Paul began to lay down the foundations of an entirely different faith. In it, salvation was to be gained not by hating one's oppressors but by loving them; not by observing the Law but by faith in Jesus Christ. With the Revolt and the destruction of Jerusalem and the Temple in 70 C.E., the original Jewish "Messianic" movement was gradually wiped out. But Paul's heretical variation continued to spread and gain adherents among the gentile "Christian" communities all over the Greco-Roman world.

I do not mean to misrepresent the fact that just about every Qumran scholar with whom I have spoken considers Eisenman's theories to be pure nonsense. When I asked Strugnell, he called Eisenman's work "totally worthless." Frank Cross shook his head and would not dignify it with a comment. Listening to one of Eisenman's early lectures, Larry Schiffman recalled that he could not help laughing. Devorah Dimant of the University of Haifa grew angry when I brought up the subject. And Jonas Greenfield of the Hebrew University has publicly branded Eisenman as "either a charlatan, a knave, or a fool." Only David Flusser seemed to take him more seriously. "You will surely feel as a Jew very well in his ideas," he assured me, noting as a caution that "I like to say that I cannot accept them, not because I cannot accept them myself but because reality cannot accept them." The reality to which he was referring was the still overwhelming earthly power of the proponents of Paul's belief.

At the time the Qumran Community was reaching its greatest size and its greatest influence in Judea, religious messengers were traveling among the bustling cities of the eastern Mediterranean, far from the tumults and conflicts of Jerusalem, with a very different gospel to spread. In contrast to the angry fundamentalism of the leaders of the Judean movement, with its demand for modesty, purity, and poverty, the Jews of the Diaspora—in the large cosmopolitan cities of Italy, Greece, and Asia Minor, with their wide circle of Gentile God-fearing supporters—were rarely eager to emphasize the strict purity laws and dietary codes that set them apart from their fellow citizens. And as Paul and his followers traveled to the cities of Ephesus, Corinth, and Philippi, they were offering the teachings of a new cult that appealed to the vast middle body of of assimilated Jews and God-fearers. It was a Bible-based cult that was both idealistic and universal—imbued with the passion and rapture of the messianic hope but stripped of its explicit demand that the earthly empire of Rome be overthrown. Despite the fact that Jesus did not return in the expected short period of time and nothing changed in the day-to-day world except their new religious identity and continuing expectations, the Christian communities of the Mediterranean began to consider themselves the True Israel. But this Israel would not insist on separating itself completely from the Roman Empire. On the contrary, in less than three hundred years church and empire would be officially joined.

Thus in Judea, for the people fighting to preserve the distinctive laws and purity codes of their nation as protection against outside political and economic encroachment, the preaching of a rival gospel that actually encouraged abandoning the Mosaic Law was seen as a mortal threat. The coming of the Kingdom of God was dependent on the proper observance of the Law by the People of Israel. That was what the Qumran sect was predicated on: the fulfillment of the Torah under the strictest possible criteria. The observance of the Law was therefore regarded as central to the continued existence of the People of Israel. And even after the destruction of the Temple and the reformation of Jewish ritual by the rabbis, Judaism still bore the messianic hope that perfect observance of the Torah would bring about a far-reaching transformation of the world.

Yet for Christians, the rejection of the Law became a central tenet of their faith that a New Covenant had been established in which an incarnated, crucified, and resurrected messiah had atoned for the sins of all. Though this new messianic religion might aspire to the highest ideals of behavior, it was, for the Jews and for all those who refused to abandon their faith in an as-yet-unarrived revolutionary leader and warrior savior, a faith that would, all too often, preach love and practice hate. At the time of the Emperor Constantine's adoption of Christianity, the deified Caesar Augustus was replaced by the heavenly Christ Jesus as the legitimation for Roman power and imperial expansion. The Cross now replaced the emperor's image on the legionary battle standards. And as a result of this will to world dominion, the bully boys and enforcers of both High Church and world empire would make the Jews—with their strange ways and stubborn demand for independence—objects of disdain and hatred for centuries to come.

"I don't see Jesus at all," Robert Eisenman admitted candidly, when I finally got around to asking him the inevitable, obvious question about the role that a historical personality named Jesus of Nazareth may have played in the creation of a distinctively Christian faith. In recent years, a group of liberal Christian scholars, who call themselves the "Jesus Seminar," have been gathering for meetings at which they vote on the historical reliability of the various recorded sayings of Jesus, giving each a numerical reliability quotient. For Eisenman, however, the New Testament is itself part of the problem, not the source of a solution, statistical or otherwise.

"I really don't see him because the material we have about him has been so artificialized and worked over and mythologized and undergone retrospective theological transformation that to get to any human being called Jesus with any substantiality is, as I've said from the beginning, an impossibility." While acknowledging that there might very well have been a personality named Jesus, who was somehow involved in the political and religious upheavals in Judea, the gospels are, to his mind, far too tendentious and theologically motivated to be relied upon as sound historical evidence. "Jesus could represent Athronges for all I know," Eisenman continued, referring to an obscure and quickly quashed messianic pretender mentioned by Josephus Flavius, "Hellenized, pax-romanicized, turned into the lover of Gentiles, the lover of the Pax Romana, the lover of the Roman Empire, the lover of Roman centurions, the lover of tax collectors, the lover of prostitutes. What can I say about any of that material? It's all preposterous."

It is a measure of how out of touch with reality Robert Eisenman was when he arrived in Jerusalem in the summer of 1985 as the National Endowment for the Humanities Fellow at the Albright Institute of Archaeological Research that he naively assumed that he would be welcomed into the fraternity of Dead Sea Scroll scholarship. He far underestimated the intensity of religious belief that often lies just beneath the surface of historical and archaeological discussions in Jerusalem. The origins of Christianity and the historicity of Jesus were not issues taken lightly—nor were they apparently suitable subjects for a no-holds-barred historical debate. Tradition has it that every visiting professor or academic fellow at the Albright Institute give a public lecture on his research; scholars from local universities and the other foreign archaeological institutions are invited. It is a coming-out party and academic audition rolled into one. Eisenman recalls looking forward to the opportunity of presenting his Qumran theories. But he did not realize that he was about to blow up all the academic bridges that he might ever have been able to build.

"All the guys from the Ecole were invited," he remembered too vividly for comfort, "Benoit, Puech, Murphy-O'Connor, and so on—all these so-called pseudo-experts. And I packed every-

thing into the paper I gave there. I forget the title. It was the connections or the parallels between the Jerusalem community and
the Community at Qumran, and some of the weakness of the paleography and history and archaeology. Well, they came in as a
group and they walked out as a group. Totally stonefaced, in total
silence. They didn't even come up and say 'Good paper . . .' 'Good
try . . .' 'Interesting . . .' They just walked out with totally blank
faces. And I think that was the first time they were ever aware that
I existed. They never read my work, I don't think.''

Eisenman also mistakenly assumed that he would be granted
free access to the unpublished Cave 4 manuscripts that were relevant to his research. At the time, he still believed that historical
scholarship was about the search for the truth, no matter what the
implications, and even if his colleagues detested his theories, they
had an obligation to facilitate, not hinder, legitimate study and
research. But as the weeks and months passed, Eisenman found
himself being treated politely by everyone he talked to but getting
no closer to seeing new material than if he had remained at home
in Long Beach. "The moment I went to the Department of Antiquities I got the great stone wall approach," he told me. "You
know: 'We can't help you, go to Father Benoit.' '' And at a polite
meeting at the Ecole Biblique, at which he gratefully accepted
copies of Eisenman's books and offprints, Father Benoit informed
Eisenman that since he was merely editor-in-chief of the publication project, not physical custodian, Eisenman really should go
back and apply to the Department of Antiquities.

This was all, of course, a search in total darkness, for Eisenman, like all other outsiders, did not have an accurate idea of just
how much or what kinds of material was still being held by the
team. His awakening was rude and unexpected. After a frustrating
visit to the Rockefeller Museum to meet Antiquities Director Avi
Eitan and to apply—unsuccessfully—for access to the unpublished fragments, he sat dejected in one of the workrooms of the
museum and, as he describes it, an employee of the department
simply felt sorry for him. "They were just making a friendly gesture," Eisenman remembered. "I was just sitting in there, kind of

moaning and saying, 'I can't see anything, I can't do anything, this guy won't do anything for me.' " The department worker left for a moment. He returned with a full computer printout of all the unpublished Qumran manuscripts.

This was one of those low-level bureaucratic actions that sometimes have enormous effects, for as Eisenman scanned the list of hundreds of plates, he saw not only the listings for the biblical books, apocryphal works, and sectarian texts, like the Community Rule and the Damascus Document, but an astonishing wealth of prayers, visions, wisdom literature, and messianic poetry. Only the titles and the inventory numbers were listed. One could only imagine what the texts contained. It was enough to make any scroll scholar's mouth water: In Milik's lot alone were not only the famous Qumran copies of the Damascus Document but at least seven new manuscripts of the Community Rule, five of the Book of Jubilees, calendars, lists of priestly courses, and an intriguing mixture of unknown apocryphal works, biblical commentaries, and texts identified as angelogical, astronomical, and cryptogramic. Even for scholars without a new theory of Qumran origins to propound, this was a treasure. But for Eisenman, it was the key to proving his theories. He was convinced that they contained the clinching evidence of the link between the Jewish Revolt, Jewish messianism, and pre-Pauline Christianity. There it was: the authentic literature of the Judean messianic movement. But getting access to the fragments would now become more of a political challenge than a scholarly one.

Near the end of the 1985–1986 academic year, as Eisenman and his family were preparing to leave Israel after a year of runarounds and disappointment, something else happened. It was a much-mythologized confrontation that Eisenman would later insist was a major turning point in the story of the scrolls. It was a drunken toast made in the middle of the night in the garden terrace of the Albright Institute in Jerusalem—a toast about which Eisenman's and Strugnell's recollections diverge radically. According to Eisenman, he and his wife, Heather, happened to meet Strugnell at a fairly sedate academic party in West Jerusalem, and when it was over they invited him back to the Albright Institute for a nightcap and further friendly conversation about their mutual interest in the scrolls. Eisenman remembers that "I was interested in the International Team and what was going on and to hear from his perspective, so for me it was an entertaining, interesting evening.

"We were sitting in the Albright garden at three o'clock in the morning, and then he made this incredible toast to me," Eisenman continued. "I don't think he understood I was Jewish at that time, although at some point he did get the idea. He didn't understand that I was Jewish because of my wife—she had converted to Judaism and we had been married in Israel and we had lived there from sixty-eight to seventy-three—but for him, she was Scottish and British and very sophisticated and elegant, and he couldn't understand what she was doing with someone like me.

"So in the midst of all this, he turns to me," Eisenman went on, "because basically his whole intent for the evening was to go and watch the sun rise over Moab—he had this idea in his brain—he wanted to stay up all night and watch the sun rise over Moab and he wanted to basically get me out of the picture, he wanted to go with Heather . . . So he said . . . Will you drink to anyone I propose? I was interested because it was such an original toast. I said sure, make a proposal. I wanted to know who he had in mind. So he lifted his glass and said—Heather is sitting there right next to me—he says: I want to drink to the greatest living man of the latter part of the twentieth century. I said, Jesus, this is fantastic, who could this be? And then we all sat forward on our chairs listening, and he says 'Kurt Waldheim.'

"I almost fell off my chair. This was at the time of the Kurt Waldheim revelations in the Israeli press. It was obviously on his mind; he was all probably seething about this. You know, the Israeli press was probably going on about all this stuff as they usually do. So I didn't know what to do at that point, because he had just confirmed to me everything that I had thought about this International Team and its basic subconscious ethos, not necessarily its conscious motivation, but its subconscious ethos. And here is the guy that the Israeli government were going to confirm as the head of the Dead Sea Scrolls research team.

"I didn't want to show that I was upset, and I just drank my cup and put it down, but I really felt that it was an insult and I wanted to get back. I had to try to think of someone who would upset him as much as he tried to upset me. Now I happen to love Orde Wingate—he's the Jewish T. E. Lawrence—and I just loved his biblical thing, and he basically set the foundation of the Israeli army and trained all of those guys and he did it on the basis of biblical scripture . . . so he was a very able commander and he died tragically in the Chindit campaign in Indochina, and I always thought that it was a great tragedy because I thought he was killed, frankly, eliminated. He was really hated.

"So I knew Strugnell, coming from a British private school and London, and being a Brit from the Oxford circle would know things that the average Qumran researcher wouldn't know. So I said OK, I drank to whomever you asked, now you drink to whomever I ask. Well that's gentlemanly, of course, and he said sure. So I said I want to drink to Orde Wingate. He blew up. He blew up. He wouldn't drink. He smashed his glass down on the table and said—and this guy was lucid—he said I won't drink to that traitor! He knew who I was talking about. He knew what it meant. *This* is how he kept his gentlemanly bargain.

"That was it for me. That was it. No quarter after that, because nobody could call Orde Wingate a traitor as far as I am concerned. What did that mean, you see, to me, spiritually, what did that mean? That meant that someone who liked Jews, *he* was a traitor and someone who did the kinds of things that Waldheim did, *he* was a great hero. That was it for me. I had it after that. There was nothing that I wouldn't do and there was no end that I wouldn't go to to to dislodge these people from control of the most precious documents of Jewish history."

The famous toast in the garden of the Albright Institute certainly makes for a dramatic story. But it is only fair to give Strugnell's version as well. "That meeting took place," Strugnell admitted to me, "but as he is incapable of summarizing any book of the New Testament, so he shows the same skill in my after-dinner talk, you know. Some of the topics indeed were mentioned, but he got it completely wrong what I was trying to say.

"I don't remember the party, but the meeting in the garden, yes," Strugnell continued. "Everyone remembers certain things. I remember some of the topics, not others . . . The discussion about Waldheim was about whether one state has the right to interfere with the democratic processes of another. It seemed at the time it was not the business of other countries"—and here Strugnell was clearly referring to Israel. "This is the claim I make also about American foreign policy. So at the time, all I knew was that Waldheim had not been one of the worst secretaries-general of the U.N. My main point was about the role of foreign countries.

"I don't often give toasts," Strugnell insisted, "and Wingate to me is just an overgrown Boy Scout. I would never use the language of 'traitor to king and country.' That's not my style. I happen to have a trick on the rare occasions when I do have to give a toast, to use the famous toast of the Duke of Dorset, where you toast"—Strugnell paused as he tried to remember the words— "You see how *rarely* I do this . . . I toast 'to church and state, sovereign, and to the ladies.' It's a famous toast. *This* toast I cannot remember at all. All I can say is that since he's inviting me to give a toast, then my contempt for Wingate is authentic, and I can't believe that he would hoax the story. But the thing that no one seems to have noticed is that he presents himself as pandering his wife to me in order to get a chance of editing the scrolls. This is a most ungentlemanly attitude. Has he not noticed that?

"I think he's given the framework of certain elements of the story," Strugnell concluded, "but I think I hold my liquor better than he does and I think he may be confused."

Confused or not, Eisenman soon embarked on a campaign that was aimed at nothing less than the destruction of the International Team. And looking back on his subsequent attempts to break through the iron grip of the establishment on Qumran studies, you certainly have to admire his sheer doggedness. John Allegro is the only previous dissident in the history of the project who ever came close to fomenting a public uproar as potent as Eisenman's, and Allegro died a discredited eccentric, an outsider in every sense of the word. Indeed, most of the scholars who had ever challenged the traditional interpretations of the texts, or the International Team's methods of work, wisely learned from the experience of banging their heads against the stone walls of the Rockefeller Museum. And most of them eventually (and prudently) shifted their attention to scholarly issues that were not quite so sensitive.

But Robert Eisenman banged his head on those same walls, and he kept on banging, even though Magen Broshi of the Shrine of the Book reportedly told him, half-facetiously, that he would never see many of the unpublished texts in his lifetime. That might have been the definitive brush-off, but Eisenman was more determined than most. For him, the issue of the Dead Sea Scrolls gradually melded into larger issues of Jewish pride and nationalism, and resentment of the Great Powers who controlled, even now, the precious literary legacy of first-century Judean messianism. He believed that the real historical context of the birth of Christianity was being suppressed. His rage against empires—intellectual, political, and religious—drove him on. He was also more politically savvy than most scholars; he gained support for his campaign from Dr. Yuval Ne'eman, a member of Knesset and one of the most outspoken leaders of the Israeli radical Right.

"You can call him Dr. Strangelove," Eisenman told me, anticipating a negative reaction, "and I'm not necessarily interested in his political views." But Ne'eman, a theoretical physicist-turned-politician, was ready to run with the ball. Ne'eman had been Minister of Science and Development in the Begin government but had eventually left the ruling coalition to become an opposition spokesman on the extreme Right. He was fascinated with the stories that Eisenman told him: about the failure of the Israeli government to take rightful control of this precious national treasure; of the continuing power of a less-than-sympathetic International Committee; and of the Team's restriction on free scholarship. "He could embarrass the government," Eisenman remembered, "so he did."

The demand for immediate Israeli control of the Dead Sea Scrolls eventually became the subject of brief, bombastic Knesset hearings, and because the Likud government did not like to be described as incompetent or submissive in their dealings with foreigners, political pressure was soon applied through the Ministry of Education on the Department of Antiquities. In 1988, a new director had just been appointed for the traditionally sleepy department: General Amir Drori, a retired career army officer, who had been a senior commander of Israeli forces in Lebanon. Drori took charge of Israel's antiquities with a vengeance, reorganizing the structure and goals of the organization, determined to transform it into a powerful, self-supporting Antiquities Authority.

Regarding the Dead Sea Scrolls, he received a clear ruling from government lawyers that, according to international law, the Israel Department of Antiquities had authority to assume full control over the preservation and publication of the manuscripts. The ownership chain for the Cave 4 Collection was, to say the least, convoluted: It was first purchased by the Palestine Archaeological Museum, which was then partially reimbursed by the government of Jordan, which was then substantially aided by the sale of allotments of scrolls to foreign institutions, which were then cancelled when the Museum was finally nationalized in 1966. Then came the war in 1967. In such a situation, a clear-cut interpretation of the legal situation was as subjective as the historical interpretation of some of the scrolls. But with the go-ahead for action, Drori instituted a clear policy change. From now on, the Israel Department of Antiquities would reserve to itself the right to oversee and approve all major administrative actions of the International Team.

In the fall of 1988, Eisenman, like many other foreign scholars working in Israel, thought it wise for future good relations to make a get-acquainted appointment with Drori, to go to his office at the Rockefeller Museum and pay his respects. That office, with its paneled wooden door, stone walls, and incongruous little fireplace, had been the locus of archaeological power in the country for more than half a century. From the time of Gerald Lankester Harding to Abdel Karim al-Gharayabah to Awni Dajani, Avraham Biran, and Avi Eitan, its occupants had played central roles—by their action or inaction—in determining the fate of the scrolls. That is why Eisenman was so intent on the meeting. Since he had heard of the change of policy regarding the scrolls, Eisenman wanted to go on record, to urge Drori to fire Strugnell immediately and abolish the monopoly of the International Team.

"I told him the whole thing about the scrolls, about Strugnell," Eisenman said, recalling that first meeting with Drori in the director's office in the Rockefeller Museum, "and then he told me, 'That's interesting what you say because we're just in the process of going to sign a contract with Strugnell for editing of the scrolls.' I said 'What!?' This was the total opposite of everything I had been working with Ne'eman to achieve. They were not only going to reconfirm these guys in power but give them absolute control and license through a contract. I said this is the absolute opposite of everything I had worked for. I said, 'You can't do this. This is ridiculous.' And then I told him the story of the Waldheim thing, and it made no impression on him whatsoever. He said uh-huh, yeah, OK, what do we care?"

Now I have to say that Amir Drori is not what you would describe as a bubbly personality. He embodies in his husky frame, short-cropped gray hair, deep voice, and slow, deliberate way of speaking the indelible stamp of his years of military service—years of overseeing the operational planning of Israeli forces, years of regimenting officers and soldiers to look to objectives larger than their individual uncertainties and pain. And thus it was that the Dead Sea Scrolls came to be for him a logistical rather than an emotional matter. Even today, Amir Drori maintains that the private political or religious orientation of scroll scholars is of no interest to the Israel Antiquities Authority in the fulfillment of its responsibility to bring the scrolls publication project to a successful conclusion. "I know that some of the people who decide about the material are not exactly great Zionists," he told me, "but I don't judge them by their Zionism—only by their ability to publish the texts. I don't check anyone to see if they are a priest or anti-Semite. My only question is whether he *can* publish and *will* publish. Those are the only criteria."

But for Eisenman, who considered the scrolls to be precious historical evidence that was being suppressed, misinterpreted, neutered, or delayed precisely *because* of the scholars' religious orientation, Drori and the Antiquities Authority were part of the problem, not the solution. And while Larry Schiffman and others were working quietly on the inside to coax out new material little by little, Eisenman decided that desperate times required desperate measures. He decided that he had to do whatever he could to break up what he saw as collusion between the Antiquities Authority and the International Team.

In March 1989, Eisenman joined Professor Philip Davies of Sheffield University in England in making a formal request to John Strugnell that they be granted permission to examine, for the purposes of their private research, the texts whose great historical importance Milik had enthusiastically announced more than thirty years before, but which had remained unpublished and inaccessible. "We and *many others*," Eisenman and Davies wrote, "feel that thirty-five to forty years is enough time to wait for these materials to become generally available on a scientific basis to the scholarly community." They sent a similar letter to Amir Drori and requested that both Drori and Strugnell respond to this formal request within thirty days.

Strugnell claims that he knew very well what Eisenman was up to. From the tone of the letter (which had, in the meantime, been leaked to the press in Israel and in America), Strugnell naturally assumed that it "was not meant to get manuscripts but to set the foundation for the legal battle." Yet in his reply to Eisenman and Davies, Strugnell did not seem to grasp how dangerous an opponent he had. He acted as if he were dealing with some impertinent working-class lad who had barged into Jesus College at Oxford and banged on the door of the master's rooms.

"As a rule I do not write answers to public letters," Strugnell admonished. "I make just this one exception in your case, hoping that it will inspire you in any further letters to follow politer and more acceptable norms." The normal procedure, he informed them, was to write directly to the assigned editor; that "has been the way that such requests for access have been handled in the past." The truth was—proper procedure or not—no outsider had *ever* been given access unless the specific editor wanted to grant it. The editor-in-chief had never intervened because there was no possibility of appeal. Yet at the same time, Strugnell recognized that there was a problem. Under the mounting behind-the-scenes pressure of the Antiquities Authority, he persuaded Milik to unload two important groups of material to other scholars: the several manuscripts of the Book of Jubilees and Jubilee-type compositions to James VanderKam, then of North Carolina State University, and the much sought after manuscripts of the Damascus Document to Joseph Baumgarten of the Baltimore Hebrew University. When Eisenman learned of these reassignments several months later, he was livid. The power of the International Team remained unbroken despite all he had done.

Both of Strugnell's designees were dependable, conventional scholars. VanderKam was a student of Cross, who had worked extensively in the Enoch and Jubilee literature and would certainly produce competent editions of those texts. The choice of Baumgarten for the Damascus Document, though, was more pointed. With his younger colleague Larry Schiffman, Baumgarten had emerged as a leader of the *halakhic* approach to the Qumran material, seeing the legal discussions of the sect as a unique (and characteristically Judean) style of religious expression that would find its fullest expression in the legal debates of later Rabbinic Judaism.

Eisenman was constructing quite a different historical picture—in which Rabbinic Judaism, like Christianity, was a distinctive variation of the biblical religion that had survived primarily because of its adherents' eventual accommodation with Rome. Neither Schiffman nor Baumgarten had ever taken Eisenman very seriously. Back in 1977, Eisenman had given his first paper, "James the Just as Righteous Teacher," at a meeting of the Society of Biblical Literature. "Schiffman saw me for the first time," Eisenman remembered, "and burst out laughing at my paper, which startled me and really amazed me and offended me." Eventually, Eisenman's colleague Philip Davies wrote to Baumgarten directly, asking him for access to the Damascus Document fragments. But he merely received a polite refusal, with Baumgarten replying that there was really nothing dramatically new in the historical sections of the document—and as for the many new laws it included ("which you and other writers have not treated"), he was working as hard as he could "to place them in some perspective from the viewpoint of *halakha.*"

That was exactly the point: Baumgarten would not put those laws into just *any* perspective. Because the task of editor and interpreter had become so intertwined, the first editions of the Qumran texts were not simple transcriptions (as the publications of the Cave 1 scrolls had been). Each one was meant to be an extensive excursus, not only presenting the letters, words, and columns transcribed from the joined fragments but also placing the text somewhere in the historical narrative that the editor considered to be the correct one. Thus some scholars, primarily interested in the early history of Christianity, would interpret their texts as Essene documents, naturally seeing hidden allusions and obscure references as background material for the study of the New Testament. Other scholars, coming from a rabbinic perspective, would interpret their texts as evidence for the kind of halakhic debates that would eventually become the basis of Rabbinic Judaism.

Yet Eisenman was convinced that the Dead Sea Scrolls offered unique evidence for a radical rewriting of the origins of both Rabbinic Judaism and Christianity, even though most scrolls scholars would not or could not recognize that fact. "From the rabbinic types you were getting *pilpul* and legal hairsplitting," Eisenman told me, "and from the Christian side you were getting total blindness as far as history and textual material went, and no critical view of Christianity at all." The irony, to his mind, was that the rabbinic scholars' general lack of familiarity with the New Testament left the standard picture of Qumran and early Christianity largely unchallenged. It also left intact the gospel image that Jesus was rejected and handed over for execution by "the Jews." Jesus and his followers were a part of the national movement; it was *Paul's* rejection, not *Jesus'*, that led to the creation of an entirely new cult. "I explained all this to Schiffman," Eisenman remembered, "but he could never understand it. By destroying me, you're actually confirming the Christian accusations against the Jewish people, and you're not allowing our people to get out from under these terrible blood libels that have been extant for nineteen hundred years."

The only answer now was complete liberation, no more halfway measures, no more teams. The only answer was to make the photographs immediately available to all scholars and, according to Eisenman, "let a thousand voices sing."

The chorus might not exactly be the Vienna Boys Choir, but wasn't that exactly the point of academic freedom? Eisenman was eager for his story to get as wide coverage as possible. Thus the battle was joined in the spring of 1989. Eisenman's unsuccessful struggle to get access to unpublished material was first covered in the pages of the *Biblical Archaeology Review* and, eventually, in the mainstream American news media. The battle for the scrolls moved from the halls of the Rockefeller Museum to the American world of investigative journalism, *People Magazine,* and CNN. After years of complete silence on the Dead Sea Scrolls, newspapers, magazine, and TV networks soon jumped on the story. There was now in America a whole generation of well-educated Baby-Boomers-turned-Middle-Agers who had grown up seeing their news and learning about their world through the narrative grammar of television, where talking heads became metaphors, not people; where an angry Colonel Oliver North, sitting gunstock-straight at a congressional hearing, became a symbol, not *just* an individual.

The Dead Sea Scrolls story had its share of good characters: a maverick scholar from Southern California, the colorful N.Y.U. professor, an imperious, Oxford-educated Harvard professor, a strong-jawed Israeli general, and hints of a shadowy ecclesiastical conspiracy. The story was soon to be hijacked and restructured. Through the collective mind's eye of *60 Minutes*-style embarrassing close-ups and hidden cameras, a classic battle was portrayed of the forces of intellectual freedom against the forces of repression, with an exotic Middle Eastern locale thrown in. The battle lines between Sons of Light and Sons of Darkness were forming, but the irony was that everyone—Larry Schiffman, Robert Eisenman, John Strugnell, and Amir Drori—were all convinced that they were the Sons of Light. Yet for the Dead Sea Scroll story to be anything more than a passing sensation—and for the scrolls monopoly to be broken—Eisenman and his occasional allies could not continue to act as individuals. And it was Hershel Shanks of the *Biblical Archaeology Review* who would soon begin to organize their separate efforts into a powerful international campaign.

7

THE FINAL BATTLE

Hershel Shanks was an unlikely rebel. A graduate of Haverford, Columbia, and Harvard Law School, a former Justice Department lawyer, and long-time partner in a prominent Washington law firm, he has always been an idealist *within* the establishment. He is soft spoken and his appearance is unassuming. With swept-over-the-top thinning hair, squarish metal-rimmed glasses, sensible shoes, and open-necked shirts, he is a familiar figure at biblical archaeology conferences from San Francisco to Jerusalem, usually sitting in the front row of the lectures, taking notes on a yellow legal pad. In the early 1980s, he left a lucrative career in the law to pursue his deep personal interest in biblical archaeology. He is clearly an admirer of great scholars and he enjoys their company. Yet Shanks himself is a force to be reckoned with in the world of digs, diggers, and biblical scholars. In a suite of offices on Connecticut Avenue in Washington, he has assembled a team of skilled and enthusiastic professionals to publish the *Biblical Archaeology Review* and *Bible Review*, slickly designed, full-color bi-monthlies with circulation in the hundreds of thousands of eager history, religion, and archaeology buffs. And magazines are only part of the Shanksian empire. The umbrella organization

of most of his activities, the Biblical Archaeology Society, orga-
nizes tours, educational cruises, and summer courses; and mer-
chandises biblical archaeology books, slide sets, video cassettes,
and Middle Eastern souvenirs.

The genius of Hershel Shanks and his Biblical Archaeology
Society has been to bring together so many different audiences
into a single readership. Israeli archaeology has long been a
source of public fascination, particularly in America, with its long
tradition of veneration for the Bible. Yet until Shanks came on the
scene, the fascination was fragmented between several quite distinct ethnic and religious groups. There were American Jews, who
found personal gratification in the rediscovery of Israel's ancient
monuments at a time of modern independence; evangelical Christians, who delighted in the unearthing of ancient cities, tombs,
and temples that provided tangible evidence of the historical reliability of the Bible; and the wide audience of armchair Indiana
Joneses of all backgrounds and persuasions, who are fascinated by
the aura of antiquity and ancient mysteries. *BAR* brought all of
them together. The letters-to-the-editor column in every issue
runs the gamut from outraged protests against any doubt being
shed on the literal truth of the Bible, to enthusiastic comments by
volunteer diggers about their once-in-a-lifetime experiences the
previous summer, to erudite critiques of scholarly hypotheses by
well-known archaeologists. *BAR* is read in the Bible Belt, in Southern California, in Jerusalem, and on Park Avenue.

No one in the archaeology game can afford to ignore Hershel
Shanks's power, yet that is exactly what happened in the case of
the Dead Sea Scrolls. In the role of chief editorialist, reporter, and
ghost rewriter of many of the articles contributed by scholars,
Shanks has made *BAR* the place where new discoveries are trumpeted, controversies are aired, and scandals exposed. *Time* magazine, the *Washington Post,* and *The New York Times* often take their
cues from the pages of *BAR* about which discoveries are important, which archaeologists are newsworthy, which issues are worth
pursuing. And with such high visibility, Hershel Shanks was able to

make the fate of the Dead Sea Scrolls the kind of emotional public issue that very few archaeological discoveries have ever become.

In the beginning, the Dead Sea Scrolls was only one of dozens of subjects that *BAR* tackled. In 1984, Shanks led a large Biblical Archaeology Society tour to attend the International Congress on Biblical Archaeology. His report on the congress—and on Qimron's presentation of MMT in particular—was not so much of criticism as surprise. In describing the importance of the new Dead Sea document, Shanks provided his readers with a synopsis of the theories of Strugnell and Qimron about MMT's possible authorship by the Teacher of Righteousness and its importance for the history of *halakha,* but he also expressed amazement that Qimron had chosen to reveal only five or six lines from the actual document while he kept the other 115 lines secret and inaccessible.

The problem became sharper for Shanks in the following year, when he was invited to attend Larry Schiffman's Dead Sea Scroll conference at New York University. His memories of that conference have a decidedly bitter edge. "These guys are sitting around the table wide-eyed," Shanks recalled, acidly mimicking the Eastern European accent of one prominent scholar, " 'Vunderful . . . vunderful!' And they can't even see the material. Inside they're seething with anger." The result was yet another of Shanks's editorial articles on the conference and on the bizarre situation in which a small group of scholars had maintained a monopoly on the scrolls and had no intention of releasing the unpublished documents until they were good and ready. More and more, Shanks was coming to see that the Dead Sea Scrolls, as the cultural and religious legacy of *both* Jews and Christians, was an object of great interest to his own ever-growing ecumenical readership. In the fall of 1985, he began to investigate a bit deeper, recognizing for the first time that the Israel Department of Antiquities had the legal authority to do something about the situation. Yet "even then," Shanks stressed to me, "it was not a campaign."

Like just about everyone else in the archaeological community in the fall of 1988, Shanks made a get-acquainted call on the newly appointed antiquities director, Amir Drori, at the Rockefeller Museum. Present at this meeting were Drori's new deputy, Rudolph Cohen, and the department's director of publications, Ayala Sussmann (who happened also to be the wife of Hebrew University Professor Yaacov Sussman, who was so influential in the recognition of the importance of MMT). The news Shanks heard at the meeting was encouraging: Drori had appointed an advisory committee of Israeli scholars to oversee the progress of the scrolls publication project; Strugnell was being pressed to come up with a definite timetable; and dozens of unpublished documents from the allotments of Starcky, Skehan, and Cross were being reassigned. Milik still held on to a great deal of material and refused to communicate directly with the Israeli authorities, but Strugnell had assured Drori that Milik would complete his work in a reasonable time. Shanks went away from that meeting satisfied with what he heard and requested that Ayala Sussman send him a copy of the schedule as soon as it was available.

Today, when you look at the "Suggested Timetable" prepared by the staff of the Department of Antiquities and sent off to Hershel Shanks in February 1989, you can see immediately what got him so upset. Under the official, formal heading "STATE OF ISRAEL, Department of Antiquities and Museums, Ministry of Education and Culture," it began with an odd little apologetic paragraph, noting that "up to now, under the preceding Editors-in-chief," seven volumes of the *Discoveries in the Judaean Desert* series had already been published, in addition to eight volumes that had appeared elsewhere, "despite many obstacles." Even more eyebrow-raising than the tacit apology was the timetable that followed, which would be—if it were taken seriously—a shockingly sudden acceleration of a publication schedule whose progress had been fitful and plodding for the previous thirty-five years.

According to the timetable, ten new volumes would be completed in the next three years alone, and ten *more* by 1996. It all had the tone of authority and uncompromising ambitiousness: Each of the coming volumes—the Greek Minor Prophets scroll from Wadi Seyyal, MMT, biblical texts from Cave 4, and so on—were numbered, briefly described, and given a precise date of "delivery to Ed-in-chief." The problems of delay and procrastination that had plagued the study of the scrolls would suddenly vanish, if this timetable was to be believed. A first edition of the long-awaited MMT was to be sent to the printer in the coming summer, and the reclusive Josef Milik—who had not come back to Jerusalem to examine any of the fragments since 1967—was scheduled to submit his final work on one hundred sixty-two Cave 4 texts by the end of the year. The official document was, in a word, unbelievable. Its deadlines could not possibly be met.

Shanks remembers his first reaction to this document vividly: "I looked at it and I was aghast: a timetable! It was a *suggested* timetable. Nobody signed it. Who's committed? Who suggested it? What happens if they don't meet it? What kind of a document is it that they're feeding me? I was at least obligated to ask some questions. So I wrote Ayala a letter and I set forth these questions. And the letter I got back was the final straw."

Ayala Sussman's "Dear Hershel" reply, in mid-April, was curt and definitive, with all appearances of being the last word. After expressing *pro forma* thanks "for the interest you are taking in the Scroll Publication Project," she went on to say that "the enclosures sent with the February letter are, in effect, the documents we wish to bring to the attention of the public. The timetable is as listed and its deadlines will be supervised closely by the appropriate authorities." Yet if Ayala Sussman hoped that this reply would satisfy Shanks, she badly miscalculated how insulted and angry he would be. By 1989, the Biblical Archaeology Society had contributed in countless ways to the unprecedented expansion of archaeology in Israel. It had provided a forum (and career boost) for many scholars; it had helped to raise funds for preservation projects; it had attracted enthusiastic volunteers to excavations all over the country; and last, but certainly not least, its exciting coverage of the ongoing search for biblical civilizations—the wellspring of Judeo-Christian tradition—had provided *modern* Israel with enormous goodwill. By 1989, therefore, Hershel Shanks felt that he was an active participant in the world of biblical archaeology who deserved to be treated as a valuable partner, not a meddler, by the Israel Department of Antiquities.

"I hit the ceiling, and ever since then . . ." Shanks's words trailed off for a moment as he recalled his anger when he opened the letter and read its six imperious lines. "I mean, first of all, it was impolite, not to say a brush-off and undiplomatic and terrible from the point of view of public relations and the public's right to know. I mean, there was no way that I could suppress the fallout from this attitude." More important was Shanks's sudden recognition that the Department of Antiquities believed that it could get along quite nicely without him—thank you very much—and that the department was conspiring with the scholars *against* him. There would now have to be a battle, and Hershel Shanks, with his readership, media contacts, and considerable legal experience, was a lawyer determined to win.

For Shanks, the Suggested Timetable was the battle banner for an all-out attack on the scrolls establishment, not merely a call for reform. Up to the spring of 1989, he had focused his attention primarily on the members of the International Team, hoping that they could somehow be persuaded to live up to their moral obligation either to publish or give up their material. Now, with righteous anger against what he considered Drori's decision to act as a shield for the International Team, he directed his attack against the Israel Department of Antiquities as well. "They will *never* do it," Shanks wrote in a stinging editorial in *BAR* in the summer of 1989, which was his open declaration of war. "They will never do it because they cannot do it. They have failed utterly and completely. The time for equivocation, explanation, and apology has passed. It is now time to face the situation squarely and unflinchingly: The team of scholars assigned more than thirty years ago to publish the Dead Sea Scrolls will *never* publish them because they cannot!" He asserted that the Israel Department of Antiquities had joined "the conspiracy of silence and obstruction." The only answer was, therefore, to abandon the entire concept of official editions and to allow free access to the scrolls to all qualified schol-ars, immediately.

In this potent mix of outrage, accusation, and mysterious, un-published documents, the Dead Sea Scrolls suddenly became a news story that the American media, in particular, eagerly gobbled up. Wire services and the major Washington, New York, and Los Angeles papers carried stories on Hershel Shanks's dramatic change of strategy, from a continuing attempt to force the Inter-national Team to publish their assigned texts as promptly as possi-ble to a demand for immediate, open access for all. At a time when the media were calling for open access to all kinds of public infor-mation—from the secret communications of the Iran-Contra schemers to the FBI and CIA archives of the Kennedy assassina-tion—did it seem too much to ask to allow unrestricted study of the documents that had been touted for forty years as "the most important manuscript discovery of the twentieth century"? In early July, an editorial in *The New York Times*, entitled "The Vanity of Scholars," gave the official imprimatur of the Newspaper of Re-cord to the idea that patience in waiting for the International Team's publications had finally run out.

Of course there were counterattacks throughout the sum-mer. Professor Frank Moore Cross branded as "presumptuous" Shanks's proposal for free access. "To give general access to plates of fragments (a shake and they are chaos)," he wrote indignantly to *BAR*, "or to original photographs (the best record of their frag-ments in their early state) would be utter folly. If nothing else, there are scholars who are not honest; even with tight controls there have been thefts and pirate editions." Urging that the ad-ministration of the scrolls be left where it was—in the hands of the International Team under the oversight of the Israel Department of Antiquities, Cross condescendingly urged the protesters to apply themselves to the study of the texts that had already ap-peared.

These arguments struck many scholars as mere rationaliza-tion. And at the same time, a new front of protests was opening in Poland, or to put it more accurately, the Polish front was being taken seriously for the first time. Eastern European Qumran studies had always been out of the mainstream, but since 1987, a tirelessly Qumran-fixated professor from Cracow, Zdzislaw Jan Kapera, had been organizing biennial Qumran conferences in the small Polish town of Mogilany. The September 1989 colloquium was an unqualified success, at least in terms of international participation. The fall of the Berlin Wall and the sudden political transformation of all of Eastern Europe encouraged a large turnout; among the guests who traveled to Mogilany was a Dead Sea Scrolls Hall of Fame—or Rogues' Gallery—depending on your point of view.

There was Norman Golb, ever anxious for a podium from which to propound his "Jerusalem Theory" of Qumran origins. There was Barbara Thiering from the University of Sydney, whose hypothesis had it that John the Baptist was the Teacher of Righteousness and Jesus, the Wicked Priest. There was John Trever, who was among the first to recognize the value of Archbishop Samuel's scrolls in 1948. There was Dr. Fred Young of Kansas City, Kansas, a retired faculty member at the Central Baptist Seminary, who had made it the goal of his retirement years to catalogue every book, article, or news story ever written about the Dead Sea Scrolls. Larry Schiffman was there, as was Philip Davies, and George Brooke from the University of Manchester. And from the *Biblical Archaeology Review* were managing editor Suzanne Singer and Hershel Shanks. At the conclusion of the meeting, the participants passed a resolution calling on Oxford University Press and the "relevant authorities in Israel" to publish the photographs of all the unpublished Cave 4 manuscripts as soon as possible.

The official reaction to the "Mogilany Resolution" was derision. The idea that the presumptuous declaration of a side-show gathering of eccentrics and scholarly sightseers would have the slightest effect on how the Dead Sea Scrolls Publication Project would be conducted seemed, to at least one unnamed Israeli participant, utterly laughable. "It will mean nothing," the *BAR* report of the conference quoted the unnamed source as saying. And, indeed, back in Jerusalem, the Department of Antiquities was finally, belatedly, making some progress toward reassignment, with Magen Broshi's announcement that a substantial number of Milik's documents had been reassigned. But the Department of Antiquities and its Scrolls Advisory Committee still clung to the fiction of the Suggested Timetable, even though by the end of 1989 Qimron, Strugnell, Cross, and Milik had already missed their first suggested deadlines. Thus, the time for mere reassignments seemed over. It was time that the scrolls be open to all. Shanks confronted Strugnell directly at a forum at Princeton in November, demanding to know whether Strugnell would agree to provide access to the unpublished scroll photographs to all qualified scholars—or at the very least release the full text of MMT.

Strugnell naturally declined both proposals and (even though a preliminary edition of MMT had been promised the previous summer) insisted that the text would be available soon. In fact, Strugnell was beginning to enjoy twitting the characters who insisted on making trouble; in his lecture on the current state of scroll studies, he announced that he would refrain from even mentioning unpublished material, since, for most of his listeners, it would be "like reading from a menu and being unable to eat from it." As the national media began to latch on to this story, Strugnell took increasing delight in ridiculing Shanks and his friends. Thus, in an early morning appearance on *Good Morning America,* when asked about his erstwhile opponents, he gave the rising nation a clever one-liner: "It seems we've acquired a bunch of fleas who are in the business of annoying us."

Thus was born the most famous and most outrageous of Hershel Shanks's *BAR* covers, one that, perhaps more than anything else in the campaign, personalized his conflict with John Strugnell and focused the animosity of the general public on the selected villain of the piece. In the center of the cover of the March/April 1990 issue was an unflattering close-up photograph of John Strugnell looking unshaven, his hair unwashed, and the corner of his mouth twisted up in a sneer. Beneath the photo— which was set into the frame of a TV monitor—was Strugnell's *Good Morning America* "fleas" quote, set in bold white type. Arranged all around the editor-in-chief and his quotation—against a striking green-blue background—were the names of sixteen prominent, respected scholars who had attacked the International Team's power. And the name of each one of them was proudly placed next to a picture of a louse.

It had been a long day—the last of my long conversations with John Strugnell in his Cambridge apartment—and he was painfully candid in relating what he saw as the betrayals and injustice that led to his removal as editor-in-chief. It was now early November 1993, and I had not seen him since the end of August. He now looked stronger and healthier and had resumed work on his autobiography, which was to be *his* definitive version of the story of the scrolls.

During our first meeting in June, he had described the project: a first-person narrative with many appendices, written in the style of the elegant travel and adventure books of the nineteenth century, beginning with his boyhood in England and his early education, and wending its way through his life among Jordanians, bedouin, Dominicans, and Israelis—concluding with the public uproar that resulted in his dismissal, and with some sober, perhaps even bitter, advice to his successor in the office of editor-in-chief. Strugnell had allowed me to read his foreword and the chapter he had written about Yigael Yadin. Though they were just preliminary drafts—"still very drafty" he had noted on the top of the first page—they were the sad and poetic expression of a man who believed that he had been unjustly robbed of his professional reputation and, in a sense, his proper role in the scholarly project that had given meaning to his life.

"You see, most of the attacks of Shanks," he told me, "are attacks on the sensible running of the project—did we do this, did we do that, did we exclude so-and-so from the project, did we let too much sunlight into the manuscripts, were we a cabal, and so on. That I put near the very end in my account of my relationship with the Israelis. But the question of anti-Semitism is one that you don't . . ." He paused. "If the answer is yes, you have no business reading this, you shouldn't trust me anyhow if you believe Shanks's statements on the topic." His memoirs were to be a chance to show how his famous newspaper interview in the Israeli daily *Haaretz* had been so widely misunderstood and misconstrued.

At this meeting, our conversation had ranged widely, as usual. He spoke proudly, even a bit defiantly, about his seven years as the editor-in-chief of the publication project, insisting, as he has always done, that due to his efforts, the most difficult scholarly problems—the reassignment of texts, the establishment of a timetable for completion, and final publication of the Qumran excavations—were well on the way to being solved. He insisted that the mounting public pressure had no effect on his performance on the job. "I read Shanks, but you see I'd always dismissed Shanks," he told me. "I'd read *BAR* back in the first numbers that attacked Kay Kenyon and I'd stopped reading. And then I started reading about eighty-two, which was when I was becoming editor-in-chief. I probably subscribed to it in eighty-three or four, and by that time he was in fairly hot pursuit of this, but my mistake was I didn't answer him at all. I think I should have written an essay, correcting every one of his mistakes every time. But one doesn't have the time to do that." He leaned forward and posed a plaintive, if rhetorical, question: "How would *you* have dealt with that campaign?"

Far more of a factor in the history of the Qumran project was the establishment of the reorganized Israel Antiquities Authority in April 1990. Strugnell was, in fact, being run over by a political steamroller long before his controversial public comments on Jews, Judaism, and Israel suddenly made his removal an international *cause célèbre*. His true nemesis was to be Amir Drori. As a former general of the Israel Defense Forces—a veteran of four wars and more than thirty years of jockeying for power within the officer corps—Drori knew about power. Now that he was out of the army, the country's archaeological establishment was his power base. Yet the transformation of the Education Ministry's small Department of Antiquities into an autonomous, self-supporting Antiquities Authority was a tricky undertaking in Israel's fractious multi-party political system, where every institutional shift or expansion of budget is interpreted by both friend and foe as a political act.

Drori could not afford to suffer embarrassing criticism at this time of delicate transition. Hershel Shanks was providing him with nothing but bad publicity, and Robert Eisenman was always liable to stir up the political waters again against the International Team. Drori, therefore, decided to act decisively. The first deadlines of the Suggested Timetable had already passed and there was no sign of the promised progress. Strugnell could do nothing but plead with his colleagues or convince them to give up some of their texts. Drori himself told me that Strugnell "had lots of information—mainly in his head—about the history of the project from 1953 and he was very involved in these things, but after four months we saw that we were not progressing with him."

Thus, by the summer of 1990, Drori decided that the best solution was to take complete, if camouflaged, control of the scrolls publication project. One of Drori's first acts on assuming directorship of the Israel Department of Antiquities in 1988 had been the appointment of a small advisory committee to help him make informed decisions about the administration of the Dead Sea Scrolls. "I needed a group that was familiar with all the problems," Drori told me, recalling his appointment of three scrolls advisors in the fall of 1988. They were Professor Shemaryahu Talmon, a professor of Bible at the Hebrew University, who had published extensively on the Qumran literature; Professor Jonas Greenfield, another Hebrew University biblical scholar, who was editor of the prestigious *Israel Exploration Journal;* and Magen Broshi, longtime curator of the Shrine of the Book. Thus was born the Israeli "Oversight Committee," which would become an important new element in the struggle for the scrolls. And in consultation with Talmon, Greenfield, and Broshi, Drori now decided to appoint a "deputy editor-in-chief" to bring some order to assignments and deadlines. A detailed and definitive inventory of all the documents in the collection would be made under his direction. The Oversight Committee would then become be the final authority in apportioning and reassigning unpublished texts. But

Strugnell would be left as a figurehead, preserving at least the fiction of the International Team.

That is why Strugnell recalls that his problems with the Antiquities Authority through the spring and summer of 1990 were far more serious than Eisenman's increasingly strident accusations or Shanks's ridicule. "You'll see that in my diary for the events of the summer, the topics I raised with the Israelis were none of these." His main struggle was to preserve the legal autonomy that the International Team had enjoyed since the days of Lankester Harding. All governments—both Jordanian and Israeli, from the Hashemite court of King Talal to the shaky Likud coalition of Yitzhak Shamir—had allowed the International Team to appoint its own members, reserving only the right to veto an appointment (but in fact, that had never been done). But now the government had decided to make an appointment itself. Instead of bowing to Shanks's calls to provide immediate access for all scholars, Drori—on the advice of his committee—was intent on enforcing deadlines and streamlining the procedures, not loosening control over them.

"I recognized we had to have an Israeli assistant for two reasons," Strugnell told me. "Because the politics demanded it and secondly because one needed such a person to be in Jerusalem for the half year when I was not in Jerusalem." Several candidates were proposed in the meetings between Strugnell and the Oversight Committee, and in the end the members of that committee (who were now clearly running things) decided to go with Professor Emanuel Tov of the Hebrew University. Tov had briefly studied with Strugnell and Cross as a graduate student. He was a well-known biblical scholar (among the first Israelis to be given Qumran documents to publish). And he was eminently qualified for the job. But qualifications were less important than the jarring new precedent his appointment had introduced—jarring, at least to the members of the International Team. "I told the Israelis that I was willing to submit their nomination to the team," Strugnell recalled, "though this was a reversal of the usual procedure." The respectful deference that local governments had always accorded the wishes and decisions of the International Team was now to be replaced by a series of authoritative dictates. But there was little he could now do to fight the new arrangements, for by this time John Strugnell's alcoholism and manic depression were impairing his ability to function as the last defender of the International Team.

It is not easy to talk to someone about their psychiatric problems, especially when those problems and subsequent hospitalization have become as public as Strugnell's had. Yet Strugnell was unblinkingly candid about his state of mind in the fall of 1991. "I was working very well, as manics very often do," he recalled. "I worked long hours into the night. Sleeplessness is one of the things that provoke a manic depression. The trouble is that a person is rarely conscious of having manic depression. It's an outsider who's needed; who asks, 'Do you really want to do that?' " Unfortunately, there was no one at the Ecole Biblique, where Strugnell kept his small room—with its cot, desk, and makeshift file cabinets made of empty beer cases—to warn him against speaking too freely to journalists. Over the past year, he had clearly enjoyed being in the spotlight, launching barbs in Hershel Shanks's direction, and chiding all the yapping scholars out there for their impatience. The team was making good progress, he repeatedly insisted. They would see their Qumran documents soon enough.

But Strugnell's interview with reporter Avi Katzman of the Israeli daily *Haaretz* was different. It was to set off a chain reaction of outrage and defensiveness from Jerusalem to America that would ultimately and profoundly alter the way Qumran scholarship was done. Over the previous year, as the struggle for the scrolls had become increasingly targeted against Strugnell, the rumors of his drinking and his anti-Zionism had only been hinted at in the press coverage and in the scholars' whispers, but when Katzman came to the Ecole Biblique for a chat with Strugnell on the morning of October 28, 1990, he was interested in getting everything on the record. And Katzman pointedly noted in his later description that "although Strugnell drank beer throughout the interview—this did not surprise me as his drinking habits were well known in Jerusalem—he did not appear to be inebriated. He was lucid and spoke in a firm voice." When I spoke with Strugnell about the interview, he seemed almost matter-of-fact.

"The man who wrote it, I found very intelligent, Mr. Avi Katzman," he said. "He was asking me how this mainly Christian project is going on on one side of the town with not too much contact on the other side of town. Is this anti-Semitism? How do you explain it, and has the project suffered from it, and so on. I thought I was addressing his questions," he concluded, "perhaps I wasn't thinking cleanly already at this time." The interview as published was typical Strugnell: witty, outrageous, and naively honest, with asides and pontifications on the present state of the publication project, the possibility of finding more scrolls, about Jordan, Israel, Judaism, and Christianity. His comments on Israel were, as might be expected from his avowedly pro-Jordanian perspective, critical. He rejected the legality of Israel's occupation of the West Bank and Jerusalem ("It's quite obvious that this was a part of Jordan") and he brought up the familiar, unflattering comparison between Israel and the short-lived Crusader Kingdom.

"The occupation of Jerusalem—and maybe the whole State—is founded on a lie, or at least a premise that cannot be sustained," he stated flatly. "That's putting it as crudely as I can. The occupation of Jerusalem cannot be sustained." These comments, and the others he made about the impossibility of deporting the entire population of Israel at this late date ("You're not going to move populations of four million. Not even the Nazis mentioned that.") and the incompetence of the Israel Antiquities Authority, would almost certainly have gotten him into trouble. Had all things been equal, a contrite apology would have permitted him to survive. But when the interview subject entered the murky waters of theology, Strugnell—in the elegant turn of phrase Frank Cross once used against John Allegro—committed "scholarly suicide."

The matter of the relationship between Judaism and Christianity was, of course, one of the central concerns of Qumran studies from the very beginning. And Strugnell—like all of the other original International Team members—had a definite religious outlook on the subject, quite apart from the day-to-day work of fitting together parchment fragments or even translating and studying the texts. They accepted the general consensus (crystallized long before any of them got to work on the Cave 4 fragments) that Qumran represented something of a missing link between Judaism and Christianity. And there was little doubt left in either their words or their religious affiliation which religion they considered to be superior. But Strugnell now spoke in a way that sealed his fate. His theological position was not particularly original, even in the field of Christian Dead Sea Scroll scholarship: It was just expressed more brutally than most.

Describing Judaism as "a folk religion," "not a higher religion," he rejected the designation anti-Semite for himself, preferring to call himself an "anti-Judaist." He went on to plead guilty to anti-Judaism by pleading guilty "the way the Church had pleaded guilty all along, because we're not guilty; we're right. Christianity," he continued, "presents itself as a religion which replaces the Jewish religion. The correct answer of Jews to Christianity is to become Christian." By this time, Strugnell was apparently so caught up in his own unbridled desire to be candid—to express his unquestioning belief in the spiritual superiority of Christianity over other religions—that he spoke in terms that a more circumspect Christian polemicist would never have used. For him, the Jewish religion was "a horrible religion," nothing more than "a Christian heresy." "You," he said to Avi Katzman, and by extension to all Jews in Israel and the Diaspora, "are a phenomenon that we haven't managed to convert."

Strugnell concluded the interview and thought nothing more of it; he was preparing to return to the States in just a few days' time and his emotional state was growing steadily worse. "I was basically sitting and doing my work, and like manics do, running out and spending money. I'd say that in those three months in Jerusalem I spent nearly about $100,000—on all sorts of things. You have no idea—Jerusalem is a robber city. So it's not the place to be." He returned to Cambridge in early November, fully expecting to leave for New Orleans toward the end of the month. A special ceremony was to be held in his honor at the Annual Meeting of the Society of Biblical Literature, where a number of his former students were to present him with a volume of essays to celebrate his sixtieth birthday. "The manic usually thinks that everything is going well, so I thought that I was going down to the SBL meeting," he recalled sadly of the missed celebration. "It would have been nice to have been there, you know." What happened instead was that he was hospitalized and remained completely out of contact with the outside world for almost a month. "I don't remember having a copy of *Haaretz* in hand," he told me, "so I don't remember anything until December when someone showed me a xerox. And by that time the shit had hit the fan, as they say in this country."

Down in New Orleans, the *Haaretz* interview had created a sensation. For some it must have seemed like a God-sent opportunity to make a dramatic change in the composition of the International Team. The appointment of Emanuel Tov as deputy editor was already a foregone conclusion, and he would now be elevated to the post of editor-in-chief. The Scroll Oversight Committee quickly contacted various International Team members, suggesting that Tov should work closely with Professor Eugene Ulrich of Notre Dame (a student of Cross, who had inherited many of Patrick Skehan's biblical manuscripts) and Emile Puech of the Ecole Biblique. Thus a new troika of efficient editors was created, with Emanuel Tov as the first among equals, eventually reassigning hundreds of long-neglected texts to a new international team of more than sixty carefully selected scholars, whose academic qualifications were of the highest possible standard—and whose adherence to deadlines would be closely supervised. The Dead Sea Scrolls Publication Project thus at last seemed to be on firm footing. The members of this new team recognized that control of the project by the Israel Antiquities Authority was not a passing, political abberation, but a permanent fact. But something else was happening behind the scenes in New Orleans, no less important for the outcome of the scrolls story. Robert Eisenman had utterly rejected the idea that the replacement of a Jordanian-appointed team by an Israeli-appointed team had accomplished anything. His goal was complete liberation. And he now had the ammunition to make that possible.

At about the time that John Strugnell was being admitted to a hospital in Boston, Robert Eisenman sensed that the tide had turned in his favor, at least temporarily. At a quiet dinner meeting in a New Orleans restaurant during the meeting of the Society of Biblical Literature, Eisenman concluded a business deal with E. J. Brill publishers of Leiden, a deal that he hoped would make the actions of the new International Team and the Israel Antiquities Authority wholly irrelevant. More than a year before, in August 1989, at the time when the Dead Sea Scrolls first became a media *cause célèbre,* Eisenman had been contacted by "people who were watching all this in the papers," as he now puts it, "and they said they would start showing me pictures because they figured I would know what to do with them." The "pictures" were photographs of the unpublished Cave 4 fragments—large black-and-white glossies of varying quality that represented every last shred of inscribed parchment and papyrus under the exclusive control of the International Team.

Although Robert Eisenman prefers not—no, refuses—to discuss his source's identity because of the continuing legal proceedings, he has assured me that he would be prepared "in four or five years to talk about these things and tell everyone who should get the proper credit." And there is no question that his shadowy source of information—his Deep Scroll—*does* deserve much of the credit. For as long as the Department of Antiquities and the International Team maintained control of physical access to the documents, the critics could do nothing but complain. But once a set of scroll photographs got into the hands of the outsiders, there would be nothing to stop them from—God forbid!—looking at any or all of the scrolls.

The debate still rages among Qumran insiders about where these pictures came from. Some claim that they come from the estate of a Jordanian photographer, Najib Albina, who worked at the Rockefeller Museum in the 1950s; others claim they come from the Huntington Library in San Marino or the Center for Ancient Biblical Manuscripts in Claremont, California—both places where copies of the scrolls photographs had been deposited under lock and key several years before for safekeeping, lest anything ever happen to the originals in the war-torn Middle East.

"They came in small batches," Eisenman recalled, "and it was only after a whole year of confidence building that everything was made over to me." But his intention was not to keep them for himself but to publish them immediately—as a defiant political act. He therefore shared the secret with Professor James Robinson of the Ancient Biblical Manuscript Center in Claremont—an internationally recognized scholar and editor of the Nag Hammadi texts from Egypt—who had come out publicly against the unconscionable delay in the publication of the Dead Sea Scrolls. Robinson agreed to help Eisenman prepare the photographs for publication and write a brief introduction. Eisenman contacted his old publisher and sketched out the idea for a daring publishing coup. And now, in New Orleans, under conditions of total secrecy, E.J. Brill's representatives came to final agreement with Eisenman for publication of a facsimile edition of all the Dead Sea Scrolls.

In the midst of his elation, Eisenman realized that the scroll monopoly was about to break open and he had not had a chance to go through any of the material—to see if, as he believed, it would provide more evidence for his own theory of Qumran's nationalistic messianism. But since Eisenman was a historian, not an epigrapher or manuscript specialist (all of his work had been done, by necessity, with published manuscripts), he needed a professional teammate to go over the pictures, and he made contact with a University of Chicago scholar named Michael Wise, whom he had met at various conferences. Wise was a colleague of the rebel-with-a-single-cause Norman Golb of the Oriental Institute, and when Wise learned that he might have a look at the entire Cave 4 collection, he agreed to provide transcripts and rough translations for Eisenman.

Thus, through the spring of 1991, Eisenman was pulled by conflicting forces. On the one hand, Robinson was anxious for the Brill publication to come out as soon as possible—before rumors spread and led to threats of lawsuits. On the other hand, Wise and his team of graduate students in Chicago were identifying among the hundreds of photographs some important texts—messianic visions, legal codes, calendars, biblical interpretation, and wisdom literature—all previously completely unknown. In many cases, Eisenman saw direct validation for his theories about the pre-Pauline character of "Christianity" in Judea—normal Jewish messianism with no hint of an actual, incarnated messiah. Wise's work so preoccupied Eisenman—with continuing requests for more and higher quality pictures—that the original date for the Brill publication, originally scheduled for March, had to be postponed.

Then Madrid happened and everything changed. The International Congress on the Dead Sea Scrolls, sponsored by the Universidad Complutense and held in El Escorial in late March, was to be a coming-out of sorts for the new International Team. In addition to the normal coterie of active scrolls scholars who were invited to give papers—Schiffman, Talmon, Dimant, and Qimron, among others—editor-in-chief Emanuel Tov met formally for the first time with his associates Emile Puech and Eugene Ulrich to discuss the reassignment of documents to new official editors. There was also to be a touch of medieval pomp and circumstance: the bow-tied éminence grise of scroll studies, Professor Frank Moore Cross of Harvard, bowed his head—amidst the general applause of his colleagues—to receive a medal of honor from Queen Sofia of Spain.

The general warm feeling of scholarly self-congratulation was, however, marred by two unpleasant incidents. By the spring of 1991, Hershel Shanks had been declared persona non grata by the Israel Antiquities Authority—the IAA went so far as to prohibit any of its archaeologists from publishing in *BAR*—and shortly before he was to fly to Spain to attend the Madrid conference he was humiliatingly disinvited by the organizing committee. He would later claim in *BAR* that this move was motivated by the members of the new committee, who wanted as little as possible to do with Shanks and his attacks. Shanks naturally made the most of this high-handed maneuver by publicizing it widely as another attempt to foster exclusiveness and secrecy by the new-style Dead Sea Scroll cabal.

And they were not reluctant to use their power. Emanuel Tov, as the new chief editor, stepped forward to discipline Professor Kapera of Poland. During the previous winter, in an effort to further the cause of free and open Dead Sea Scrolls studies, Kapera had offered subscribers to his Cracow-based *Qumran Chronicle* a copy of the full transcription and English translation of MMT that had been circulating privately among scholars for over a year. Inspired by the spirit of the Mogilany Resolution, he believed he was striking a blow for academic freedom. And Hershel Shanks, announcing Kapera's offer in the pages of *BAR,* in a slap at the closed world of Qumran studies, acidly referred to Poland as "new home of the free press." Yet for the Israel Antiquities Authority this was a very serious matter. Not since the days of John Allegro had any scholar so brazenly challenged the International Team's absolute monopoly of first publication. And this was a breach of protocol even more egregious than Allegro's, since Kapera reportedly received the document anonymously and did not claim to have made either the transcript or the translation himself.

Less than a week before the opening of the Madrid Congress, Kapera received an angry, threatening letter from Amir Drori, declaring that his unauthorized distribution of MMT was "a violation of all legal, moral, and ethical conventions and an infringement on the rights and efforts of your colleagues." Drori demanded Kapera's "immediate reply prior to further action." And just to make sure that all the appropriate bodies were fully aware of the situation, Drori sent copies of the letter to the Polish Academy of Sciences, the members of the Scrolls Oversight Committee, the International Team members, and a representative of Oxford University Press. Even more humbling was the personal dressing-down Kapera got from the scholars in Madrid. His response was to express his sincere apologies and promise to discontinue the distribution of the MMT transcript immediately.

The efficacy of the International Team's hardball approach was not lost on any of attendees at the conference, not least of all on the editorial representative of E. J. Brill. "They got frightened," Eisenman recalls bluntly and sadly, "because they saw the vicious feelings that were involved. And the representative was kind of naive and he misunderstood; he thought they were complaining about the *pictures* of MMT. He didn't realize that they were just complaining about this guy's transcription. It was all confusing to him. And he wrote a report to the bigwigs at Brill." The upshot of the entire matter was that in apparent fear of a scholarly boycott and/or legal action, Brill suddenly decided to cancel its publication agreement with Eisenman and Robinson.

For Eisenman this was a painful setback, especially when things seemed otherwise to be going so well. And it was soon coupled with the vicious reviews and outright condemnations that greeted the publication of *The Dead Sea Scrolls Deception*—the mass market exposé by Michael Baigent and Richard Leigh on the supposed Vatican conspiracy to suppress the Cave 4 material—which prominently featured Eisenman's theories about James the Just, Paul, and the *real* Judean messianic movement. In cancelling their publishing contract, Brill returned all the photographs to Eisenman, who was intent on finding another publisher. The search was not particularly successful. "Robinson used the contacts he had with the people in his field," Eisenman remembered. "But that took a couple of months and he didn't get anywhere. So we finally said, 'Oh well, let's go to Shanks.' "

In Hershel Shanks's eyes, John Strugnell's public meltdown had accomplished little. Though he put the Antiquities Authority on notice that he expected them to make the scrolls available to all scholars, Shanks soon came to see that Strugnell's fall from power merely resulted in the establishment of another scholarly clique. Each of the new editors (Tov, Puech, and Ulrich) and all three members of the Israeli Oversight Committee (Talmon, Greenfield, and Broshi) received an allotment of the reassigned scrolls. Though the quality of their scholarship was not in question, this smacked of, at least, a conflict of interest.

Shanks had, in the meantime, formulated a quite different strategy to bring down the Qumran house of cards. Some years before, he had heard about the existence of a secret concordance of all the Cave 4 material—a bound Xerox copy of a cardfile that had been compiled in the late 1950s and early 1960s by four young scholars (Joseph Fitzmeyr, Raymond Brown, Willard Oxtoby, and Javier Teixidor) on behalf of the International Team. In 1986, Avi Eitan, then serving as director of the Israel Department of Antiquities, denied knowing anything about it, but Shanks was convinced of the reliability of his sources, and he eventually learned that this concordance (duplicated and distributed privately in 1988 by John Strugnell to get the publication work moving) might be another way of getting at the unpublished Cave 4 texts.

One of the copies of this concordance had been deposited in the library of Hebrew Union College in Cincinnati (others were sent to the Shrine of the Book, Gottingen, Oxford, and, of course, the Harvard Divinity School). Sometime in the spring of 1991, Shanks had been approached by an unlikely duo: Professor Ben-Zion Wacholder, a crusty, rebellious, and nearly blind Talmudic scholar, and graduate student Martin G. Abegg—a pocket-pencil-holder type if there ever was one—who had together figured out how to use the concordance to reconstruct the scrolls. For each word used in the Qumran literature, the concordance listed every occurrence, citing the specific document, line, and phrase. Under the conditions of the late 1950s, working backward—reconstructing the texts from the card file—though possible, would have been a painfully tedious undertaking. But now in the days of personal computers it was just moderately tedious. So Abegg set to work designing software to reassemble the scattered card references into texts—and Professor Wacholder helped check and recheck the original references when the Qumranic Hebrew of the printout sheets did not make sense. Hershel Shanks was charmed by this mix of modern technology, ancient literature, and a crusade for intellectual freedom. So he quietly made plans—with financial support from the scholar and philanthropist Manfred Lehmann—to begin publishing the Wacholder-Abegg reconstructions as *A Preliminary Edition of the Unpublished Dead Sea Scrolls* under the imprimatur of the Biblical Archaeology Society.

"But simultaneously with that—and I never told Wacholder—I kept Wacholder's confidence," Shanks told me, "I get a call from William Cox, not from Eisenman. I almost hung up on him. He says 'I'm a lawyer from Los Angeles and I have a client, and I'm not at liberty to disclose who he is.' I said, 'Wait a minute, I don't even want to talk to you if you're from an undisclosed client. If you want to tell me who your client is, we'll go on talking, otherwise that's the end of the conversation.' That's my way: Let's be open and above board." But the ploy didn't work, Shanks admitted. "I *did* stay on the phone."

Cox explained that he was in possession of a complete set of Dead Sea Scroll photographs, which would be made available through Robert Eisenman, though Eisenman was neither his client nor the source. With Brill apparently frightened out of the picture by the International Team in Madrid, taking up this project offered yet another way for Shanks to strike back. The negotiations went forward with Cox, and eventually with Eisenman and Robinson. Financial support for the publication was provided through one of Eisenman's contacts, but at this point, Shanks took command. "I got the boxes and it was I who decided. We worked with my secretary one night, one Saturday night, until eleven o'-clock, sizing. I decided how big they would be. All we got was a box of pictures and their introduction and the index. We had our agreement how they would be listed. They're not listed as editors—'prepared, with an index by'—very deliberate, and the rest is history."

In the meantime, on September 4, 1991, Hershel Shanks and the Biblical Archaeology Society made headlines across the nation with the publication of the first fascicle of the *Preliminary Edition of the Unpublished Dead Sea Scrolls*. Though the reliability of the computer-assisted transcriptions was still in question, anyone who wanted to send off a check for a mere $25.00 could purchase a thin volume containing reconstructed texts of the Cave 4 copies of the Damascus Document and about twenty other unpublished documents—no questions asked. Though some Qumran scholars questioned the ethics of using the work of others without permission ("What else can you call it but stealing?" a recuperating John Strugnell told the Associated Press), Shanks, Wacholder, and Abegg were hailed as heroes. "We've broken the monopoly," Shanks proudly stated to *The New York Times*.

Then came the next great explosion, from an unexpected direction. On September 22, Dr. William A. Moffett, director of the Huntington Library in San Marino, California, gave an order that made the revolution in Qumran studies just about unstoppable. He instructed that his institution—one of the most respected private research libraries in America—would open its *own* complete set of Dead Sea Scrolls photographs to all qualified scholars, immediately. This was not just a matter of procedure, it was a step that could not easily be taken back. Under the headline "THE MONOPOLY OVER THE DEAD SEA SCROLLS IS ENDED"— stretching across the three center columns of the front page of the Sunday *New York Times* on September 22—was a picture of a white-gloved William Moffett standing next to photographer Robert Schlosser, closely examining an original scroll negative. "It will be very hard for the cartel that's controlled the scrolls to put the genie back in the bottle," Moffett said to the *Times* reporter, gloating. The jig was up for the scroll establishment, or so it certainly seemed at the time.

On September 25, the Israel Antiquities Authority and the International Team drafted articles of conditional surrender. In a dense, legal-sized, single-spaced press release, the IAA agreed "in principle to facilitate free access to the photographs of the scrolls." But the important sentence was buried down near the bottom: "While all parties involved are in favor of free access to the photographs of the Dead Sea Scrolls, it is also felt that the work of scholars who in recent years have taken it upon themselves

to publish texts should not be harmed by any new arrangements."
But even this attempt at circumlocution did not last long.

The cause of scroll liberation had some powerful allies. Two days after the IAA press release, *The New York Times* resident wordsmith-and-pontificator William Safire roared out with a bazooka blast of an op-ed piece, praising the Huntington and attacking the "insular jerks in Jerusalem's antiquities bureaucracy." Safire's voice was—and still is—a voice that is closely listened to in Washington when it comes to the public debate over billions of dollars of aid to Israel, the appointment of Defense Secretaries, and the direction of American foreign policy. So his opinion on the relatively minor international flap over the Dead Sea Scrolls carried tremendous weight. Speaking again of the objections of the insular jerks in Jerusalem, Safire simply suggested that Prime Minister Shamir should "shut them up."

A full-scale retreat was soon in progress. On October 27, 1991, editor-in-chief Emanuel Tov announced that all qualified scholars would now be granted free access to the Cave 4 materials, even though that access was meant only "for personal research." For Hershel Shanks, this was an opportunity to seize back the initiative. "It was very clear by that time," he recalled, "that they had dug in, they had been completely intransigent, uncompromising, unwilling to move." Now, he believed, was the time to begin the distribution of the *Facsimile Edition,* containing the privately obtained photographs. Any scholar who wanted at least to look at the scrolls would not have to apply anywhere for permission. All that he or she would have to do would be to leaf through the pages of the Biblical Archaeology Society's two-volume set. And now, with the tide of public opinion running strongly in his favor, Shanks felt that he had little to fear. And on November 19, he, Eisenman, and Robinson appeared at a press conference in New York City, posing for the cameras, smiling broadly, proudly holding the freshly published volumes in their hands. "This should end the controversy for all time," Eisenman told a Reuters correspondent, "Now it's time for us to all go back to work interpreting the meaning of the scrolls."

* * *

Though it might have seemed that the final battle was over, the Dead Sea Scrolls story still had at least one more ironic twist. Professor Elisha Qimron later recalled that he was shocked when he leafed through the publisher's foreword and saw his own transcription of MMT. Hershel Shanks had, in one last act of defiance to the Antiquities Authority and the scholars of the Inner Circle, composed a long and biting Publisher's Foreword to the Facsimile Edition, giving vent to the rage that he had felt over the previous two and a half years. Attacking the insistence of the IAA to maintain control of the assignments and thus continue to restrict access, he included a virtual scrapbook of his frustrated efforts to free the scrolls. Among the twenty-two "figures" appended to his foreword were the 1989 "Suggested Timetable," now a laughable dead letter; the brush-off note by Ayala Sussman; his unsuccessful letters to Strugnell, Cross, Milik, and Puech to allow other scholars access to their documents; a supportive editorial from the *Washington Post* and Safire's column; the threatening correspondence received by the Huntington Museum; and to show the extent to which the IAA had acted as a bully, Shanks included Drori's threatening letter to Zdzislaw Kapera and a copy of the privately circulated transcription of MMT. And he did not even mention Qimron's name in connection with the text, describing the transcription of MMT simply as the work of Strugnell and "a colleague."

Here was the problem: Shanks did not—or preferred not to—recognize that MMT was not a text that could be read clearly like a newspaper, but was a highly fragmentary document with almost half of the words missing. Qimron's hypothetical reconstructions, placed between square brackets, were inserted in many of the gaps. Shanks had recognized that there was a potential copyright problem with the English translation of MMT which had been published by Kapera, so he consciously left that out. But as a lifelong admirer of high scholarship, he never stopped to consider that philological reconstruction could be considered creative writing. "I didn't give a thought," he told me. "I mean, I knew that you could make a claim about the translation, but here was a transcript and I just didn't think of the reconstructions." How could the words of an ancient author—presumably reconstructed correctly—be claimed by a modern scholar under his own copyright?

Over the years the rights to the unpublished Qumran documents had been treated like legal tender by the International Team members—tradable, bequeathable, and transferrable. The monopoly might be broken for the future, but Qimron was now determined to defend at least *his* hard-won property. Elisha Qimron proved not to be another John Strugnell when it came to fighting back against Hershel Shanks. Where Strugnell might have responded haughtily and imperiously, Qimron went on the offensive. He hired Attorney Yitzhak Molho and on January 14, 1992, filed suit in the Jerusalem District Court against Hershel Shanks, Robert Eisenman, James Robinson, and the Biblical Archaeology Society.

Court papers filed on behalf of Qimron claimed that his legal copyright on the MMT transcription had been infringed by its unauthorized publication. And at the end of the month, Judge Dalia Dorner issued an injunction against further distribution of the Facsimile Edition and agreed to adjudicate Qimron's claim for the equivalent of $200,000 in damages. Qimron remained adamant that the unauthorized, uncredited publication of the MMT transcript "has caused me and my family a great deal of suffering." It had become a matter of honor, not historical discussion. "A major achievement of my career has been stolen from me."

During the months of intensive legal preparation by both sides for the trial in Jerusalem—from January 1992 to the February 1993 court date—Robert Eisenman refused to allow his ideas to be silenced by the threat of legal action, and, as usual, had gone his own way. The goal of his struggle had always been far wider than the abstract ideal of academic freedom; from the beginning of his involvement with Qumran studies he had attempted to discredit the historical conclusions—as well as the exclusivist methods—of the International Team.

Now, with the entire Cave 4 collection available to him, he found what he believed to be dramatic, confirming evidence for his main historical hypothesis—that Christianity had begun entirely within the context of militant Jewish messianic resistance to the Roman Empire, and that the later images of Jesus Christ (that formed the centerpoint of Christianity outside Judea) were the product of a conscious, politically inspired reworking of Jewish messianic themes to produce an opposite ideological objective: undermining, not furthering, the goal of Judean independence, and the melding, not separation, of Jewish and Hellenistic ways of life.

Eisenman's participation with Hershel Shanks in the publication of the Facsimile Edition in the fall of 1991 offered him a chance to convey his revolutionary ideas to a far wider public. Just before the publication press conference, Shanks had published at two-page layout in *BAR* containing three "Long Secret Plates from the Unpublished Corpus," with translations and brief commentaries by Eisenman. Although it later became evident—to Shanks's great embarrassment—that two of the documents had been previously published by Baillet and Milik and that the third was about to be published by Puech, Eisenman's *interpretation* was stolen from no one. He pointed out that these representative examples of Qumran testaments, prayers, and visions expressed a militant resistance to foreign oppressors and the fervent expectation of a Davidic-style messiah, who would be coming soon to heal the wounded, resurrect the righteous dead, and to bring glad tidings to the poor.

That was just the start of additional revelations. Eisenman had been working closely with Wise and his team at the University of Chicago, and he had identified a number of texts among the unpublished Cave 4 materials that he saw as additional indications that the Christian messiah was merely the Jewish expectation that had been given a name, a mythologized earthly existence, and stripped of its necessary connection to the Jewish law. In this, Eisenman now went much further than Allegro had ever dreamed of going (at least in his pre-mushroom theories). In Eisenman's thinking, the New Testament accounts of Jesus' life were not merely innocent retellings of Qumran's messianic message. They were a conscious transformation of a highly political, anti-imperial ideology into an essentially apolitical, devotional belief.

Thus when he revealed to the world the existence of the "Pierced Messiah" text in early November 1991, the news media was excited and some of his fellow scholars were aghast. The text in question was 4Q285, that tiny, six-line fragment, not much bigger than a large commemorative postage stamp. It was long buried among J. T. Milik's holdings and had recently been reassigned to Oxford professor Geza Vermes. Maybe that is why Vermes took such great exception to the Eisenman-Wise reading of this highly fragmentary passage of messianic expectation. According to Eisenman's press release, "the text is of the most far-reaching significance because it shows that whatever group was responsible for these writings was operating in the same scriptural and messianic framework as early Christianity." While most scholars had considered Qumran's messiah to be the usual triumphant biblical redeemer, Eisenman and Wise read a crucial line of this text as foretelling that the messianic "Branch of David" would suffer wounds or "piercings" and would ultimately be put to death.

Here, Eisenman believed, was additional proof (as if any was needed) that the original International Team had been sitting on explosive material for decades, material that would show that the passion of the messiah (most probably by crucifixion, as it was carried out with such brutal regularity by the Roman Sons of Darkness) was a common expectation, not a historical event. In general, important ancient texts are not announced first in the newspapers, but Eisenman was by this time regarded as a dangerous troublemaker and a slapdash scholar by many of his colleagues, and soon after his initial announcement, Geza Vermes summoned what amounted to a tribunal of twenty Qumran scholars to Oxford to judge Eisenman's claims for this document—without, of course, allowing Eisenman to defend himself.

Their conclusion was predictable: Eisenman was off his rocker. Because of the frequent ambiguity of Hebrew words that are written mostly in consonants, the crucial word in line 4, *hmytw,* could be translated either "he killed him" (referring to the messiah's action, presumably against some sinful figure), or "they put to death" (referring to the messiah's own grisly fate). The distinguished invitees to the Oxford seminar, all of them convinced of the distinctiveness of Qumran messianism, saw no reason to see a suffering messiah in this scrap of parchment. And although there were arguments that could and would be mustered on both sides of the argument, Hershel Shanks clearly distanced himself from the theories of his erstwhile publishing partner. The *BAR* report on the Oxford seminar was given the deceptively definitive headline "The 'Pierced Messiah' Text—an Interpretation Evaporates."

There were to be more sensations with the publication of Eisenman and Wise's book *The Dead Sea Scrolls Uncovered* in November 1992. Advertised as "The First Complete Translation and Interpretation of 50 Key Documents Withheld for Over 35 Years," the book was filled with terse, dense commentaries and highly fragmentary Hebrew texts. Here was Eisenman's chance, as he would later express it, to level the playing field. Since he had seen how the International Team had long used the right of first publication to establish and maintain an orthodox interpretation, he saw his chance to produce the first published versions of many unknown documents—contextualizing them in *his* historical framework.

Thus the book included a transcription and translation of MMT, now renamed "Letter on Works Reckoned as Righteousness," placing it not in the Hasmonean religious squabbles of the second century B.C.E.—as Strugnell and Qimron would have it—but in the political agitation for the purification of the Temple from accommodationist priests and Roman defilement in the first century C.E. And in discussing a long wisdom text that they called "The Children of Salvation and the Mystery of Existence" (which John Strugnell had been working on for almost forty years), they pointed to the variant uses of the word "salvation," expressed by the Hebrew word *Yesha,* or the variant "His salvation," *Yeshuato.*

Now as any of the Jews for Jesus can tell you, the Hebrew name of Jesus is usually rendered as *Yeshua*. The implication here—implicit and unspoken—was that Jesus was merely an abstract theme that was later given a specific earthly incarnation by Paul and his followers.

The last document transcribed and translated in the *Dead Sea Scrolls Uncovered* would have significance only to those readers who were aware of how innocently and uncritically Qumran scholars had always assumed that the Qumran sect loathed the Hasmonean kings. As I have mentioned, the whole history of the sect—and the date of the establishment of a communal religious settlement at Qumran—was predicated on the faith that the heirs of the Maccabean family were seen by the most pious among the population as degenerate, Hellenized potentates. As the archaeological explorations of Pesach Bar-Adon in the Dead Sea region had shown, this area was one of particular importance to the Hasmonean kingdom, and it was unlikely to be the chosen place of refuge for anti-Hasmoneanists. Eisenman had, as early as 1983, ridiculed the credulity of the established scholars in just parroting the anti-Hasmonean line. It had become an article of faith—applied even to MMT—and yet in the unpublished corpus was a document that lavished blessings and praise on "King Jonathan" (apparently the Hasmonean king also known as Alexander Janneus), which apparently indicated that Eisenman, not the consensus, might be right.

But here is one of the places where Eisenman and Wise got into trouble: in April 1992, a feature story by veteran reporter Abraham Rabinovich appeared in the *Jerusalem Post*, describing the circumstances by which Israeli doctoral student Ada Yardeni had been the first to decipher the cramped, cursive handwriting of this document. And Eisenman and Wise, though referring to the *Post* article, neglected to mention Yardeni's name. That later became one of the examples used to show Eisenman and Wise's bad faith and lack of ethics, but here, too, the historical point was lost. Eisenman believed that the Hasmoneans always had a loyal, pious following, and it was only when the Hasmonean line was wiped out in the bloody rise to power of the Roman client-king

Herod that the nation felt itself to be leaderless. "Messianism arose just when you would expect it to," Eisenman stressed to me in one of our conversations. "When the Maccabean family was destroyed by the Herodian family, a new principle of leadership emerged."

The entire Eisenmanian hypothesis about messianism, Judaism, and Christianity has—as I have repeatedly said—its bitter, disdainful detractors, and they love to depict Eisenman as a crank and a troublemaker who simply doesn't have the linguistic skill or experience to understand the admittedly difficult Qumran texts. But in their dismissal of his arguments, the burden of proof is always placed on *him*. The consensus view of Qumran history and dating is an untouchable, sanctified Mount Rushmore of Hasmonean-period Wicked Priest, Man of Lies, and Teacher of Righteous. In most cases, scholars prefer to scoff rather than take anything that Eisenman has said at all seriously. If he could be wished away, there is no question in my mind that the vast majority of established scholars would sit down and start wishing.

Thus the outraged open letter of the nineteen prominent Qumran scholars against *The Dead Sea Scrolls Uncovered* became the writ of accusation against Eisenman and Wise at the December 1992 New York Conference on the Dead Sea Scrolls. There were certainly errors of judgment made in the use of other scholars' transcriptions, but as Eisenman stated in his defense, there was no way that this new interpretation could be seen as intellectual theft from anyone. The inquisition in New York City over the supposed instances of plagiarism and errors and imprecisions of interpretation in the *Dead Sea Scrolls Uncovered,* although humiliating, was inconclusive. The book continued to sell widely in America and Europe. The real confrontation was yet to come.

8

JUDGMENT DAY

The trial that began in a stark Jerusalem courtroom on the first day of February 1993 was a private, civil action—a claim for monetary compensation and vindication of injured personal honor. Yet Professor Elisha Qimron's quarter-million-dollar copyright infringement suit against Hershel Shanks, Robert Eisenman, James Robinson, and the Biblical Archaeology Society clearly had a symbolic and emotional significance that far transcended the specific claims. Among the expert witnesses called by the plaintiff were Antiquities Authority director Amir Drori and Shrine of the Book curator Magen Broshi, both of whom had long been primary targets of Shanks's editorial attacks.

Also on the witness list were Professor Yaacov Sussmann, who had worked closely with Qimron in analyzing MMT's historical significance, Professor Larry Schiffman, who had also been consulted by Strugnell and Qimron; and Professor Norman Golb, who disagreed with just about everything most other Qumran scholars had to say. The trial was thus eagerly anticipated as the scholarly equivalent of a steel-cage match between the Dead Sea Scroll rebels and the Dead Sea Scroll establishment. And while the two long days of the trial's direct testimony and cross-examination often proved more tedious than gripping, seats on the hard wooden benches of the spectators' section in the Jerusalem court-room became some of the hottest tickets in town.

Hershel Shanks had no alternative but to defend himself against the lawsuit. Mobilizing his faithful readers for a new crusade to defend intellectual freedom, he announced the establishment of a legal defense fund and voiced his objections to both the aggressive tactics employed by Qimron's lawyers and the very contention (in light of the wide circulation of the pirated MMT transcription and its previous publication by Kapera in Poland) that the text had never been published before. Particularly galling to Shanks was Qimron's claim that he owned the copyright on the transcription. For Shanks, this claim was laughable. Copyright implied some act of inspiration and creativity, and if Qimron's transcription included correctly restored words and letters, the inspiration and creativity was completely that of the ancient author, *not* Elisha Qimron.

In coldly translating his scholarly work into property rights that had a definable monetary value, Qimron was attempting something that the International Team had never, in all of its thirty-eight years of existence, suggested. In the creation of the team in 1953, Père De Vaux and Lankester Harding had hoped to facilitate the editing process by restricting it to a small circle of dependable scholars, who would presumably publish the texts in the *Discoveries in the Judaean Desert* series without expectation of direct personal reward. (The Palestine Archaeological Museum itself received no royalties from the first volumes.) There is no question that the International Team members achieved great professional prestige and, in some cases, professional advancement, but if they sometimes greedily claimed more texts than they could ever publish, if they selfishly held onto those texts while there were plenty of younger scholars who would have eagerly jumped at the chance to work on them, none of them ever—so far as I am aware—considered their reconstructed transcripts to be private property.

If Qimron's suit prevailed in the court in Jerusalem, the official editors' reconstructions of *all* Qumran texts (and by extension, all fragmentary ancient texts discovered in the country) would be regarded as copyrightable, ownable intellectual property. Once the exclusive right of first publication was granted to a scholar (no matter if it was granted through personal connections, under political pressure, or even by a fair evaluation of the skill of the scholar), his or her eventual reconstruction would become a personal possession defendable in a court of law. Thus a dangerous precedent would be established in a determination that Elisha Qimron held the copyright on MMT: For the text to be legally reproduced, it would have to be done with Qimron's express permission. And as a copyright holder he had absolutely no legal requirement to grant that permission to everyone.

Would he be likely to grant that permission to some rival whose theories he despised and whose personal manner he detested? How would he be likely to react to an angry, impolitic letter from someone like Robert Eisenman? What would then happen to the ideal of open discussion of ideas among the fellowship of scholars? These were precisely the questions that Shanks now used to formulate a new campaign for academic freedom. "If anything is worse than refusing to allow the public to see the photographs of the fragments," he insisted in a *BAR* editorial in the autumn, "it is giving exclusive rights in a transcription of the ancient text to the scholar who transcribes it."

The Dead Sea Scroll story had taken many strange twists since the sudden good fortune of Ahmad Muhammed, Khalil Musa, and Muhammed edh-Dhib in the winter of 1946–47, but none of the reversals of fortune was as ironic as this. What would Père De Vaux or Lankester Harding, both faithful partisans of the Hashemite Kingdom of Jordan, have thought of the idea that the exclusive rights of the International Team members would eventually be confirmed in a court of law in the State of Israel—with arguments, petitions, and summations delivered in modern Hebrew, presided over by a judge who readily admitted that she had taken the case because it concerned the heritage of the People of Israel?

Neither Eisenman nor Robinson was present at the trial;

Shanks had from the beginning taken full responsibility for the Publisher's Foreword, ready and determined to argue that Dead Sea Scroll texts did not belong to Qimron or to any individual scholar, but were the intellectual legacy of the entire world. For Shanks, this legal battle was now about more than free access to the Dead Sea Scrolls; it had become a struggle for the free interplay of ancient literature and modern ideas. Unfortunately, neither Shanks nor his lawyers could persuade Judge Dorner to sympathize with that transcendent ideal.

The first witness was Magen Broshi, curator of the Shrine of the Book and member of the Scrolls Oversight Committee, who explained to the court how he had first introduced Qimron to Strugnell around 1980; how Strugnell had been utterly stymied in his study of MMT owing to his lack of halakhic understanding; and how Qimron had spent ten years of his life toiling over the fragments of the various copies of MMT in order to assemble the reconstructed text. When asked about the historical significance of the manuscript, Broshi had no doubt that Qimron had divined its true context, and he asserted—in an imaginative, if implausible, speculation—that if the contents of the text had not been revealed by others and Qimron had written a book for the general public about it, it might well have sold tens of thousands of copies by now. It was an assertion that strained even a willing suspension of disbelief. This, about an ancient text that contained no sex, violence, or heretical secrets—by a scholar whose specialty was historical grammar and whose writing style was as dry as the Judean wilderness. As Eisenman's attorney Amos Hausner later implied pointedly during his summation, MMT was not Masada and Elisha Qimron was no Yigael Yadin.

Then came Professor Yaacov Sussmann, Qimron's long-time associate, with another story to tell. Sussmann rehearsed the significance of Qimron's work and MMT's interpretation: as precious evidence of halakhic discussion in the Hasmonean period. The irony is that everyone in the courtroom accepted that opinion as a definitive "scientific" explanation, a matter of indisputable fact. But at issue here was not history but money. Sussmann raised eyebrows throughout the courtroom when he asserted just how significant he believed Qimron's monetary loss to have been from the whole MMT affair. Its premature publication, Sussmann claimed, had robbed Qimron of acclaim and thereby damaged his reputation. And since—Sussmann maintained in an enormous exaggeration—first-rank scholars with international reputations could earn as much as $5,000–$10,000 per lecture, Qimron's loss was obvious.

The sideshow went on for two full days from morning until late in the evening, with Qimron offering his heartrending story of a life of privation in the name of scholarly dedication and how he now felt that his life's work had been stolen from him and his world had collapsed. Yet it was Shanks himself who sealed his own fate, being unblinkingly candid about his intentions and his beliefs. Admitting that he had made a mistake in not acknowledging Qimron's contribution and in not paying enough attention to the restored words between the square brackets, he refused to concede that Qimron could claim any copyright. If any copyright should be granted, Shanks suggested, it should be granted to the Teacher of Righteousness. At this point, Judge Dorner directly intervened to ask Shanks what was perhaps the single most telling question: If he had known about the amount of painstaking work that went into Qimron's work of transcription and restoration, would he still have published the text? Shanks could have been contrite. He could have taken the easy way out and told everyone in the small courtroom what they wanted to hear. But it is to the credit of Hershel Shanks—especially in light of the later cost and humiliation—that he stated plainly that, under the same circumstances, he would certainly do it again.

The forty-four-page judgment issued by Judge Dorner on March 30 could hardly have been more stinging. "This judge obviously didn't like me," Shanks later told me in a breathtaking understatement, "and had no sympathy for the campaign." Although Dorner acknowledged that Qimron's losses of book royalties and lecture fees were entirely hypothetical, she awarded him the maximum of the equivalent of $7,400 in punitive damages, because she resented the fact that Shanks saw this publication as part of an ethical battle and refused to acknowledge the damage he had caused Qimron. In addition, she awarded Qimron the equivalent of $29,600 for mental anguish, which was the largest ever awarded in Israel for a copyright case. Shanks would also be liable for about $18,500 for Qimron's legal fees. The tone of the judgment against Shanks was openly critical and the sums were just large enough to be painful for the Biblical Archaeology Society. Yet even worse for the future of Qumran scholarship, was the fact that Judge Dorner significantly expanded the legal copyrights of the editorial team.

Despite Shanks's contention that a text, once published, could be used freely by other scholars as the essential foundation for further scholarly discussion and research, Judge Dorner ruled that "There is no evidential support for the scholarly convention, and even if there were, there would be no support in law. Publication does not cancel copyright. Neither law nor custom allow the unauthorized reproduction of material that has already been published. And when it is legally used, it must be used as a quotation, citing the original author." What all this meant, of course, was that the first editor of a text could control its future use. Thus coldly turning her back on her avowed interest in the shared heritage of the People of Israel, she cast into doubt the new regime of open access that Shanks had fought so hard to achieve. Qimron was now in a position to sue anyone who published unauthorized transcriptions of MMT that resembled his own. Rumors spread of his intention to sue Abegg and Wacholder and Eisenman and Wise.

If you want to talk about a chilling effect, this was certainly one. The ominous mix of copyright law and Qumran scholarship was a subtle way of preserving the hierarchy of power, by making the publication of alternative reconstructions of Qumran texts by any outsiders a matter of some legal sensitivity. With copyright now an issue, an unauthorized editor would have to prove that he or she was completely unaware of the official editor's views on a particular document—and that would be impossible in the small world of Qumran scholarship. Scrolls editor-in-chief Emanuel Tov, reacting to Judge Dorner's decision, was clearly gratified that the critics and usurpers had been put in their place. "This will serve as a precedent for the future," he declared to *The New York Times* correspondent Joel Greenberg. "It justifies the work of our team, and I hope that other people planning to make improper use of our group's material will now think twice."

If Hershel Shanks had been put in his place, at least temporarily, Robert Eisenman continued to be ostracized. The reviews by Qumran scholars of *The Dead Sea Scrolls Uncovered* continued to be vicious, and his historical ideas continued to be dismissed out of hand. In late May, when I spoke with Tov about the progress of the publications project, he expressed clear regret that the uproar of the previous few years had ever occurred. "I think that in many ways it would be much better for us had this not taken place," he told me, with a definitiveness I doubted. "I have a feeling, or I know, I would say that all of us members of the team would have done exactly the same scholarly work and in a much better way had these external disturbances not taken place."

There is no question that Tov has succeeded in organizing and supervising the work of the publications project in a manner that will ensure the publication of all the remaining Qumran Cave 4 material within just a few years. Already, several new volumes of the *Discoveries in the Judaean Desert* series are in advanced stages of preparation. It is his hope that all the material will be submitted to him by 1997. In sharp contrast to the wide variation in length and detail of the earlier Qumran publications, Tov has tried to establish uniform guidelines—at least in the style of transcription, translation, and commentary—for the material to be received from the dozens of scholars in Europe, America, and Israel who have been allotted unpublished texts. And now, in an age of personal computers and desktop publishing, he has been able to prepare camera-ready pages of scroll texts and commentary to be sent directly to Oxford University Press.

Yet as editor-in-chief, Emanuel Tov still clings to the idea that a select fraternity of scrolls scholars, whose experience and expertise are entirely in paleography and biblical studies, are the only scholars qualified to speak with authority about the scrolls—even if they are relatively isolated from developments in the wider disciplines of social history, sociology, and historical anthropology. For all that he has achieved, Tov still seems resentful of the divergent interpretations of outsiders, whom he and his colleagues are quick to brand as mere gadflies or cranks. And when I spoke to him in May 1993, he seemed to have a certain maverick scholar in mind. "See the way it goes in scholarship," he told me, "is if you are writing a wild theory, it's there—you can't eradicate it anymore. The so-called Pierced Messiah, you live with him. I live with him. He never was there. Every journalist asked me about the Pierced Messiah, but he never was there. You can't eradicate him anymore. Had it been the other way around, had we first seen an organized, good publication of that particular fragment and had the theory of the Pierced Messiah appeared afterwards, it would be much easier for scholars to say, 'Who cares? Let's read the organized, good scholarly commentary, the first publication of that text by Geza Vermes.' And then you can laugh about what Eisenman thinks."

The scrolls might now be available to all scholars, but the efficient new International Team was still very much the center of power. Despite Hershel Shanks's expensive and exhausting campaign for complete freedom of scroll study; despite John Strugnell's ouster and Robert Eisenman's passionate fight for recognition, the orthodox interpretation of the Dead Sea Scrolls had prevailed.

Looking back on the long, twisting course of the Dead Sea Scrolls story, we've come to a situation where access to the documents is open, but the acceptability of new ideas is strictly limited. Since the great upheaval in 1991, many new documents have become known to the scholarly public, but precious little progress has been made in understanding the literature of Qumran as an expression of protest, as an alternative vision of the Judean past and future that was discredited and forgotten—not because it was morally or spiritually inferior, but because it was apparently part of a wider movement that was systematically and coldly destroyed in the suppression of the Jewish Revolt by the legions of Rome.

The Qumran literature, in its militant, xenophobic intensity, offers us a glimpse at the mindset of an ancient people on the receiving end of Roman oppression and exploitation. It may help us to hear the silenced voices of the many peoples subjugated, sold into slavery, and culturally marginalized by the Grandeur That Was Rome. The chief obstacle to understanding that message is a scholarly frame of mind in which a self-interested fear of straying too far from the respectable consensus masquerades as caution and objectivity. The study of the Dead Sea Scrolls is a potentially sensitive matter. Millions of Jews and Christians all over the world have been brought up from childhood with the traditional histori- cal outlooks of their respective religions in which each is seen as the inevitable and purest expression of God's intervention in human history. In the recognition that apocalypticism and mes- sianism were not merely theological phenomena but expressions of intensifying popular protest against economic dislocation and political disenfranchisement, the Dead Sea Scrolls can uncover for us another source of our shared western religious tradition. Who can deny the resemblance between the rage-filled visions of the War of the Sons of Light Against the Sons of Darkness and the fervent calls for jihad among the scattered cells of Radical Islam? Who can deny the messianic and eschatological fervor that led David Koresh and his followers to create their own fiery apoca- lypse at Mount Carmel in Waco, Texas, as a final act of defiance toward the Sons of Darkness who had surrounded their commu- nity?

Up to now, most Dead Sea scholars have had no time or no interest in universal religious behaviors. They have prided them- selves, first and foremost, on being specialists in paleography and textual analysis. Yet the Dead Sea Scrolls are not just raw material for learned dissertations: They are that message that has been left for us in the hope that we would be able to read. In their apocalyp- tic message, the scrolls give a voice to a group that felt dispossessed and disenfranchised in a world turned upside down. They express a rage against invaders and contempt for collaborators, who are only interested in personal gain. In reaction and in defense, they wrap their community in a defensive cocoon of national laws and traditions. And they express the timeless dreams of the powerless for a day when this upside-down world will be righted—when the wicked will suffer, not be rewarded, for their wickedness, and when the poor, the scorned, and the downtrodden will be recognized as the Elect of God.

History has shown that these are all pretty dangerous notions when they are put into action. In this upside-down world, the weak and the dispossessed will almost always be defeated by the strong. It is the fate of true religious protest to exist on a knife edge, sustainable in all its passion for only a brief moment before its adherents must submit either to compromise or death. Yet the Judean messianic movement, with its seemingly impossible quest for the Kingdom of God on earth, has never been entirely silenced. And despite the inclination of most scrolls scholars to dissect, analyze, and render the Dead Sea Scrolls utterly harmless, those thousands of scraps of darkened inscribed parchment recovered from the caves of the Judean Wilderness bear eloquent witness to the timeless rage against injustice and oppression that lies at the hidden heart of both Judaism and Christianity.

The courtyards, cisterns, and workshops of the Qumran settlement are now just sunbaked, tumbledown ruins, gawked at by tourists and argued over by scholars, but in their silence they symbolize a powerful yearning for independence that was violently and tragically extinguished by the legions of Rome. The ancient settlement, perched on the high white plateau by the Dead Sea shore, was, for almost two centuries, a living link in an ever-changing network of Judean and Galilean towns, villages, neighborhoods, brotherhoods, and sisterhoods, which could not and would not ever calmly accept foreign rule. It was an amorphous movement composed of zealots, idealists, soldiers-of-fortune, visionaries, farmers, priests, and servants who had watched a few fellow Judeans prosper at the expense of all the others by learning to play by the new economic, social, and political rules. Though their rage may have been phrased in biblical-style poetry or apocalyptic oracles, it was nonetheless powerful political ideology. It gave voice to the faith that no foreign oppressor—no matter how technologically advanced or aggressive—could escape total destruction on Judgment Day.

Their vision of the future was precise and coldly cruel. God had decreed that there would soon be a Day of Vengeance, and nothing—neither the tortured screams of the dying nor the sickening gore of bloody, hacked bodies—would deter the Sons of Light from fulfilling their God-given destiny. Every aspect of their equipment and tactics was set out in meticulous detail, from the permitted ages of soldiers and camp functionaries, to the precise dimensions of the swords and shields the soldiers would carry, to the engraved inscriptions on the battlefield trumpets that would sound the call for advance. After being called back from the Wilderness of the Nations, the Sons of Light would be arrayed in battle against the army of Belial on the outskirts of Jerusalem. In the enemy ranks would be the same roster of oppressors and bad neighbors that the Judean highlanders had suffered since the coming of Rome. Among the Sons of Darkness would be "the troop of Edom and Moab, and the sons of Ammon" (the Greek settlers and Nabatean traders of Transjordan), "the army of the dwellers of Philistia" (Hellenized merchants and financiers of Gaza, Ascalon, and the other port cities), "the Kittim of Asshur" (the Roman legions in Syria who were sent southward to put down the sporadic disturbances in Judea), and local collaborators and turncoats whom they called "the offenders against the covenant."

What is so striking in this description is that it features not a vague, mythic biblical encounter but a strangely down-to-earth plan for a great liberating war. On the appointed day of battle, the army of the Sons of Light shall be arrayed in seven formations. At a divine signal, the company of angels would join the Sons of Light—"going forth for a carnage in battle"—to annihilate the spirits and Sons of Darkness. Three times the Sons of Light would press hard on their enemies, almost overcoming their defenses. Three times the Sons of Darkness would counterattack, sending the Sons of Light into a retreat. But on the seventh clash between the two armies, "the great hand of God shall subdue Belial and all the angels of his dominion." And the Sons of Darkness—Romans, hostile neighbors, and local collaborators—would be hacked down, to the last one.

The victory in the Battle of Jerusalem would be just the first step in conquest. Following the first encounter outside Jerusalem, the Sons of Light would march south and defeat the Romans in the rich province of Egypt, and then retrace their steps and wage war against the lands of the north. In the first year of campaigning, they would conquer the headwaters of the Tigris and the Euphrates (the modern Syria and Iraq). During the next year they would conquer Turkey, and in the year after that they would subdue the Armenians and the other peoples of the Caucasus. According to their plan, they would then press on to conquer the mountainous regions of Iran, Afghanistan, and Pakistan, all the way to India.

Having thus secured the Middle East and access to the Indian Ocean, the Sons of Light would then break up into independent units and spend twenty years subduing Africa and Europe as well. These were all steps to the eventual goal—the destruction of the Roman Empire with its detestable methods of exploitation and penchant for idolatry. The destruction of that evil empire would be, according to the War Scroll, the turning point in the history of all mankind:

> This shall be a time of salvation for the people of God, an age of dominion for all the members of His company, and of everlasting destruction for all the company of Satan. The confusion of the sons of Japheth shall be [great] and Assyria shall fall unsuccoured. The dominion of the Kittim shall come to an end and iniquity shall be vanquished, leaving no remnant; [for the sons of] darkness there shall be no escape.

This was not idle daydreaming but an ideological preparation for rebellion. And when the time came for action, there were many who answered the call. In the spring of 66 c.e., in an atmosphere of intensifying violence, the actions of procurator Gessius Florus in confiscating funds from the Temple treasury and ordering his soldiers to attack the Temple provoked a violent response from the people of Jerusalem. The small Roman force was driven out of the city and the rebel leadership and their priestly allies declared the independence of Judea with an act of enormous symbolism: an immediate halt to the hated daily sacrifice for the Roman emperor. Here was certainly a giant step along the divine timetable— the prohibition of Gentile sacrifices had been prominent themes in works like MMT and the Temple Scroll. How far the rebellion was being guided by a single doctrine is impossible to know. But the worldview of the Qumran community was certainly typical of, if not central to, the theological rationalization of the revolt.

The signs of redemption must have seemed unmistakable through the first four years of the revolt. In the autumn of 66 c.e., Cestius Gallus, the Roman governor of Syria, marched southward with his armies to quell the rebellion. After initial victories, Cestius's forces were defeated in open battle by a makeshift muster of Jewish volunteers, and in a panicked retreat from Jerusalem the fleeing Romans were massacred. Just as in the detailed vision of the War Scroll, the Sons of Light seemed to have been aided by heaven-sent forces. And thus it must have seemed with the arrival of General Vespasian with an even larger army in the spring of 67 c.e. Even though Vespasian's forces quickly quashed the rebellion in Galilee and moved relentlessly southward, reducing rebel strongholds and slowly capturing back large areas of the country, he was unable to mount an attack on Jerusalem. In the spring of 68, his forces made their way down the Jordan Valley, and it was during this campaign—according to De Vaux—that the settlement at Qumran was destroyed and burned.

That attack did not necessarily mean the end of habitation in the area. It did not even necessitate the final hiding of the scrolls. For God seemed to have intervened once more just at the time that Vespasian was about to move for a final attack on Jerusalem. In the late summer of 68 c.e., Vespasian received word of the death of Emperor Nero—and for the next year, he was too deeply involved in the internal politics of the empire to make further inroads against the Judean rebels. It was only in the spring of 70 c.e. that Vespasian—now emperor of Rome—empowered his son Titus to undertake the reduction of Jerusalem. Within three months of death and destruction, the Temple was in ruins and the once beautiful city of Jerusalem destroyed.

How could God permit such a thing? Were the heaven-sent revelations that had nurtured a sense of national independence so mistaken? Here and there small groups of rebels apparently maintained the armed resistance long after the outcome of the war was clear. In this atmosphere of desperate, doomed resistance, the last of the scroll jars may have been deposited in the caves around Qumran. By this time, the only possible escape from the Kittim and the other Sons of Darkness was in remote places in the wilderness, hidden desert enclaves. The last of them to fall was the fortress of Masada—occupied by a group of rebels who apparently preferred sure resurrection in the World to Come as self-made martyrs than the certain prospect of Roman execution or slavery. How could the signs of imminent redemption have been so completely misread? The scroll of the Songs of the Sabbath sacrifice—found at both Masada and Qumran—expresses the mystery of how the Wicked are allowed to triumph and the righteous condemned to defeat:

> ... From the God of knowledge (comes) all that exists forever, [and from] His [plan]s (come) all the eternally appointed. He produces the former things in their appointed times, and the latter things in their seasons. None among those who know the [wonderfully] revealed things can comprehend them before He makes them. When He makes them, none of [the doers of righteous]ness can understand His plan; for they are His glorious works.

In Rome, the people had never before witnessed such a triumph. Crowds lined the city's main thoroughfares from early in the morning on this summer day in 71 C.E. Slave and free, men, women, and children, enjoying an official holiday from their labors, jammed together laughing, singing, cheering, and occasionally surging forward to hiss and jeer the villains and to celebrate their empire's greatest victory. Hours before, in the predawn darkness, thousands of foot soldiers and cavalry troops had been marshalled in parade formation on the Field of Mars by the Tiber. Their helmets, breastplates, and greaves were finely polished. Their arms and standards proudly bearing the image of the emperor were decorated with campaign trophies and were ready for display.

With the first streaks of light appearing in the sky across the river, the bald and corpulent Emperor Vespasian and his handsome son Titus, wreathed and dressed in crimson togas, took their seats on ivory thrones among the senators and civic leaders, who had gathered in the shadow of a looming marble colonnade. Fate had favored the empire. The Jews' God was defeated and humbled by Roman skill and might.

A booming cheer went up from the formations of tough veterans recruited from all across the empire as they caught a glimpse of their commanders. Vespasian rose and motioned for silence. With his son Titus beside him, he recited the time-honored prayers to the gods and goddesses who ensured Rome's great fortune and prosperity. It was a spectacle of naked arrogant power and violence, masquerading as divine favor. Latter-day tyrants would attempt to emulate this splendor in places like Nuremberg and Red Square. But none would ever taste of victory so complete and so longlasting. The world had entered a period of "peace" because of the ultimate victory of tyrants; the unimaginable had happened. Evil had triumphed over righteousness. And on this day, after the troops had been given their morning provisions and the sacrifices had been made to the gods at the Porta Triumphalis, the Emperor and Titus donned the robes of triumphant generals, mounted gilded chariots, and drove off toward the Temple of Jupiter on the Capitol to bask in the adulation, admiration, and raucous cheers of the people of Rome.

There has been no empire on earth that has succeeded so thoroughly in its exploitation, and which survives today behind its mask of strong foundations and impressive aqueducts. Yet engineering marvels, elaborate law codes, and architectural orders are in themselves no more valuable than trains running on time. For the Roman Empire that swept over all of southern and western Europe, forming the basis of its civilization, conceals within its heart a horrible genocidal mission of conquest, slavery, and cruelty that is all the more evil for the skill with which it is concealed. Behind every bank building with its Roman style, behind every aqueduct, and behind every Latin terminology lies the cruelty of power that would allow no other consciousness or sensibility to exist independently. The triumphal processions may now be over, but the triumph of that great power endures.

For the far-flung peoples and cultures annihilated with gory, inhuman relish in the gladiatorial arenas, mines, and slave galleys, Rome was a thousand-year Reich that succeeded. It was a tyrannical power that had no Allied Expeditionary Force to attack it; no battle of El Alamein to stop its progress in North Africa; no Battle of Britain to prevent its conquest of Londinium; no Normandy Invasion to roll back its conquest of Gaul. Over the centuries, the peoples of its empire adapted themselves to a kneeling submission or died resisting its power. Our modern cultures and our modern religions have been shaped by the experience of Rome. And if Judaism and Christianity initially represented a force of resistance to oppression and suffering, they have come down to us in only those forms that were permitted, or at least tolerated, by the rulers of the Roman Empire. All other systems of belief were destined to be destroyed.

During the years following the fall of Masada and the end of the war in Judea, the Tenth Legion was permanently stationed in Jerusalem, defiling yet further the ruined city and Temple with its detestable boar's head emblem and the smoke of its soldiers' pagan sacrifices. Tens of thousands of Judean captives were shipped off as slaves across the Mediterranean. The former Judean aristocrats and civic leaders who had surrendered and were deemed politically harmless were resettled in specially designated areas, where their actions could be closely monitored. Priests were sent northward to the village of Gophna; scribes and others were relocated at the former royal estate town of Iamnia, or Yavne, on the Mediterranean coast. And since the Emperor now claimed vast tracts of valuable land in the Jordan Valley and as far south as the rich oasis of En-Geddi, there was now little chance that any independent community could exist in the vicinity of Qumran.

Throughout the countryside of Judea—over which the Roman forces had marched, foraged, and destroyed the military power of the rebels—there were enormous disruptions in traditional patterns of daily life and trade. The years of famine, the slow consolidation of small farms into large plantations, and the swelling of the urban populations had changed Judea's time-honored rural landscape forever. And now, in the wake of so much killing and destruction, the prophetic images of fertility and prosperity in a restored Land of Israel must have seemed hopelessly distant. The belief in the imminent coming of the messiah and the Kingdom of God was no longer a spur to action. With Judea under the heel of the newly reinforced Roman administration, those distant dreams must rather have been a source of confusion and despair.

The most devastating change, of course, was the sudden termination of the Temple service, whose strict observance had for so long been regarded as the primary instrument for national redemption—in its meticulously observed rituals and absolute separation from all forms of idolatry, and all that the worship of Caesar and the gods and goddesses had come to represent. The Romans had recognized that the Temple of Jerusalem was as much a political symbol of the independence of the Judeans as a place of worship for just another bizarre oriental cult. Yet now no sacrifices could be offered on an altar that had been defiled and destroyed by Roman soldiers. And to add insult to injury, the Romans now made all Jews pay for the rebelliousness of Judea. For the first time in all of Jewish history, both Diaspora Jews and Judeans were forced to pay an annual tax of two drachmae—equivalent to the yearly half-shekel long payable to the Temple—to the temple of Jupiter Capitolinus in Rome. All Jews had become rebels in the eyes of the empire, and the land of the Jews a completely subjected country—*Iudaea capta*—as Vespasian's newly struck commemorative coins arrogantly proclaimed.

Yet if the god of Rome had apparently triumphed over the God of Israel, there were still some in Judea who believed that the victory was only temporary, just one last test for the faithful. If the complex treasure lists and figures recorded on the Copper Scroll are any indication, surviving priests who were schooled in the rituals of the Temple continued to collect voluntary offerings and compulsory tithes, in the secure belief that God would miraculously restore his House if only His people kept the faith. The Temple ritual now had to be kept secret; the gifts collected according to biblical law had to be hidden throughout the countryside. The recent destruction of the Temple by the Romans was perhaps only setting the stage for an even more miraculous rebuilding—as documents like the Temple Scroll had always maintained.

In these times of near genocide and Roman conquest, perfect faith in the down-to-earth reality of the messianic future was hard to maintain. And it is not surprising that many Judeans, who had survived the revolt and had evaded a life of enslavement, began to turn to less dangerous religious alternatives. For Romanized Judean aristocrats like Josephus, the verdict of history had to be accepted: God Himself had decreed the victory of Rome. For him, Jewish history had culminated in a great period of (sinful) rebellion which had cost the Jews the religious independence they had enjoyed under the beneficent tolerance of the emperors. Josephus had no suggestions for the future; he was merely a political propagandist for the Flavians—Vespasian and Titus—who had spared his life, so he informed his readers, in gratitude for his prediction that Vespasian would become emperor. Josephus had proclaimed that the crusty old veteran of the Roman conquest of Britain and now Judea, was the "star from Jacob, the scepter from Judah" mentioned in the biblical prophecies.

What sheer blasphemy that kind of talk must have seemed to those Judeans who were ready for martyrdom to help bring on the messiah. How could a Jew dare to suggest that the leader of the Sons of Darkness was anointed by God? Yet Josephus was not alone in his craven pandering to Rome's power. Rabbinic legend has it that Rabbi Yohanan ben Zakkai, leader of the sages at Yavne, made a similar prediction about Vespasian's glorious destiny. And under the patronage, or at least tolerance, of the Roman Occupying Forces, Rabbi Yohanan ben Zakkai became one of the founders of a new kind of Israelite religion, enacting legislation that made Judaism into a religion without a Temple—in which local, not centralized, courts were empowered to make religious decisions without the recourse or even need for Temple sacrifices or priests.

We have all been brought up to think that modern Judaism and Christianity represent the culmination of a natural, almost inevitable, evolution from the earlier Israelite cult of live sacrifice and Temple offerings to universal faiths of prayer, study, and piety. Yet the new religion established by the rabbinic sages settled in the Roman reeducation camp of Yavne survived not because it was superior or more spiritual but because—in Roman eyes—it was tolerable. If the Copper Scroll is to be taken seriously, it is a clear indication that many Judeans rejected the religious innovations being discussed in Yavne. The people who contributed gold and silver to the priests to hide them in the tombs, water channels, caves, and tunnels of Judea had no interest in changing their ways; the need for a Temple remained a central fact of their national existence. Even though its sanctuary and courts were destroyed and the campfires of the Roman camp fouled the air of the once sacred city, faith in the Temple did not die.

The Copper Scroll may have been one of the last documents of Temple-centered Judaism, but the political implications of its insistence on national centralization led to its suppression as an element in Judean politics. The Copper Scroll was deposited, never to be reclaimed, sometime in the late first century C.E., before the messianic, Temple-oriented Israelite religion was effectively terminated by rabbinic legislation and the force of Roman arms. And in a way, the early rabbis of Yavne and the Roman commanders became the unlikely partners in the creation of an acceptable faith for the people of Israel, in which the demand for political as well as spiritual independence no longer played a role.

For a while, the image of the Temple and its political and religious significance continued to smolder beneath the surface— flaring up a generation later with the Diaspora revolt of 115–117 C.E. and then again in its last major explosion in Judea in the Bar Kokhba revolt of 132–35 C.E. Yet the expectation of an imminent Holy War between Light and Darkness gradually faded. Over the centuries, the rabbinic tradition did its best to reduce the image of the coming messiah to a harmless slogan or folk custom—like the leaving of an extra cup of wine on the seder table and the door left ajar for Elijah the Prophet. In the case of Christianity, the original messianic gospel underwent an even more thorough reworking, with the national savior transformed by the Apostle Paul into a transcendent being—with faith taking the place of the meticulous observance of ritual law. Christianity, moving from its Judean base to the wider Mediterranean world, offered divine grace through a transcendent Davidic messiah. Rabbinic Judaism, accepting the destruction of the Temple as an historical event that could not be reversed by human efforts, dispensed with the need for Temple sacrifices, rearranged and reinterpreted Jewish law for synagogue worship, scriptural interpretation, and universal purity codes.

Over the centuries, some of the old messianic themes, long dormant, rose to the surface, appearing in various forms in Judaism, Christianity, and Islam. Visions of a hidden messiah appearing to lead the long-suffering poor in a Holy War against the wicked served as the spark for popular unrest and sometimes hysteria; modern reinterpretations of biblical prophecies identified kings, popes, and sultans as the final embodiments of evil, soon to be swept away by the unfolding of God's secret plan for history. It is uncertain to what extent these recurrent themes were inherited or independently reinvented. Perhaps the Jewish Karaites of the Middle Ages—religious dissidents and bitter opponents of Rabbinic Judaism—did actually come into possession of some scrolls from the Dead Sea region in the chance discovery of the ninth century C.E. reported by the Nestorian Patriarch Timotheus. It was, after all, in the geniza of the Cairo synagogue, long used by Karaites, that copies of the Damascus Document were first found. There may have been other such discoveries, but none are recorded. While religious orthodoxy eventually triumphed, the message of the Judean messianic movement was suppressed and driven underground.

Then, in the winter of 1946–47, came the discovery of ancient manuscripts by three Taamireh bedouin in a cave on the western shore of the Dead Sea. And in the Dead Sea Scrolls, we have once again come into possession of a vast collection of ancient religious literature, polemic, and prophecy that was composed, collected, and studied with the absolute faith that the Kingdom of God was at hand. It was—and is—a message of direct challenge to the forces of empire, a message of resistance and independence, capable of summoning all the puritanical rage, deadly violence, and disastrous defeat that the rebellion of subject people against imperial masters almost always entails. In their own time, the people of the scrolls were unable to bring about the reign of the messiah and the establishment of the Kingdom of God. Yet in the hundreds of documents they left behind them, in their hope for a world renewed by righteousness and divine order, the forgotten, radical message of the Dead Sea Scrolls—even today—lives on.

BIBLIOGRAPHICAL NOTES

CHAPTER 1: A WAY IN THE WILDERNESS

For recent studies of the period immediately after the suppression of the Jewish Revolt, see Goodblatt, "The Jews of Eretz-Israel"; Smallwood, *The Jews Under Roman Rule*, chapter 13; and Martin Goodman, *The Ruling Class*, chapter 10. For the Romans' use of resettlement camps for surrendered Judeans, see Alon, "Rabban Johanan B. Zakkai's Removal to Jabneh."

My account of the deposit of the scrolls in Cave 1 is intentionally speculative, but the distinction between this cave, with its jars and complete manuscripts, and other caves at Qumran such as Cave 4, which might have served as a community library or *geniza*, has been noted by many scholars. The highly fragmentary and deteriorated state of the Cave 4 texts and the very dubious identification of the large holes observed in the walls of the cave as anchors for the supports of "shelves" make it likely, in my opinion, that this cave was in fact a *geniza*. In any case, its closeness to the site of the settlement makes it unlikely that the scrolls were completely unconnected with the settlement as some recent theories have suggested. For a survey and evaluation of the theories of De Vaux, Golb, and Donceel, see Shanks, "The Qumran Settlement." But for another possibility—that of a dual use of the site, as both a military/ commercial outpost and a communal settlement—see the references to Bar-Adon below.

The identification of Khirbet Qumran as Secacah was first proposed by John Allegro, *The Treasure of the Copper Scroll.* For De Vaux's suggestion of Ir Ha-Melach, see his *Archaeology and the Dead Sea Scrolls.* On the later exploration of the region and the identification of sites along the north-western coast of the Dead Sea, see Bar-Adon, *Excavations in the Judean Desert.*

I am also indebted to Bar-Adon for the hypothesis that the settle-ment at Khirbet Qumran was, in fact, established as part of the royal building program of the Hasmoneans—*not* as a refuge from Judean soci-ety, as most scholars still claim. See the archaeological findings of Bar Adon in "Hasmonean Fortifications," and the historical evidence for precisely this type of military settlement in Bar-Kochva, "Manpower, Eco-nomics, and Internal Strife." It is intriguing that Reich has seen the sud-den appearance of ritual baths at Gezer (which are also so prominent at Qumran) as a sign of the official Hasmonean settlement policy; see his "Archaeological Evidence." For the wider historical implications of Has-monean expansion in the Dead Sea Region (and the unlikeliness of its being a suitable place for anti-Hasmonean refuge in this period), see Fo-erster, "On the Conquests of John Hyrcanus," and Stern, "Judea and Her Neighbors." All the geographical arguments against the strategic importance of the Qumran site (i.e., the apparent impossibility of over-land communications southward, owing to the obstruction of the Ras Feshka promontory), are obviated if Qumran is seen as a point on a net-work of water-borne commercial exchange across or along the coasts of the Dead Sea.

In my reconstruction of the history of the Qumran Community, I have made a crucial distinction between the use of the settlement in Level I (an officially sponsored fortress or border settlement) and Level II (an independently founded religious community—with its clear politi-cal orientation). There is no hard archaeological evidence that the initial level of occupation was in any sense religious. Communal yes, but not necessarily any more religious than Maccabean settlements like those at Gezer or Beth Zur. Note also the evidence of a concerted Hasmonean building program in this region in Netzer, "The Hasmonean Palaces in Eretz-Israel." Thus, the destruction of the Qumran settlement at the time of the civil war between the pro-Hasmonean supporters of Aristob-ulus II or Antigonus and the forces of Herod makes sense—as does the reoccupation of the site only after the death of Herod. This crucial politi-cal dimension of the occupational history of the site has been overlooked by all Qumran scholars except Robert Eisenman. The pro-Maccabean orientation of the Qumran community is, of course, one of the main arguments of Eisenman's *Maccabees, Zadokites.*

(The statements above were written before publication of the most recent archaeological reassessments of the Khirbet Qumran site. From preliminary press announcements, it seems that both Dr. Jean-Baptiste Humbert of the Ecole Biblique and Dr. Yitzhak Magen, and Director Amir Drori of the Israel Antiquities Authority have uncovered evidence that the settlement's beginnings in the Hasmonean period were unconnected with the activities of the Dead Sea sect. For a brief summary of their preliminary conclusions, see Rabinovich, "Operation Scroll." Additional scholarly discussion of this question will undoubtedly be forthcoming in the near future.)

The identification of the site as *Metzad Hasidim,* The Fortress of Pious Ones, is based on a passing reference in the Wadi Murrabat Bar Kokhba Letters. For the identification and relevant bibliography, see Mor, *The Bar Kokhba Revolt,* p. 137.

On the economic pressures of Herodian and Roman rule in Judea, see Applebaum, "Economic Life," and Goodman, "The Problem of Debt," and *The Ruling Class of Judea.* Although the archaeological evidence for the growth of economic inequality is obvious in this period (see Netzer "Herod's Building Projects," and Avigad, *Discovering Jerusalem,* for example), there has yet to be a serious integration of the archaeological data with the literary evidence for serious social breakdown during this period.

On the messianic and apocalyptic movements of the first century, see especially Hengel, *The Zealots;* Crossan, *The Historical Jesus,* especially chapter 10, and Horsley, *Jesus and the Spiral of Violence.* On the social implications of apocalypticism, see the classic work of Norman Cohn, *The Pursuit of the Millennium,* and his more recent *Cosmos, Chaos, and the World to Come.*

By the "consensus" reconstruction of the history and nature of the Qumran Community and the significance of the Dead Sea Scrolls, I refer to the classic works of Cross, *Ancient Library;* Milik, *Ten Years of Discovery;* Burrows, *The Dead Sea Scrolls;* Vermes, *The Dead Sea Scrolls in English;* and, of course, De Vaux, *Archaeology and the Dead Sea Scrolls.* See also the important, and in some respects distinctive, reconstruction of the sect's history and theology in Talmon, *The World of Qumran from Within.* Note particularly Talmon's reticence to accept any identifications of the Qumran sect with groups known from Josephus or other historical sources.

The recent controversy over the control of the scrolls has been most thoroughly reported in *Biblical Archaeological Review.* For other perspectives on the early phases of the story, see Baigent and Leigh, *The Dead Sea Scrolls Deception;* Ron Rosenbaum, "Riddle of the Scrolls"; Stephen Fried, "Scroll Man"; and Rabinovich, "Dead Sea Fever."

My account of the 1992 New York Dead Sea Scrolls conference is based on the notes I took and the interviews I conducted there. The text of the scholars' letter of protest against *The Dead Sea Scrolls Uncovered* was published in *Biblical Archaeology Review* 19:2 (March/April 1993): 66–67. Schiffman's statement of condemnation is contained in his "Ethical Issues."

CHAPTER 2: DISCOVERY AT QUMRAN

Cross's account of the original discovery of the scrolls appears in his *Ancient Library*, p. 4.

On the history and cultural ecology of the Taamireh, see Shmueli, "The Desert Frontier," and Couroyer, "Histoire d'une tribu semi-nomade de Palestine." On their earlier archaeological experience and activities, see a clear reference in Vincent, "Une grotte." The story of the repeated offers of the bedouin to the workers at the Palestine Potash Works was told to me by the late Arieh Chechik of Jerusalem in the mid-1970s. The work of the Taamireh with Neuville was described to me in an interview with Professor Jean Perrot.

By far the most complete account of the discovery of Qumran Cave 1 is found in Trever, *The Untold Story* and "When Was Qumran Cave I Discovered?" For another, partially contradictory account, see Brownlee, "Muhammad ed-Deeb's Own Story" and "Edh-Dheeb's Story." In the several cases where there are inconsistencies in the various versions, I have generally followed Trever's extensively researched account of the events.

For a description of early discoveries of manuscripts in the Dead Sea Region, with full bibliographical references, see Rowley, *The Zadokite Fragments*, 22–26, 49–50.

On the Shapira manuscripts, see Silberman, *Digging For God and Country*, chapter 13, and Allegro, *The Shapira Affair*.

My account of Archbishop Samuel's involvement with the Dead Sea Scrolls is based on two long interviews I conducted with him at his home in New Jersey; on his own account, see *The Treasure of Qumran;* and on the other usual sources, including Trever, *The Untold Story*, and Burrows, *The Dead Sea Scrolls*.

On Sukenik's recognition of the importance of the scrolls and the negotiations for their purchase, see Silberman, *A Prophet From Amongst You*, and Yadin, *The Message of the Scrolls*. My account of the involvement of Judah Magnes in the purchase is also based on material in the Central Zionist Archives and Hebrew University Archives.

For the role of the Americans in the early study, photography, and negotiations regarding Archbishop Samuel's scrolls, I have based my account primarily on the detailed chronology in Trever, *The Untold Story;* with additional details from Burrows, *The Dead Sea Scrolls;* Samuel, *The Treasure of Qumran;* and from my interviews with Samuel, Trever, and Cross.

For more details on Yadin's secret purchase of the scrolls, see Silberman, *A Prophet From Amongst You,* chapter 10, with bibliography. For the recent revelation of the role of another character involved in the negotiations with the archbishop, see Isaacs, "The Man Who Bought the Dead Sea Scrolls."

Except where otherwise noted, I have used Geza Vermes's translations of Qumran texts from *The Dead Sea Scrolls in English.* The quotation from the Genesis Apocryphon comes from column 12; the quotations from the Commentary on Habakkuk come from columns 11–12.

On Solomon Schechter and his discoveries in the Cairo *Geniza,* see Bentwich, *Solomon Schechter,* and Levy, "First Dead Sea Scroll." Schechter's own publication of the text appeared as *Fragments of a Zadokite Work.* For a new transcription and commentary, see Broshi, *The Damascus Document Reconsidered,* and for a detailed discussion of conflicting theories about the text over the decades, see Davies, *The Damascus Covenant.*

The quotations from chapter 1 of the Book of Habakkuk come from the Revised Standard Version.

CHAPTER 3: THE INNER CIRCLE

In addition to the personal details and impressions contained in my interviews with Cross and Strugnell, my account of the early activities at the Palestine Archaeological Museum in connection with the scrolls is based on archival material at the Israel Antiquities Authority and on preliminary reports published in *Revue Biblique* and *Biblical Archaeologist.*

For a bibliography and listing of the Cave 4 material published up to 1990, see Fitzmyer, *The Dead Sea Scrolls.* For the listing of the remainder of the Cave 4 material, see Tov, "The Unpublished Qumran Texts." Photographs of the entire collection have been reproduced in Eisenman and Robinson, *A Facsimile Edition,* and Tov, *Microfiche Edition.*

The letter from Sir Thomas Kendrick to Harding is in the administrative archives of the Israel Antiquities Authority.

On the long fascination of Christian scholars with the Essenes long before the discovery of the Dead Sea Scrolls, see, for an early example, Ginsburg, *The Essenes.* On the nineteenth and early twentieth-century fascination with the Essenes, see Beskow, *Strange Tales,* chapter 7. For a highly enlightening survey of the religious biases and/or orientations that have affected the course of Qumran studies, see Schiffman, "Confessionalism."

A basic source on the paleological study of the scrolls and other ancient Hebrew and Aramaic inscriptions is Cross, "The Development of Jewish Scripts." For his evolving ideas of the historical context of the Qumran community, see his *Ancient Library,* "Early History," and "The Historical Context."

Zeitlin's longstanding and long-winded attacks on mainstream scroll scholarship were published in 1948 in the *Jewish Quarterly Review.* Eisenman's critique of the standard dating of the composition of the Qumran biblical commentaries was clearly expressed in *Maccabees, Zadokites,* pp. 28ff.

The basic published source on the Khirbet Qumran excavations (with full bibliography of relevant literature up to the late 1960s) is De Vaux, *Archaeology and the Dead Sea Scrolls.* See also Cross, *The Ancient Library;* Milik, *Ten Years of Discovery,* and Van der Ploeg, *Excavations.* For highly critical evaluations of the Qumran excavations, see Davies, "How Not to Do Archaeology"; Eisenman, *Maccabees,* chapter 8; and Golb, "Khirbet Qumran."

The history of the Rockefeller involvement with the Palestine Archaeological Museum in general and the Dead Sea Scrolls Project in particular can be traced in the administrative archives of the Israel Antiquities Authority and in the Rockefeller Family Archives, Records Group 3 (Rockefeller Family and Associates), Box 40 (Palestine Archaeological Museum File) at the Rockefeller Archive Center. Especially relevant in this connection is correspondence between Professor Carl Kraeling of the University of Chicago and Dana S. Creel of the Rockefeller Foundation.

For Hershel Shanks's 1991 op-ed piece in *The New York Times,* see "Scholars, Scrolls, Secrets."

CHAPTER 4: SECRET MESSIAH

On the complex, contentious, and ever-fascinating issue of messianism in general and of the messianism of the Dead Sea Scrolls in particular, see the collected essays in Charlesworth, *The Messiah;* and Neusner, Green, and Frerichs, *Judaisms and Their Messiahs;* and Collins, *The Apocalyptic Imagination,* pp. 122–126. There are naturally many other sources that could be mentioned, but nearly all of them, in their unquestioning belief that a two-messiah pattern prevailed at Qumran, must be reevaluated in light of the significant body of messianic literature and references in the Cave 4 material. See especially Wise and Tabor, "The Messiah at Qumran," for an enlightening discussion of just how uncertain some of the most time-honored hypotheses of Qumran messianism really are.

For the parallel theological and administrative terms at Qumran and in early Christianity, see Burrows, *The Dead Sea Scrolls,* pp. 111–118; Milik, *Ten Years of Discovery,* pp. 99–101, 142–3; and the collected essays in Stendahl, *The Scrolls and the New Testament.* On the cited quotations regarding the relationship of the Dead Sea Scrolls to Christianity, see Cross, *Ancient Library,* p. 149, n. 6; Burrows, *The Dead Sea Scrolls,* p. 327; Milik, *Ten Years of Discovery,* p. 143; VanderKam, "The Dead Sea Scrolls and Christianity," p. 201.

For a valuable history of the Ecole Biblique et Archéologique in Jerusalem, see Viviano, "Ecole Biblique"; on the role played by its faculty in modern New Testament studies, see Murphy-O'Connor and Taylor, *The Ecole Biblique.*

The Dead Sea Scroll holdings of the Rockefeller Museum are described in detail in Reed, "Survey of the Dead Sea Scrolls," and Tov, "The Unpublished Qumran Texts."

Emile Puech's original publication of 4Q521 appeared in *Revue de Qumran* 15 (1991). For his wider understandings of the Qumran belief in the coming of the messianic age, see *La croyance des esséniens.* I have used the English translation of Wise and Tabor of lines 1–8, column 2 of 4Q521, as it appears in their article, "The Messiah at Qumran," pp. 62–63. A slightly different transcription and translation was published in Eisenman and Wise, *The Dead Sea Scrolls Uncovered,* p. 23.

For the Testament of Qahat (4Q542), see Puech, "La Testament," and Eisenman and Wise, *The Dead Sea Scrolls Uncovered,* pp. 145–151. For The Wisdom Text with Beatitudes (4Q525), see Puech, "4Q525," and Viviano, "Beatitudes." Compare these interpretations with Eisenman and Wise, *The Dead Sea Scrolls Uncovered,* pp. 168–177, where the text is named "The Demons of Death."

On the centrality of the "Star Prophecy" in the messianism of Judea in the first century c.e., see Hengel, *The Zealots,* pp. 236–240, and Eisenman, *Maccabees, Zadokites,* p. 25, and throughout. For the possible ideological impact of Roman emperor worship on the rise of Jewish messianism, see Hengel, *The Zealots,* pp. 99–107; Hopkins, *Conquerors and Slaves;* and Frend, *The Early Church,* pp. 4–6.

The nostalgic and patriotic Maccabean themes of the first-century Judean resistance movement were long ago stressed by Farmer in *Maccabees, Zealots and Josephus.* Eisenman, *Maccabees, Zadokites,* applies this ideological background directly to Qumran.

On Edmund Wilson and his connection with the Dead Sea Scrolls story, see Edel, "Edmund Wilson in the Fifties," and Castronovo, *Ed-*

mund Wilson, chapter 7. Wilson's research notes on his first trip to Israel are published in Wilson, *The Fifties,* pp. 213–247. For his later visits to Israel and subsequent reflections on the scrolls, see Wilson, *Israel and the Dead Sea Scrolls.*

For syntheses of Dupont-Sommer's early historical interpretation of the scrolls, see *The Dead Sea Scrolls* and *The Jewish Sect of Qumran and the Essenes.*

Wilson's quoted summations on the Essenes can be found in *The Scrolls,* pp. 97–98. His colorful description of David Flusser appears on pp. 77–83.

Flusser's collected work on the scrolls and early Christianity was published in the volume, *Judaism and Christianity.* See also his *Spiritual History of the Dead Sea Sect.* The affair of the "Son of God" text is clearly described in Collins, "A Pre-Christian 'Son of God.' " Flusser's own publication is "The Hubris of Antichrist." I have used his translation here.

An English translation of Anatole France's story "The Procurator of Judaea" (by Frederic Chapman) was published in Benjamin, *Great French Short Stories,* pp. 856–871.

Allegro's publications on the scrolls are extensive. See, among them, *The Dead Sea Scrolls, The People of the Dead Sea Scrolls, The Treasure of the Copper Scroll,* and *The Mystery of the Dead Sea Scrolls.* For his more general religious critique, see *The Chosen People, The End of a Road,* and *The Sacred Mushroom and the Cross.* In contradiction to the now-conventional scholarly ridicule, the index of this last work does *not* read like the index of a sex manual. This highly exaggerated and patently ridiculous charge—based on a single scholar's offhand comment—has become one of the "clarifications" utilized by Betz and Riesner in their polemical tract, *Jesus, Qumran, and the Vatican,* p. 14, to discredit Allegro's entire body of work. Betz adopts a similarly inflammatory tone in his condemnation of other admittedly unconventional scholars and writers with whom he disagrees.

The letter to the London *Times,* signed by De Vaux, Milik, Skehan, Starcky, and Strugnell, was published on March 16, 1956. The responses of Allegro to the criticism of De Vaux and the other International Team members were described in Baigent and Leigh, *The Dead Sea Scrolls Deception,* pp. 46–60. Allegro's quote on the necessity for religious reevaluation come from the *Mystery of the Dead Sea Scrolls,* p. 176.

The passage from the War Scroll, column 11, was translated by Geza Vermes in *The Dead Sea Scrolls in English.* The biblical passage containing the "star" prophecy is Numbers 24:17–19.

CHAPTER 5: THE TREASURE

The most thorough translation and commentary on the Copper Scroll is Lefkovits, *The Copper Scroll—3Q15,* with complete bibliography of earlier publications. For recent examinations of the political and ideological context of the interpretation of the Copper Scroll, see Wolters, "Apocalyptic" and "History." See also McCarter, "The Mystery," and Goranson, "Sectarianism, Geography, and the Copper Scroll." Manfred Lehmann was a pioneer in understanding the significance of the Copper Scroll through the use of rabbinic parallels. See his articles, "Identification of the Copper Scroll" and "Where the Temple Tax Was Buried."

For general surveys of the Jerusalem Temple, its priesthood, and its services, see Safrai, "The Temple"; Jeremias, "Jerusalem," chapter 8, and Stern, "Aspects." For an intriguing and characteristically iconoclastic reconstruction of the early history of the Second Temple, see Smith, "Palestinian Parties."

For the economic implications of the Judean way of life and the impact of Hellenism on it, see Hengel, *Judaism and Hellenism,* chapter 1, and Applebaum, "Economic Life." An early testimony to the distinctive economic and land-tenure system of the Judeans was given by Hecataeus of Abdera around 300 B.C.E. It is quoted in Stern, *Greek and Latin Authors:* I, 28. On the possible social context of developing religious ideology, see Hanson, *The Dawn of Apocalyptic.*

The Holy War aspect of the Maccabean revolt and the religious character of the subsequent Hasmonean expansion is stressed in Efron, "Studies," and Bar-Kochva, "Manpower, Economics."

Through the first century B.C.E. and the first century C.E., many Judeans grew progressively more concerned with the purity of the Temple, not less concerned; see Hengel, *The Zealots,* pp. 206–224; Mendels, *Rise and Fall,* pp. 277–301; Goodman, *The Ruling Class.* The Essenes' special relationship with the Temple is described by Josephus, yet recent scholarly discussion about the identity of the Dead Sea sect makes the issue of Temple observance in the scrolls even more problematic; see Yadin, *The Temple Scroll,* pp. 232–239. For the supposed buried "sacrifices" in the courtyards of Khirbet Qumran, see De Vaux, *Archaeology,* pp. 12–15.

The quotation on the rejection of sacrifices comes from column 11 of the Community Rule, translated by Geza Vermes in *The Dead Sea Scrolls in English.*

For the best accounts of the political background of the early interpretation of the Copper Scroll, see Wolters, "Apocalyptic" and "History." For the general background of the period, see Dann, *King Hussein.* There is considerable discussion of the turbulent political situation and its likely effect on the future of Dead Sea Scroll studies in the correspondence between Kraeling and Harding and Kraeling and Creel in the archives of the Israel Antiquities Authority and the Rockefeller Archives Center. Gerald Lankester Harding resigned as director of the Jordanian Department of Antiquities in the summer of 1956 and left the country in the autumn. He later briefly served as an advisor to the Department of Antiquities after the nationalization of the Palestine Archaeological Museum in late 1966.

Allegro's role in the unrolling and decipherment of the Copper Scroll is recorded in his book *The Treasure,* and extensively documented in Lefkovits, *The Copper Scroll.* For Allegro's subsequent archaeological expeditions, see his *Search in the Desert,* a book with considerably more personal than archaeological detail.

An English translation of the 1960 article in *ad-Difa'a* is in the administrative archives of the Israel Antiquities Authority.

The account of the unrecorded negotiations between the Israeli authorities and the international team has been reconstructed from my interviews with Biran, Strugnell, and Broshi.

Allegro's allotment of Cave 4 material was published in *Qumran Cave 4.* For Strugnell's stinging review of Allegro's volume, see his "Notes en marge."

For the early, fitful negotiations for the purchase of the Temple Scroll, see Yadin, *The Temple Scroll,* pp. 24–39, and Shanks, "Intrigue and the Scroll." The description of the parallel negotiations in Beirut comes from my interviews with Cross and Dr. James Swauger of the Carnegie Museum in Pittsburg. Swauger also generously allowed me to see relevant entries in his journal from the spring of 1967. The account of the arrest of Kando and the confiscation of the Temple Scroll came from Sitton, *Men of Secrets,* pp. 261–278, the details of which were largely corroborated in a background interview I conducted in June 1993 with a former intelligence officer in the Israel Defense Forces. For another version of the events and the unrolling of the document, see Silberman, *Prophet,* pp. 304–310.

The major scholarly publication of the Temple Scroll is Yadin, *The Temple Scroll.* For a detailed review of Yadin's conclusions and suggested alternatives, see Levine, "The Temple Scroll." For a new translation, see Vermes, *The Dead Sea Scrolls,* pp. 128–158, and for a new interpretation, see Wise, *A Critical Study.* See also Wacholder, *The Dawn of Qumran,* and Stegemann "Is the Temple Scroll a Sixth Book of the Torah."

On the visions of the Temple, and their literary and historical significance, see the essays in Brooke, *Temple Scroll Studies,* and, for a survey of their historical development, see Maier, "The Temple Scroll and Tendencies."

On the architecture and construction of Herod's Temple, see Mazar, *The Mountain of the Lord,* and Ben-Dov, *In the Shadow of the Temple Mount.* For a recent, highly detailed study of the economic and technological aspects of the huge construction project, see Warszawski and Peretz, "Building the Temple Mount." For the Temple's impact on the economy of Jerusalem, see Jeremias, *Jerusalem,* and Goodman, "The First Jewish Revolt."

On the religious opposition to the High Priesthood during the first century, see Smallwood, "High Priests and Politics"; Horsely, "High Priests and Politics"; and Goodman, *The Ruling Class.*

My account of the history of the study of MMT is based on my interviews with Strugnell. Professor Strugnell also generously provided me with a draft of the paper on MMT that he presented at a scrolls conference at the University of Notre Dame in the spring of 1993. See also Kapera, *Qumran Cave IV and MMT.*

For the first publication of the text, see Qimron and Strugnell, "An Unpublished Halakhic Letter." Pending the full publication of this document, the best general accounts of MMT's contents and significance are Schiffman "The New Halakhic Letter," and Sussmann, "The History of Halakha," and Qimron, "Halakhic Terms." The final benedictory lines of the text are quoted in Schiffman, "The New Halakhic Letter," p. 71.

But see also Eisenman and Wise in *The Dead Sea Scrolls Uncovered,* pp. 182–200, for an alternative division, reading, and dating of the text. So far the controversy surrounding the Eisenman-Wise publication of this document has centered on the originality of the transcription. As far as I am aware, there has been no serious scholarly discussion of the central historical problem brought up by their interpretation: namely, that MMT addresses religious issues known to have been debated extensively and bitterly in the first century C.E. (e.g., the permissibility of Gentile offerings to the Temple, priestly intermarriage, and the permissibility of niece-marriage, as was extensively practiced by the Herodians) while there is no evidence that these issues were of particular concern during the rule of the early Hasmonean dynasty in the second century B.C.E. According to most scholars, the reason for the Qumran "separation" from the Judean mainstream is the genealogical (i.e., non-Zadokite) illegitimacy of the Hasmonean High Priests. This issue is never explicitly addressed in the Qumran literature. In fact, the "Wicked Priest" is described in the Habakkuk Commentary as having originally been "called by the name of Truth" and only later did he reportedly abandon the Law and become corrupt. This change of behavior, rather than his family background, is apparently the sect's main religious objection to his holding the office of High Priesthood.

The importance of Rabbinic discussion of halakhic matters for determining the identity of the authors of scrolls was demonstrated by Joseph Baumgarten in his article, "The Pharisaic-Sadducean Controversies." See also Sussmann, "The History of Halakha," and Schiffman, "The Sadducean Origins."

Hershel Shanks's account of the announcement of MMT at the 1984 Congress was in his article, "Jerusalem Rolls Out Red Carpet."

CHAPTER 6: SONS OF LIGHT, SONS OF DARKNESS

Lawrence Schiffman has produced an impressive body of scholarly work on the scrolls. See, in addition to works cited above, among many others, his *Halakhah at Qumran; Sectarian Law;* "4QMiqsat Ma'aseh Ha-Torah and the Temple Scroll"; "The Temple Scroll"; and "New Light on the Pharisees." His general history of the period is *Text and Tradition.* The 1985 New York University Dead Sea Scrolls symposium was edited by Schiffman and published under the title *Archaeology and History and the Dead Sea Scrolls.*

On the escalating tensions in Judea during the period of direct Roman rule, see Smallwood, *The Jews,* and Hengel, *The Zealots.* The incident of the Roman standards in Jerusalem and the beating of the Temple crowds under Pilate appears in Josephus Flavius, *The Jewish War,* Book II: 169–177.

The issue of the ancient Jewish belief in the resurrection of the dead is a complex and bitterly argued one, especially in its connection with the beginnings of Christian belief. For two views, see Collins, *The Apocalyptic Imagination,* and Puech, *Croyance.* The archaeological evidence of burial practices in this period are suggestive, though not without their own controversies of interpretation. See Meyers, *Jewish Ossuaries,* and Rachmani, "Ancient Jerusalem's Funerary Customs," and his review of Meyers in the *Israel Exploration Journal* 23 (1973): 121–126.

For discussions of the cemetery at Qumran and its religious and historical significance, see De Vaux, *Archaeology,* pp. 45–48, 57–58; Laperrousaz, *Qoumran,* pp. 19–25.

On the general literary and religious trends of the late Second Temple period, see Stone, *Scriptures, Sects, and Visions,* and Collins, *The Apocalyptic Imagination.*

The intellectual and social history of the quest for the Historical Jesus has been traced by Georgi, "Interest in Life of Jesus." For the basic history of the research, see Schweitzer, *The Quest,* and Robinson, *A New Quest.* Among the recent works on this subject, see Crossan, *The Historical Jesus;* Horsley, *Jesus and the Spiral of Violence;* and Wilson, *Jesus.* In all of these works, the authors utilize the Qumran scrolls as general background and take at face value the conventional scholarship regarding the basic isolation and uniqueness of the Qumran sect.

On the early identifications of the Community with Judeo-Christians on the basis of the Damascus Document, see, for example, Margoulioth, "The Sadducean Christians," and Teicher "The Dead Sea Scrolls." For an entirely different Christian identification, see Thiering, *Jesus and the Riddle.* On the identification of the earliest Christians with the Zealots, see Eisler, *The Messiah Jesus,* and Brandon, *The Fall of Jerusalem.* On the identification of the Qumran Community with the Zealots, see Roth, *The Dead Sea Scrolls,* and Driver, *The Judean Scrolls.*

There is no question in my mind that Robert Eisenman's work has been unfairly dismissed as baseless crankery, as in Greenfield, "Scrolls Book Shunned." A close reading of Eisenman's two books, *Maccabees, Zadokites* and *James the Just,* will demonstrate that he addresses issues of ideology, public discourse, and political resistance that are utterly absent in most studies of the scrolls. In my opinion, the correctness of his specific identifications of historical characters (for which he is often attacked) is far less important than his general hypotheses on the place of Qumran literature at the very center (or at least in the mainstream) of the political and religious agitation in Judea in the first century C.E. For Eisenman's views on Paul's activity, I have relied on an unpublished paper, "Paul as Herodian," which he delivered at an annual meeting of the Society for Biblical Literature.

A version of the doctrinal discussions at the Apostolic Council in Jerusalem are recorded in Acts 15:4–29; James's quotation on the observance of the Law can be found in the Letter of James 2:10. On the spread of Pauline Christianity, see Meeks, *The First Urban Christians,* and on Christianity's later amalgamation with concepts of Empire, see Fowden, *Empire to Commonwealth.*

On the methodology and work of the Jesus Seminar, see Funk, Hoover et. al., *The Five Gospels.*

My account of Eisenman's early attempts to contest the authority of the International Team is based primarily on interviews with Eisenman, Drori, and Strugnell, checked against the running accounts of the controversy published in the *Biblical Archaeological Review.*

CHAPTER 7: THE FINAL BATTLE

In addition to *Biblical Archaeology Review* and *Bible Review,* Hershel Shanks also edits *Moment Magazine,* a journal of contemporary Jewish thought, news, and culture.

Shanks's account of the 1984 conference was published as "Jerusalem Rolls Out Red Carpet." His account of the 1985 Conference was published as "Failure to Publish."

The Suggested Timetable of the Department of Antiquities was published in Shanks, "Dead Sea Scrolls Scandal," p. 20, and as figure 3 of the publisher's foreword to Eisenman and Robinson, *Facsimile Edition*, p. xxvi. Ayala Sussmann's reply of April 17, 1989 was also published in Eisenman and Robinson, *Facsimile Edition*, as figure 4, p. xxvii.

Hershel Shanks's official campaign against the monopoly of the scrolls establishment began with his article "The Dead Sea Scandal." For subsequent positive reactions to his efforts in the popular press, see, for example, Wade, "Editorial Notebook," and Ostling, "Secrets of the Dead Sea Scrolls."

Frank Cross's letter to *BAR* appeared under the headline, "Pere De Vaux Was a Dead Sea Scroll Hero."

On the activities of Zdzislaw Kapera, see the various issues of the periodical he edits, *The Qumran Chronicle*. For the text of the Mogilany Resolution and the proceedings of the 1989 Mogilany conference, see *The Qumran Chronicle* 1 (1990): 3–12. Shanks's report on the Mogilany conference appeared in the *Biblical Archaeology Review* 16:1 (January/February 1990): 10. The confrontation between Shanks and Strugnell was covered in the same issue of *Biblical Archaeology Review* and was covered extensively in the popular press; see, for instance, Franklin, "Scholarly Clash."

The famous *Biblical Archaeology Review* "louse" cover appeared on the March/April 1990 issue.

The chronology of the actions of the Israel Antiquities Authority with the regard to the scrolls is based on my conversations with Drori, Tov, Strugnell, and Broshi.

The Katzman interview with Strugnell was published in *Haaretz* on November 9, 1990. An edited English version of the interview appeared in Katzman, "Chief Dead Sea Scroll Editor." For the news accounts of Strugnell's removal, see, for example, Rabinovich, "Dead Sea Scrolls Editor," and Wilford, "Dead Sea Scroll Editor's Exit."

The official proceedings of the Madrid conference have been published in Barrera and Montaner, *The Madrid Congress*. Shanks's indignant report of his exclusion from the conference was reported in *Biblical Archaeology Review* 17:3 (May/June 1991): 12. The letter from Tov and Drori to Kapera was reproduced in the publisher's foreword to Eisenman and Robinson, *Facsimile Edition*, figure 9, p. xxxii.

The publication of the Wacholder and Abegg *Preliminary Edition* caused a great sensation in the international press because of unique combination of high-tech ingenuity and biblical scholarship. See, for example, Wilford, "Computer Hacker," and Specter, "Renegades Bring Dead Sea Scrolls to Light."

The press release of the Israel Antiquities Authority marking the beginning of the end of the monopoly of the International Team was reprinted in Eisenman and Robinson, *Facsimile Edition,* figure 1, p. xxiv. Safire's column was entitled "Breaking the Cartel." The press conference announcing the publication of the *Facsimile Edition* was reported in Spiegelman, "Rest of the Dead Sea Scrolls." On the involvement of the Huntington Museum in the last phase of the struggle, see Sanders, "What Can Happen in a Year?" and Wilford, "Monopoly Over Dead Sea Scrolls Is Ended."

The chronology of the court actions were recorded in the official decision of Judge Dalia Dorner in the Jerusalem District Court, dated March 30, 1993. Qimron's personal comments come from an open letter published in *Biblical Archaeology Review* 18:4 (July/August 1992): 76.

The first publication of the "long secret plates" was in *Biblical Archaeology Review* 17:6 (November/December 1991): 64–65. The first news report on the "Pierced Messiah" text appeared in Wilford, "Link to Messianic Christianity." The hostile verdict of the Oxford Seminar was published in Vermes, "The Oxford Forum" and "The 'Pierced Messiah' Text." But note also the reply of Tabor, "A Pierced or Piercing Messiah?"

The Dead Sea Scrolls Uncovered includes Eisenman and Wise's interpretation of the "Letter on Works Reckoned as Righteousness," (pp. 180–200); "Children of Salvation" (pp. 241–254); and the "Paean to King Jonathan." (pp. 273–280). The first report of this last text appeared in Rabinovich, "A Prayer for King Yonaton." For a far more detailed, scholarly treatment, see Eshel, Eshel, and Yardeni, "A Qumran Composition."

Jonas Greenfield's scathing review of *The Dead Sea Scrolls Uncovered* was entitled "Scrolls Book Shunned." For a more temperate, if no less scathing review, see Harrington and Strugnell, "Critical Note." For the text of the scholars' letter and Hershel Shanks's account of the 1992 New York Scrolls Conference, see his "Blood on the Floor." I received xerox copies of the scholars' protest and the replies of Golb and Wise during the New York Conference.

CHAPTER 8: JUDGMENT DAY

My account of the trial in Jerusalem is based on interviews with Broshi, Schiffman, and Shanks; on Judge Dorner's decision, issued in Jerusalem on March 30, 1993; on contemporary press clippings from Israel including Rabinovich, "Dead Sea Fever," Katzman, "Cave Men," and Segev, "Who Stole the Scroll?"; on Shanks's published account, "Lawsuit Diary;" and on extensive notes taken for me at the summation hearing by Janet Amitai.

On Hershel Shanks's moral and intellectual justification for pursuing the case against Qimron and his view of the dangerous implications of the lawsuit on scroll studies, see, for example, his articles "Why Professor Qimron's Lawsuit Is a Threat to Intellectual Freedom" and "Paying the Price."

Emanuel Tov's reaction to Judge Dorner's verdict was quoted in *The New York Times* in Greenberg, "Court Supports Editor." On the tremendous expansion of the membership of the International Team under the direction of Professor Tov, see his article, "Expanded Team of Editors Hard at Work." Tov's success in this important aspect of the work should not be underestimated or minimized.

For an interesting statistical study of the conservative character of Dead Sea Scroll studies (up to the mid-1980s), see Heisey, "Paradigm Agreement."

For general works on the history of apocalyptic literature and thought, see Cohn, *Cosmos, Chaos* and *The Pursuit of the Millennium;* Collins, *The Apocalyptic Imagination;* and for an intriguing study of this phenomenon in American religious life, see Boyer, *When Time Shall Be No More.* For an intriguing sociological study of subtle literary and cultural forms of political resistance that may have some relevance in understanding the suggested "radicalization" of the Qumran sect, see Scott, *Domination and the Arts of Resistance.*

There are some striking parallels between the political context of religious protest movements in first-century Judea (including the ideology expressed in the scrolls) and the ideology of modern radical Islam. See, for example, Sivan, *Radical Islam,* where the militant calls for a reassertion of Islamic law and traditional values throughout the Muslim world are seen as popular responses to the failed promise of industrialization. Particularly suggestive for a potential comparative study of the scrolls are Sivan's concepts of a "Conservative Periphery" within society that forms a support group for the most radical activists; the high educational level and feelings of alienation and disenfranchisement shared by the activists; and the belief that the defeat of the invading satanic forces can be achieved by political terrorism. Only further study can explain whether these behaviors are unconnected, universal behaviors—or whether some common themes have survived through the centuries in certain mystical or heretical sects of Judaism or Islam. Eisenman implies this far-reaching possibility in the introduction to *Maccabees, Zadokites.*

In my description of the Qumran Community and its literature, I do not want readers to overlook the violent, puritanical, and xenophobic aspects of the community's ideology. To the members of the Judean aristocracy and to those Judeans not completely hostile to Roman culture, the resisters and religious fundamentalists must often have seemed like cranks, thugs, and terrorists. This is precisely how the Judean resistance movement was depicted in the writings of Josephus Flavius. I intend neither to condone nor romanticize the uncontrolled violence and intolerance that is often characteristic of a movement like that which produced the Qumran literature. My intention is rather to shift attention away from the purely religious, otherworldly interpretation of the scrolls, which strips their study of an important political dimension.

On the tactics and strategic plan of the War Scroll, see Yadin, *Scroll of the War*, pp. 18–37, 141–197. The quotation from Column 1 of the War Scroll was translated by Geza Vermes in *The Dead Sea Scrolls in English*.

It is surprising that few scholars have recognized how the seemingly miraculous victories of the rebels at the outbreak of the rebellion might have been interpreted at the time as divine intervention. See Gihon, "Cestius Gallus"; Smallwood, *The Jews Under Roman Rule*, chapters 11 and 12; and Rappaport, *Judea and Rome*. De Vaux's very dubious presumptions about the date of destruction of the Qumran settlement and the supposed discovery of the Tenth Legion coin in its ruins have been very effectively countered in Eisenman, *Maccabees, Zadokites*. The evidence of continued messianic agitation and political activity in Judea *after* 70 C.E. (as described in Goodblatt, "The Jews of Eretz-Israel," and Smallwood, *The Jews Under Roman Rule*, chapter 13) make the presumption that the scrolls had to be deposited by 68 C.E. utterly untenable.

For the publication of the Songs of the Sabbath Sacrifice fragment from Masada, see Newsom and Yadin, "The Masada Fragment." I have, however, used Geza Vermes's translation here, from *The Dead Sea Scrolls In English*, p. 223. The traditional explanations for the presence of Qumran-type documents at Masada (i.e., that they were the property of individual "Essenes" who had fled from the destruction of Qumran to find shelter with the Sicarii) should be reconsidered. Although I have written approvingly in the past about the recent scholarly criticism of the famous suicide story, I now recognize that the theme of righteous martyrdom in a Holy War is both prominent and common to the Maccabees and the "zealot" movement (see Hengel, *The Zealots*, pp. 256–271). It may also be implied by some of the problematic allusions to resurrection in the War Scroll, the Thanksgiving Hymns, and other Qumran texts. For an early discussion of the idea of martyrdom at Qumran, see Cross, *The Ancient Library*, pp. 117–118.

The account of the triumph in Rome is to be found in Josephus, *The Jewish War*, Book VI, 119–158. For a penetrating study of the bases of

Roman imperial power and the nature of Roman society, see Hopkins, *Conquerors and Slaves.*

For the reconstruction of the period immediately after the suppression of the Jewish Revolt, see Goodblatt, "The Jews of Eretz-Israel"; Smallwood, *The Jews Under Roman Rule,* chapter 13; and Martin Goodman, *The Ruling Class,* chapter 10. For the use by the Romans of resettlement camps for surrendered Judeans, see Alon, "Rabban Johanan B. Zakkai's Removal to Jabneh."

Manfred Lehmann's reconstruction of the general historical context of the Copper Scroll is enlightening and persuasive. See his "Identification" and "Where the Temple Tax Was Buried." I believe that he has, however, overlooked the polemical intent of the rabbinic passages that suggest that offerings for the (destroyed) Temple be disposed of; this suggests that there were those who were *not* disposing of the offerings, and I would suggest that these were the rival priestly circles—precisely like those who presumably produced the Copper Scroll. Note also the hostile reactions to Lehmann's theories in subsequent issues of the *Biblical Archaeology Review.* In every case, the critics refer only to his specific interpretation of a coin of the Emperor Nerva; his general historical reconstruction is ignored.

On the possible avenues of contact between the Qumran literature and the later literature of the Jewish Karaite movement, see Erder, "When did the Karaites First Encounter Apochryphic Literature" and Ben-Shammai, "Some Methodological Notes."

SOURCES CONSULTED

ARCHIVES

Central Zionist Archives, Jerusalem
Hebrew University of Jerusalem, Jerusalem
Israel Antiquities Authority, Jerusalem
Rockefeller Archive Center, North Tarrytown, New York.
Yad Izhak Ben-Zvi, Jerusalem

INTERVIEWS

Nahman Avigad, Jerusalem, July 2, 1990
Sarah Ben-Arieh, Jerusalem, June 9, 1992.
Avraham Biran, Jerusalem, October 16 and 21, 1990
Magen Broshi, Jerusalem, February 16, 1992
Frank Moore Cross, Lexington, Massachusetts, January 19, 1992.
Devorah Dimant, Philadelphia, May 11, 1992
Amir Drori, Jerusalem, May 27, 1993
Robert Eisenman, New York, December 14, 1992; Huntington Beach,
    California, August 14, 21, 1993
David Flusser, Jerusalem, May 25, 1993.
Avraham Harman, Jerusalem, June 12, 1991
Anton Hazou, Jerusalem, February 21, 1992

Harry Orlinsky, New York City, November 1, 1990
Jean Perrot, Jerusalem, June 7, 1993
Emile Puech, Jerusalem, February 21, 1992; June 6, 1993
Athanasius Yeshue Samuel, Lodi, New Jersey, December 26, 1991; June 15, 1993
Lawrence Schiffman, New York City, April 3, 1992; September 21, 1993
Hershel Shanks, Washington, D.C., July 27, 1993
John Strugnell, Cambridge, Massachusetts, June 18, August 28, and November 4, 1993.
James Swauger, Pittsburgh, Pennsylvania, September 15, 1993.
Jacques-Raymond Tournay, Jerusalem, February 21, 1992.
Emanuel Tov, Jerusalem, May 27, 1993.
John Trever, Laguna Hills, California, May 7, August 31, September 7, 1993.
Benedict Viviano, Jerusalem, February 21, 1992.

PUBLISHED WORKS

Allegro, John Marco. *The Chosen People*. London: Hodder and Stoughton, 1971.
———. *The Dead Sea Scrolls*. Harmondsworth: Penguin Books, 1956.
———. *The End of a Road*. London: MacGibbon and Kee, 1970.
———. *The Mystery of the Dead Sea Scrolls Revealed*. New York: Gramercy Publishing Co., 1981
———. *The People of the Dead Sea Scrolls*. London: Routledge and Kegan Paul, 1959.
———. *Qumran Cave 4. I (4Q158-4Q186). Discoveries in the Judaean Desert of Jordan*. Volume 5. Oxford: Clarendon Press, 1968.
———. *The Sacred Mushroom and the Cross*. Garden City, New York: Doubleday, 1970.
———. *Search in the Desert*. Garden City, New York: Doubleday 1964.
———. *The Shapira Affair*. Garden City, New York: Doubleday, 1960.
———. *The Treasure of the Copper Scroll*. London: Routledge and Kegan Paul, 1960.
Alon, Gedalyah. "Rabban Johanan B. Zakkai's Removal to Jabneh." Pp. 269–313 in Alon, Gedalyah, *Jews, Judaism and the Classical World*. Jerusalem: Magnes Press, 1977.
Applebaum, Shimon. "Economic Life in Palestine." Pp. 631–700 in *The Jewish People in the First Century*. Volume 2. Edited by Shmuel Safrai and Menachem Stern. Assen: Van Gorcum, 1974–6.
Avigad, Nahman. *Discovering Jerusalem*. Nashville, TN: Thomas Nelson, 1983.

Baigent, Michael, and Richard Leigh. *The Dead Sea Scrolls Deception*. New York: Summit Books, 1991.

Bar-Adon, Pesach. *Excavations in the Judean Desert. Atiqot Hebrew Series*. Volume 9. Jerusalem: Israel Antiquities Authority, 1989. [In Hebrew].

————. "The Hasmonean Fortifications and the Status of Qumran in the Northern Dead Sea Region." *Eretz Israel* 15 (1981): 349–352. [In Hebrew]

Bar-Kochva, Bezalel. "Manpower, Economics, and Internal Strife in the Hasmonean State." Pp. 167–194 in *Armées et fiscalité dans le monde antique*. Edited by Henri van Effenterre. Paris: Editions du CNRS, 1977.

Barrera, Julio Trebolle, and Luis Vegas Montaner. *The Madrid Qumran Congress: Proceedings of the International Congress on the Dead Sea Scrolls*. Leiden: E. J. Brill, 1992.

Baumgarten, Joseph M. "The Pharisaic-Sadducean Controversies about Purity and the Qumran Texts." *Journal of Jewish Studies* 31 (1980): 157–170.

Ben-Dov, Meir. *In the Shadow of the Temple Mount*. Jerusalem: Keter, 1985.

Benjamin, Lewis Saul, ed. *Great French Short Stories*. New York: Boni and Liveright, 1928.

Ben-Shammai, Haggai. "Some Methodological Notes Concerning the Relationship between the Karaites and Ancient Jewish Sects." *Cathedra* 42 (1987): 69–84. [In Hebrew]

Bentwich, Norman. *Solomon Schechter: A Biography*. Philadelphia: Jewish Publication Society of America, 1938.

Beskow, Per. *Strange Tales about Jesus: A Survey of Unfamiliar Gospels*. Philadelphia: Fortress Press, 1983.

Betz, Otto, and Rainer Reisner. *Jesus, Qumran, and the Vatican: Clarifications*. New York: Crossroad, 1994.

Boyer, Paul. *When Time Shall Be No More: Prophecy Belief in Modern American Culture*. Cambridge, Mass: Harvard University Press, 1992.

Brandon, S. G. F. *The Fall of Jerusalem and the Christian Church*. London: Society for Promoting Christian Knowledge, 1951.

Brooke, George J., ed. *Temple Scroll Studies*. Sheffield: JSOT Press, 1989.

Broshi, M., ed. *The Damascus Document Reconsidered*. Jerusalem: Israel Exploration Society and Shrine of the Book, 1992.

Brownlee, William H. "Edh-Dheeb's Story of His Scroll Discovery." *Revue de Qumran* 3 (1961–62): 483–494.

————. "Muhammad ed-Deeb's Own Story of His Scroll Discovery." *Journal of Near Eastern Studies* 16 (1957): 236–239.

Burrows, Millar. *The Dead Sea Scrolls*. New York: The Viking Press, 1956.

————. *More Light on the Dead Sea Scrolls*. New York: The Viking Press, 1958.

Castronovo, David. *Edmund Wilson*. New York: F. Ungar Publishing Company, 1984.

Charlesworth, James, ed. *The Messiah: Developments in Earliest Judaism and Christianity*. Minneapolis: Fortress Press, 1992.

Cohn, Norman. *Cosmos, Chaos, and the World to Come: The Ancient Roots of Apocalyptic Faith*. New Haven: Yale University Press, 1993.

————. *The Pursuit of the Millennium*. New York: Oxford University Press, 1970.

Collins, John J. *The Apocalyptic Imagination*. New York: Crossroad Publishing Company, 1992.

————. "A Pre-Christian 'Son of God' Among the Dead Sea Scrolls." *Bible Review* 9:3 (June 1993): 34–38, 57.

Cross, Frank Moore, Jr. *The Ancient Library of Qumran and Modern Biblical Studies*. Garden City, New York: Doubleday, 1958.

————. "The Development of Jewish Scripts." Pp. 133–202 in *The Bible and the Ancient Near East*. Edited by G. Ernest Wright. New York: Doubleday, 1961.

————. "The Early History of the Qumran Community." Pp. 70–89 in *New Directions in Biblical Archaeology*. Edited by David Noel Freedman and Jonas C. Greenfield. Garden City, New York: Doubleday, 1971.

————. The Historical Context of the Scrolls." Pp. 20–32 in *Understanding the Dead Sea Scrolls*. Edited by Hershel Shanks. New York: Random House, 1992.

————. "Pere De Vaux Was a Dead Sea Scroll Hero." *Biblical Archaeology Review* 16:1 (January/February 1990): 18, 62.

Crossan, John Dominic. *The Historical Jesus: The Life of a Mediterranean Jewish Peasant*. San Francisco: Harper, 1991.

Couroyer, Bernard. "Histoire d'une tribu semi-nomade de Palestine." *Revue Biblique* 58 (1951): 75–91.

Dann, Uriel. *King Hussein and the Challenge of Arab Radicalism: Jordan 1955–1967*. New York: Oxford University Press, 1989.

Davies, Philip R. *The Damascus Covenant: An Interpretation of the "Damascus Document."* Sheffield: JSOT, 1983.

————. "How Not to Do Archaeology." *Biblical Archaeologist* 51:4 (December 1988), 203–207.

De Vaux, Roland. *Archaeology and the Dead Sea Scrolls*. London: The British Academy, 1973.

Driver, G. R. *The Judean Scrolls*. Oxford: Basil Blackwell, 1965.

Dupont-Sommer, Andre. *The Dead Sea Scrolls: A Preliminary Survey*. Oxford: Basil Blackwell, 1952.

————. *The Jewish Sect of Qumran and the Essenes.* New York: The Macmillan Company, 1955.

Edel, Leon. "Edmund Wilson in the Fifties." Pp. xiii–xxx in Wilson, Edmund, *The Fifties: From Notebooks and Diaries of the Period.* New York: Farrar, Straus, and Giroux, 1986.

Efron, Joshua. *Studies in the Hasmonean Period.* Leiden: E. J. Brill, 1987.

Eisenman, Robert H. *James the Just in the Habakkuk Pesher.* Leiden: E. J. Brill, 1986.

————. *Maccabees, Zadokites, Christians, and Qumran.* Leiden: E. J. Brill, 1983.

Eisenman, Robert H., and James M. Robinson. *A Facsimile Edition of the Dead Sea Scrolls.* Washington, D.C.: Biblical Archaeology Society, 1991.

Eisenman, Robert, and Michael Wise. *The Dead Sea Scrolls Uncovered.* Rockport, Massachusetts: Element, 1992.

Eisler, Robert. *The Messiah Jesus and John the Baptist.* New York: The Dial Press, 1931.

Erder, Yoram. "When did the Karaites First Encounter Apochryphic Literature Akin to the Dead Sea Scrolls?" *Cathedra* 42 (1987): 54–68. [In Hebrew].

Eshel, Esther, Hanan Eshel, and Ada Yardeni. "A Qumran Composition Containing Part of Ps. 154 and a Prayer for the Welfare of King Jonathan and his Kingdom." *Israel Exploration Journal* 42 (1992): 199–229.

Farmer, W. R. *Maccabees, Zealots, and Josephus: An Inquiry into Jewish Nationalism in the Greco-Roman Period.* New York: Columbia University Press, 1956.

Fitzmyer, Joseph A. *The Dead Sea Scrolls: Major Publications and Tools for Study.* Atlanta: Scholars' Press, 1990.

Flusser, David. "The Hubris of Antichrist," *Immanuel* 10 (1980): 31–37.

————. *Judaism and the Origins of Christianity.* Jerusalem: Magnes Press, 1988.

————. *The Spiritual History of the Dead Sea Sect.* Tel Aviv: MOD Books, 1989.

Foerster, Gideon. "On the Conquests of John Hyrcanus in Moab and the Identification of Samaga." *Eretz-Israel* 15 (1981): 356–60. [In Hebrew]

Fowden, Garth. *Empire to Commonwealth: Consequences of Monotheism in Late Antiquity.* Princeton, New Jersey: Princeton University Press, 1993.

Franklin, James L. "Scholarly Clash for Dead Sea Scrolls." *The Boston Globe,* 15 November 1989: 2.

Frend, W. H. C. *The Early Church.* Philadelphia: Fortress Press, 1982.

Fried, Stephen. "Scroll Man," *The Washington Post Magazine,* 10 May 1992: 20–23; 35–37.

Funk, Robert W., Roy W. Hoover et al. *The Five Gospels: The Search for the Authentic Words of Jesus.* New York: Macmillan Publishing Company, 1993.

Georgi, Dieter. "Interest in Life of Jesus Theology as a Paradigm for the Social History of Biblical Criticism." *Harvard Theological Review* 85 (1992): 51–83.

Gihon, Mordecai. "Cestius Gallus' Campaign in Judaea." *Palestine Exploration Quarterly* 113 (1981): 39–62.

Ginsburg, Christian David. *The Essenes: Their History and Doctrines.* New York: The Macmillan Co., 1865.

Golb, Norman. "The Dead Sea Scrolls—A New Perspective." *The American Scholar* 58 (1989): 177–207.

———. "Khirbet Qumran and the Manuscripts of the Judean Wilderness: Observations on the Logic of their Investigation." *Journal of Near Eastern Studies* 49 (1990): 103–114.

Goodblatt, David. "The Jews of Eretz-Israel in the Years 70–132 C.E." Pp. 155–184 in *Judea and Rome: Revolts of the Jews.* Edited by Uriel Rappaport. Tel Aviv: Am Oved, 1983. [In Hebrew]

Goodman, Martin. "The First Jewish Revolt: Social Conflict and the Problem of Debt." *Journal of Jewish Studies* 33 (1982): 417–27.

———. *The Ruling Class of Judea.* Cambridge: Cambridge University Press, 1987.

Goranson, Stephen. "Sectarianism, Geography, and the Copper Scroll." *Journal of Jewish Studies* 43 (1992): 282–287.

Greenberg, Joel. "Court Supports Editor on Rights to Dead Sea Text." *New York Times,* 31 March 1993.

Greenfield, Jonas C. "Scrolls Book Shunned by Well-Known Presses." *Jerusalem Post International Edition,* 20 March 1993: 20.

Hanson, P. D. *The Dawn of Apocalyptic.* Philadelphia: Fortress Press, 1975.

Harrington, Daniel J., and John Strugnell. "Critical Note—Qumran Cave 4 Texts: A New Publication." *Journal of Biblical Literature* 112 (1993): 491–499.

Heisey, Terry M. "Paradigm Agreement and Literature Obsolescence: A Comparative Study in the Literature of the Dead Sea Scrolls." *The Journal of Documentation* 44 (1988): 285–301.

Hengel, Martin. *Judaism and Hellenism.* Philadelphia: Fortress Press, 1974.

———. *The Zealots.* Edinburgh: T. & T. Clark, 1989.

Hopkins, K. *Conquerors and Slaves.* Cambridge: Cambridge University Press, 1978.

Horsley, Richard A. "High Priests and the Politics of Roman Palestine: A Contextual Analysis of the Evidence in Josephus." *Journal for the Study of Judaism* 17 (1986): 23–55.

———. *Jesus and the Spiral of Violence: Popular Jewish Resistance in Roman Palestine.* Minneapolis: Fortress Press, 1993.

Isaacs, Marty. "The Man Who Bought the Dead Sea Scrolls." *Contemporary Review* 261:1522 (November 1992): 257–260.

Jeremias, Joachim. *Jerusalem in the Time of Jesus.* London: SCM Press, 1969.

Kapera, Zdzislaw J. *Qumran Cave IV and MMT.* Krakow: The Enigma Press, 1991.

Katzman, Avi. "Cave Men." *Haaretz Supplement,* 29 January 1993. [In Hebrew]

———. "Chief Dead Sea Scroll Editor Denounces Judaism, Israel." *Biblical Archaeology Review* 17:1 (January/February 1991): 64–65, 70, 72

Laperrousaz, E. M. *Qoumran: l'établissement essénien des bords de la mer morte.* Paris: A. and J. Picard, 1976.

Lapp, Paul W. *Palestinian Ceramic Chronology, 200 BC–AD 70.* New Haven, CT: American Schools of Oriental Research, 1976.

Lefkovits, Judah K. "The Copper Scroll—3Q15, A New Reading, Translation and Commentary." Ph.D. dissertation, New York University, 1993.

Lehmann, Manfred R. "Identification of the Copper Scroll Based on Its Technical Terms." *Revue de Qumran* 6 (1964): 97–105.

———. "Where the Temple Tax Was Buried." *Biblical Archaeology Review* 19:6 (November/December 1993): 38–43.

Levine, Baruch A. "The Temple Scroll: Aspects of its Historical Provenance and Literary Character." *Bulletin of the American Schools of Oriental Research* 232 (1978): 3–24.

Levy, Raphael. " 'First Dead Sea Scroll' Found in Egypt Fifty Years Before Qumran Discoveries." Pp. 63–78 in *Understanding the Dead Sea Scrolls.* Edited by Hershel Shanks. New York: Random House, 1992.

McCarter, P. Kyle, Jr. "The Mystery of the Copper Scroll." Pp. 227–241 in *Understanding the Dead Sea Scrolls.* Edited by Hershel Shanks. NY: Random House, 1992.

Maier, Johann. "The Temple Scroll and Tendencies in the Cultic Architecture of the Second Commonwealth." Pp. 67–82 in *Archaeology and History in the Dead Sea Scrolls.* Edited by Lawrence H. Schiffman. Sheffield: JSOT Press, 1990.

Margoulioth, G. "The Sadducean Christians of Damascus," *Bibliotheca Sacra* 69 (1912): 412–437.

Mazar, Benjamin. *The Mountain of the Lord.* Garden City, NY: Doubleday and Co., 1975.

Meeks, Wayne A. *The First Urban Christians: The Social World of the Apostle Paul.* New Haven, CT: Yale University Press, 1983.

Mendels, Doron. *The Rise and Fall of Jewish Nationalism.* NY: Doubleday and Co., 1992.

Meyers, Eric M. *Jewish Ossuaries: Reburial and Rebirth, Secondary Burials in their Near Eastern Setting.* Rome: Biblical Institute Press, 1971.

Milik, J. T. "The Copper Document from Cave III." *Biblical Archaeologist* 19 (1956): 60–64.

———. *Ten Years of Discovery in the Wilderness of Judea.* London: SCM Press, 1958.

Mor, Menachem. *The Bar Kochba Revolt, Its Extent and Effect.* Jerusalem: Yad Izhak Ben-Zvi, 1991 [In Hebrew]

Murphy-O'Connor, Jerome, and Justin Taylor. *The Ecole Biblique and the New Testament: A Century of Scholarship (1890–1990).* Gottingen: Vandenhoeck and Ruprecht, 1990.

Netzer, Ehud. "The Hasmonean Palaces in Eretz-Israel." Pp. 126–136 in *Biblical Archaeology Today 1990.* Edited by Avraham Biran and Joseph Aviram. Jerusalem: Israel Exploration Society, 1993.

———. "Herod's Building Projects: State Necessity or Personal Need?" Pp. 48–80 in *Jerusalem Cathedra.* Volume 1. Detroit: Wayne State University Press, 1981.

Neusner, Jacob, William S. Green, and Ernest Frerichs. *Judaisms and Their Messiahs at the Turn of the Christian Era.* Cambridge: Cambridge University Press, 1987.

Newsom, Carol, and Yigael Yadin. "The Masada Fragment of the Songs of the Sabbath Sacrifice." *Israel Exploration Journal* 34 (1984): 77–88.

Ostling, R. N. "Secrets of the Dead Sea Scrolls," *Time,* 14 August 1989: 71–2.

Puech, Emile. *La croyance des esséniens en la vie future: immortalité, résurrection, vie éternelle? Histoire d'une croyance dans le judaïsme ancien.* Paris: J. Gobalda, 1993.

———. "4Q525 et les péricopes des béatitudes en Ben Sira et Matthieu." *Revue Biblique* 98 (1991): 80–106.

———. "Le testament de Qahat en araméen de la grotte 4." *Revue de Qumran* 15 (1991): 23–54.

Qimron, Elisha. "Halakhic Terms in the Dead Sea Scrolls and Their Contribution to the History of Early Halakha." Pp. 128–138 in *The Scrolls of the Judaean Desert: Forty Years of Research.* Edited by Magen Broshi et. al. Jerusalem: The Bialik Institute, 1992. [In Hebrew]

Qimron, Elisha, and John Strugnell. "An Unpublished Halakhic Letter from Qumran." Pp. 400–407 in *Biblical Archaeology Today*. Edited by Janet Amitai. Jerusalem: Israel Exploration Society, 1985.

Rabinovich, Abraham. "Dead Sea Scrolls Editor Accused of Antisemitism Removed for 'Health,' " *Jerusalem Post International Edition*, 12 December 1990.

———. "Dead Sea Fever," *Jerusalem Post Magazine International Edition*, February 1993: 9–11.

———. "Operation Scroll," *Jerusalem Post Magazine International Edition*, 21 May 1994: 9, 12, 14.

———. "A Prayer for King Yonaton," *Jerusalem Post Magazine*, 23 April 1992: 8–11.

Rachmani, L. Y. "Ancient Jerusalem's Funerary Customs and Tombs." *Biblical Archaeologist* 44 (1981): 171–177, 229–235; 45 (1982): 43–53, 109–119.

Rappaport, Uriel, ed. *Judea and Rome: Revolts of the Jews*. Tel Aviv: Am Oved, 1983. [In Hebrew]

Reed, Stephen A. "Survey of the Dead Sea Scrolls Fragments and Photographs at the Rockefeller Museum." *Biblical Archaeologist* 54 (1991): 44–51.

Reich, Ronny. "Archaeological Evidence of the Jewish Population at Hasmonean Gezer." *Israel Exploration Journal* 31 (1981): 48–52.

Robinson, James. *A New Quest of the Historical Jesus*. London: SCM Press, 1961.

Rosenbaum, Ron. "Riddle of the Scrolls," *Vanity Fair* (November 1992): pp. 222–228; 286–294.

Roth, Cecil. *The Dead Sea Scrolls: A New Historical Approach*. New York: W. W. Norton & Co., 1968.

Rowley, H. H. *The Zadokite Fragments and the Dead Sea Scrolls*. Oxford: Basil Blackwell, 1956.

Safrai, S. "The Temple and the Divine Service." Pp. 282–337 in *The World History of the Jewish People: The Herodian Period*. Edited by Michael Avi-Yonah and Zvi Baras. Jerusalem: Massada Publishing Co., 1975.

Safire, William. "Breaking the Cartel," *The New York Times*, 26 September 1991.

Samuel, Archbishop Athanasius Yeshue. *Treasure of Qumran: My Story of the Dead Sea Scrolls*. Philadelphia: The Westminster Press, 1966.

Sanders, James A. "What Can Happen in a Year?" *Biblical Archaeologist* 55 (1992): 37–42.

Schechter, Solomon. *Fragments of a Zadokite Work*. Cambridge: Cambridge University Press, 1910.

Schiffman, Lawrence H., ed. *Archaeology and History and the Dead Sea Scrolls*. Sheffield: JSOT, 1990.

————. "Confessionalism and the Study of the Dead Sea Scrolls."
Jewish Studies 31 (1991): 3–14.

————. "Ethical Issues in the Publication of the Dead Sea Scrolls," in
*Proceedings of the New York Academy of Science: Methods of Investigation
of the Dead Sea Scrolls and the Khirbet Qumran Site: Present Realities and
Future Prospects.* Forthcoming.

————. "4QMiqsat Ma'aseh Ha-Torah and the Temple Scroll." Pp.
435–457 in *The Texts of Qumran and the History of the Community.*
Volume 2. Edited by F. Garcia Martinez. Paris: Gabalda, 1990

————. *The Halakhah at Qumran.* Leiden: E. J. Brill, 1975.

————. "The New Halakhic Letter (4QMMT) and the Origins of the
Dead Sea Sect." *Biblical Archaeologist* 53 (1990): 64–73.

————. "New Light on the Pharisees." Pp. 217–224 in *Understanding the
Dead Sea Scrolls.* Edited by Hershel Shanks. New York: Random
House, 1992.

————. "The Sadducean Origins of the Dead Sea Sect." Pp. 35–49 in
Understanding the Dead Sea Scrolls. Edited by Hershel Shanks. New
York: Random House, 1992.

————. *Sectarian Law in the Dead Sea Scrolls: Courts, Testimony, and the
Penal Code.* Chico, CA: Scholars Press, 1983.

————. "The Temple Scroll and the Systems of Jewish Law of the
Second Temple Period." Pp. 245–251 in *Temple Scroll Studies.*
Edited by George J. Brooke. Sheffield: JSOT Press, 1989.

————. *Text and Tradition: A History of Second Temple and Rabbinic
Judaism.* Hoboken, NJ: Ktav, 1991.

Schweitzer, Albert. *The Quest of the Historical Jesus.* New York: Macmillan
Co., 1968.

Scott, James C. *Domination and the Arts of Resistance.* New Haven, CT:
Yale University Press, 1990.

Segev, Tom. "Who Stole the Scroll?" *Haaretz,* 2 February 1993. [In
Hebrew]

Shanks, Hershel. "Blood on the Floor at the New York Dead Sea Scrolls
Conference." *Biblical Archaeology Review* 19:2 (March/April 1993):
63–68.

————. "Dead Sea Scrolls Scandal." *Biblical Archaeology Review* 15:4
(July/August 1989): 18–21, 55.

————. "Failure to Publish Dead Sea Scrolls Is Leitmotif of New York
University Scroll Conference." *Biblical Archaeology Review* 11:5
(September/October 1985): 4.

————. "Intrigue and the Scroll." Pp. 116–125 in *Understanding the
Dead Sea Scrolls.* Edited by Hershel Shanks. New York: Random
House, 1992.

————. "Jerusalem Rolls Out Red Carpet for Biblical Archaeology

Conference." *Biblical Archaeology Review* 10:4 (July/August 1984): 12–18.

———. "Lawsuit Diary." *Biblical Archaeology Review* 19:3 (May/June 1993): 69–71.

———. "Paying the Price for Freeing the Scrolls." *Biblical Archaeology Review* 19:4 (July/August 1993): 65–68.

———. "The Qumran Settlement: Monastery, Villa, or Fortress?" *Biblical Archaeology Review* 19:3 (May/June 1993): 62–65.

———. "Scholars, Scrolls, Secrets, and 'Crimes.'" *New York Times*, 7 September 1991.

———. "Why Professor Qimron's Lawsuit Is a Threat to Intellectual Freedom." *Biblical Archaeology Review* 18:5 (September/October 1992): 67, 70

Shmueli, Avshalom. "The Desert Frontier in Judea." Pp. 17–38 in *The Changing Bedouin*. Edited by Emanuel Marx and Avshalom Shmueli. New Brunswick, New Jersey: Transaction Books, 1984.

Silberman, Neil Asher. *Digging for God and Country*. New York: Alfred A. Knopf, 1982.

———. *A Prophet From Amongst You: The Life of Yigael Yadin*. New York: Addison-Wesley, 1993.

Sitton, Rafi. *Men of Secrets, Men of Mystery*. Tel Aviv: Edanim, 1990. [In Hebrew]

Sivan, Emmanuel. *Radical Islam: Medieval Theology and Modern Politics*. New Haven, CT: Yale University Press, 1985.

Smallwood, E. Mary. "High Priests and Politics in Roman Palestine." *Journal of Theological Studies* 13 (1962): 14–34.

———. *The Jews Under Roman Rule*. Leiden: E. J. Brill, 1976.

Smith, Morton. *Palestinian Parties and Politics That Shaped the Old Testament*. New York: Columbia University Press, 1971.

Specter, Michael. "Renegades Bring Dead Sea Scrolls to Light," *The Washington Post*, 5 September 1991.

Spiegelman, Arthur. "Rest of the Dead Sea Scrolls Are Published, Breaking Monopoly of Group of Scholars." *The Boston Globe*, 20 November 1991.

Stegemann, Hartmut. "Is the Temple Scroll a Sixth Book of the Torah—Lost for 2500 Years?" Pp. 126–136 in *Understanding the Dead Sea Scrolls*. Edited by Hershel Shanks. New York: Random House, 1992.

Stendahl, Krister, ed. *The Scrolls and the New Testament*. New York: Harper & Row, 1957.

Stern, Menachem. "Aspects of Jewish Society: the Priesthood and Other Classes." Pp. 561–630 in *The Jewish People in the First Century*. Volume 2. Edited by S. Safrai and M. Stern. Assen: 1976.

————, ed. *Greek and Latin Authors on Jews and Judaism.* Jerusalem: Israel
  Academy of Sciences and Humanities, 1974.
————. "Judea and Her Neighbors in the Days of Alexander
  Jannaeus." Pp. 128–150 in Stern, Menachem, *Studies in Jewish
  History: The Second Temple Period.* Jerusalem: Yad Izhak Ben-Zvi,
  1991. [In Hebrew]
Stone, Michael E. *Scriptures, Sects, and Visions: A Profile of Judaism from
  Ezra to the Jewish Revolts.* Philadelphia: Fortress Press, 1980.
Strugnell, John. "Notes en marge du volume V des 'Discoveries in the
  Judaean Desert of Jordan.' " *Revue de Qumran* 7 (1969–71):
  163–276.
Sussmann, Yaacov. "The History of the Halakha and the Dead Sea
  Scrolls." Pp. 99–127 in *The Scrolls of the Judaean Desert: Forty Years of
  Research.* Edited by Magen Broshi et. al. Jerusalem: The Bialik
  Institute, 1992. [In Hebrew]
Tabor, James D. "A Pierced or Piercing Messiah—The Verdict Is Still
  Out." *Biblical Archaeology Review* 18:6 (November/December 1992):
  58–9.
Talmon, Shemaryahu. *The World of Qumran from Within.* Jerusalem:
  Magnes Press, 1989.
Teicher, Joel L. "The Dead Sea Scrolls: Documents of the
  Jewish-Christian Sect of Ebionites." *Journal of Jewish Studies* 3
  (1951): 67–99.
Thiering, Barbara. *Jesus and the Riddle of the Dead Sea Scrolls.* San
  Francisco: HarperCollins, 1992.
Tov, Emanuel. "Expanded Team of Editors Hard at Work on Variety of
  Texts." *Biblical Archaeology Review* 18:4 (July/August 1992): 69,
  72–75.
————, ed. *The Dead Sea Scrolls on Microfiche: A Comprehensive Facsimile
  Edition of the Texts from the Judean Desert.* Leiden, E. J. Brill, 1993.
————. "The Unpublished Qumran Texts from Caves 4 and 11."
  Biblical Archaeologist 55 (1992): 94–104.
Trever, John C. *The Untold Story of Qumran.* Westwood, NJ: Fleming H.
  Revell Company, 1965.
————. "When Was Qumran Cave I Discovered?" *Revue de Qumran* 3
  (1961–2): 135–141.
VanderKam, James C. "The Dead Sea Scrolls and Christianity." Pp.
  181–202 in *Understanding the Dead Sea Scrolls.* Edited by Hershel
  Shanks. New York: Random House, 1992.
Van der Ploeg, J. P. M. *The Excavations at Qumran.* London: Longmans,
  Green, and Co., 1958.
Vermes, Geza. *The Dead Sea Scrolls in English.* New York: Penguin Books,
  1990.

———. "The Oxford Forum for Qumran Research: Seminar of the Rule of War from Cave 4 (4Q285)." *Journal of Jewish Studies* 43 (1992): 85–90.

———. "The Pierced Messiah Text—An Interpretation Evaporates." *Biblical Archaeology Review* 18:4 (July/August 1992): 80–83.

Vincent, Louis-Hughes. "Une grotte funéraire antique dans l'Oudy et-Tin," *Revue Biblique* 54 (1947): 29–35.

Viviano, Benedict T. "Beatitudes Found among the Dead Sea Scrolls." *Biblical Archaeology Review* 18:6 (November/December 1992): 53–55.

———. "Ecole Biblique et Archéologique Française de Jérusalem." *Biblical Archaeologist* 54 (1991): 160–167.

Wacholder, Ben Zion. *The Dawn of Qumran: The Sectarian Torah and the Teacher of Righteousness.* Cincinnati, OH: Hebrew Union College Press, 1983.

Wacholder, Ben Zion, and Martin G. Abegg. *A Preliminary Edition of the Unpublished Dead Sea Scrolls: The Hebrew and Aramaic Texts from Cave Four.* Washington, D.C.: The Biblical Archaeology Society, 1991.

Wade, Nicholas. "Editorial Notebook: The Vanity of Scholars," *The New York Times,* 9 July 1989: 26.

Warszawski, Abraham, and Abraham Peretz. "Building the Temple Mount: Organization and Execution," *Cathedra* 66 (1992): 3–46. [In Hebrew]

Wilford, John Noble. "Computer Hacker Bootlegs Version of the Dead Sea Scrolls," *The New York Times,* 5 September 1991.

———. "Dead Sea Scrolls Editor's Exit Tied to Anti-Jewish Remarks," *The New York Times,* 12 December 1991.

———. "Link to Messianic Christianity Is Found in Scrolls," *The New York Times,* 8 November 1991.

———. Monopoly Over Dead Sea Scrolls Is Ended," *The New York Times,* 22 September 1991.

Wilson, A. N. *Jesus: A Life.* New York: Fawcett Columbine, 1992.

Wilson, Edmund. *The Fifties: From Notebooks and Diaries of the Period.* New York: Farrar, Straus, and Giroux, 1986.

———. *Israel and the Dead Sea Scrolls.* New York: Farrar, Straus, and Giroux, 1978.

———. *The Scrolls from the Dead Sea.* New York: Oxford University Press: 1955.

Wise, Michael O. *A Critical Study of the Temple Scroll from Qumran Cave 11.* Chicago: Oriental Institute, 1990.

Wise, Michael O., and James D. Tabor. "The Messiah at Qumran." *Biblical Archaeology Review* 18:6 (November/December 1992): 60–65.

Wolters, Al. "Apocalyptic and the Copper Scroll." *Journal of Near Eastern Studies* 49 (1990): 145–154.

————. "History and the Copper Scroll." Paper presented at the 1992 New York Academy of Sciences Dead Sea Scroll Conference, December 16, 1992.

Yadin, Yigael. *The Message of the Scrolls.* New York: Simon and Schuster, 1957.

————. *The Scroll of the War of the Sons of Light Against the Sons of Darkness.* Oxford: Oxford University Press, 1962.

————. *The Temple Scroll.* volumes 1–3. Jerusalem: Israel Exploration Society, 1983.

————. *The Temple Scroll: The Hidden Law of the Dead Sea Sect.* London: Weidenfeld and Nicholson: 1985.

INDEX